D0817329

ART
FOR CHILDREN
A STEP-BY-STEP GUIDE FOR
THE YOUNG ARTIST

ART
FOR CHILDREN
A STEP-BY-STEP GUIDE FOR
THE YOUNG ARTIST
DIANA CRAIG · MOIRA BUTTERFIELD · LYNSY PINSENT
CHARTWELL
BOOKS, INC.

A QUARTO BOOK

ISBN: 0–7858–0510–9

This book was designed and produced by
Quarto Children's Books Limited
The Fitzpatrick Building
188–194 York Way
London N7 9QP

Manufactured in Hong Kong by
Regent Publishing Services Limited.

Published by Chartwell Books
A Division of Book Sales, Inc.
P.O. Box 7100
Edison, New Jersey 08818–7100

Contents

How to Draw and Paint Pets

Face Painting

How to Draw and Paint The Outdoors

Getting started

Before you start to work, you should get together all the things you will need – then you can enjoy making your pictures without having to stop to find something you've forgotten. But first, have a look through this book. It may give you some new ideas for different materials and tools to try out.

The best place to store all your materials safely is in a cupboard. Drawing pads and paper can be stored flat, and you can organize your things so that you can find what you need quickly. It will also give you somewhere to keep, or display, the work you have done.

A place to work

Where you work will depend on what materials you are using. You can draw in a hardcover sketchbook almost anywhere, but if you are using a loose sheet of paper you will need a firm surface to work on. A tabletop will do, but fixing your paper to a drawing board is even better because it keeps the paper firmly in place. You can buy ready-made boards, or make your own from chipboard or plywood. Fix your paper to the board with paper clips or thumbtacks.

Brushes

The better your brushes, the better the results they will give – and the easier they will be to use. The brushes that come in paint sets are thin and floppy and it is very hard to control them properly. You can buy good-quality brushes in art stores. Nylon and bristle brushes are not too expensive. Nylon is soft and good for thin paint such as **watercolor**. Bristle is stiffer and good for thicker paint such as **poster paint**. For painting details, you will need a small, pointed nylon brush, and one or two larger brushes, either nylon or bristle, for painting bigger areas.

Paper

There are all kinds of paper for different uses. Drawing paper has a smooth surface that is good for pencil drawing. Rougher and softer paper is good for **pastels** or **powder paints. Water-colors** contain a lot of water, so they need a thick paper that does not wrinkle too much. It's a good idea to have a small sketchbook to carry around with you so that you can do sketches whenever you want.

Palettes

It isn't necessary to have a real artist's palette for mixing up your colors. You can use an old plate or small tray. An old muffin tin is also useful because you can mix good quantities of different color in each of the hollows.

Water pots

Use a sturdy container to keep water in, or it may fall over. A clean glass jar or an old saucepan is ideal. Make sure it is not too small, or the water will quickly get dirty and spoil your colors, and remember to change the water frequently. Keep your water container away from the edge of your work surface, on your right side if you are right-handed and on your left if you are left-handed – that way, you are less likely to knock it over.

Keep it clean

Covering your clothes and your work surface will protect them from marks and stains that might not wash off. Wear an apron or old shirt to protect your clothes, and cover your work surface with newspaper.

Look after it

If you look after your materials, they will last much longer and be easier to use. Always wash your brushes after use, or old paint will clog the hairs and make the brushes hard. After painting, rinse brushes out in cold or lukewarm water (hot water melts the glue that holds the hairs in place). Then wash them gently with soap or dishwashing detergent, and finally rinse them clean. Store your brushes in jars with the heads upward. Always remember to put the tops back on paint pots and felt-tip pens, too, or they will dry out.

Save it

Keep a lookout for anything that you think might be useful, and save it! The backs of old business letters can be used for painting pictures as they are often written on good, thick paper (but check that nobody needs them first). Old jars can be used for holding water, and plastic cups can be used for mixing paint in (make sure they are not too light, or they may fall over). And of course any small objects, such as buttons, scraps of wrapping paper or foil, cotton, twigs, pasta shapes, or pictures cut from old magazines, are ideal for making collages.

Black and white drawings

Different drawing materials make different marks. Generally, soft materials such as crayon or pastel look rough and smudgy; harder ones such as pencil or ballpoint pen make thinner, neater marks and lines. Try them out and choose the best ones for your picture.

Charcoal is good for big, quick drawings, but it can get messy and is not so good for details. If you want to do a detailed picture, try pen and ink. Thin felt-tip pen is also good for neat lines; thick felt-tip is best for wide lines or marks, or filling in.

Experiment with how you use your materials – drawing in smooth, even lines isn't the only way to make a picture. Try scribbling to show, say, a shaggy coat, or use zigzag lines for the scales on a fish or lizard. Or you could build up your picture with lots of little dots and short lines, or crisscrossing lines (this is called *cross-hatching*): the more crisscrossing lines you do, the darker your picture will be. Smudge or rub out part of your picture and see what that looks like.

Hard pencils make thin, neat, light lines. Hard pencils are marked "H," with a number. The higher the number, the harder the pencil.

Soft pencils make wider, softer, darker lines. They are marked "B," with a number. The higher the number, the softer the pencil. (Medium pencils are marked "HB" or "F.")

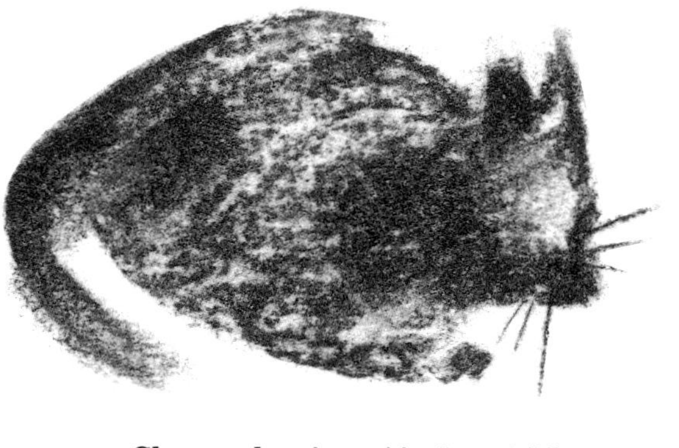

Charcoal makes wide, "rough" lines, and smudges easily.

Chalks give a nice crumbly line, and are perfect for filling in.

Thick felt-tip pens can make broad lines or dots, and are good for filling in.

Thin felt-tip pens make an even line. They are available with very fine points for detailed drawing.

Pen and ink makes a strong, black line.

What shall I use for cats?

Choose the drawing material that will look most like your pet. For a cat with short fur, lots of little lines in thin felt-tip pen could look like individual hairs, and you could fill in with thicker pen if you liked. If your cat is fluffy, a smudgy material like pastel or charcoal would be good.

Patch says... You can make symmetrical shapes, such as a butterfly, by putting an ink blob on paper and folding it over.

Lydia used soft pencil to draw her rabbit. See how she has used the pencil to show the way the fur grows.

Cheryl chose black felt-tip pen to draw a simple outline of her dog and for filling in the details.

Colored pencils, pastels, and crayons

There are many wonderful colored drawing materials to choose from, all with their own special qualities.

You have probably already used colored pencils. Their sharp points are good for drawing details, and if you press lightly, you can also color in bigger areas. They make soft, delicate pictures. But did you know that you can also "paint" with certain pencils and crayons? Watercolor pencils and crayons are just like ordinary colored pencils except that, if you paint over them with water, the color spreads like paint.

Pastels and oil pastels all make similar marks. Pastels are soft and smudge easily, so you can blend colors by rubbing them with your finger or a piece of absorbent cotton. Oil pastels give stronger colors, and won't smudge.

If you have used ordinary pastels for your picture, be especially careful with it when you have finished. Hold the paper by the edges or it may smudge.

Wax crayons won't smudge and you can't rub them out, but you can "blend" colors by putting one on top of another – some of the color beneath will show through.

colored pencil

watercolor pencil

pastels, chalks (use their ends to draw with: hold them on their sides to color in)

oil pastel

wax crayon

Making highlights

Eyes and noses will look much more real if you give them highlights to make them look shiny.

In pencil drawings, leave a white space.

In pastel drawings, a blob of white on top looks especially effective.

In crayon drawings, you can scrape away with a pen nib to the white paper beneath.

Patch says... Look carefully to see how many different colors there are on your pet. There may be subtle changes of color that you haven't yet noticed – say, around its nose, or on its paws.

Rabbit in pastels
This picture was done in pastels, on special pastel paper (you can use any slightly rough paper instead). See how the pastel has been lightly smudged to blend the colors. Using the colored paper makes the picture more interesting, and you can allow some of the paper color to show through.

Rabbit in colored pencil Another picture of the same rabbit was done with colored pencil. Here, the pencil has been used to color in lots of short lines to look like the rabbit's fur. See how the lines change direction, just like fur. Colored pencil drawings stand out best on white paper.

Drawing with colored pens

Felt-tip pens are very different from colored pencil or pastel, so you should not try to use them in the same way. They make much stronger lines and marks, so they are not suitable for soft, delicate pictures. To get the best from felt-tips, the trick is to work boldly!

Another difference is that felt-tip pen marks cannot be rubbed out, but don't be afraid of making mistakes. A slightly "wrong" outline will just make your picture look more unusual and interesting – or you can draw over the line again, and this will also add interest. Remember that the more practice you have, the more confident you will become.

You can also do colored drawings with ballpoint pens and old-fashioned "dip" pens, but they both have disadvantages. Ballpoints come in so few colors that your drawing would not look very exciting, and it is somewhat of a waste to use colored ink just to draw fine lines or dots. The colors are so rich and beautiful you would enjoy them much more if you painted them on with a brush, in broad strokes, so you could really *see* them.

Big, round felt-tip pens make broad lines and dots.

Wedge-tip marker pens give bold, even lines.

Dip pens can make bold or spidery lines, depending on how hard you press.

Fine felt-tip pens make even, fine lines.

Ballpoint pens make spidery lines – but keep the tip clean or the ink may blob.

Fountain pens give a clean, strong line.

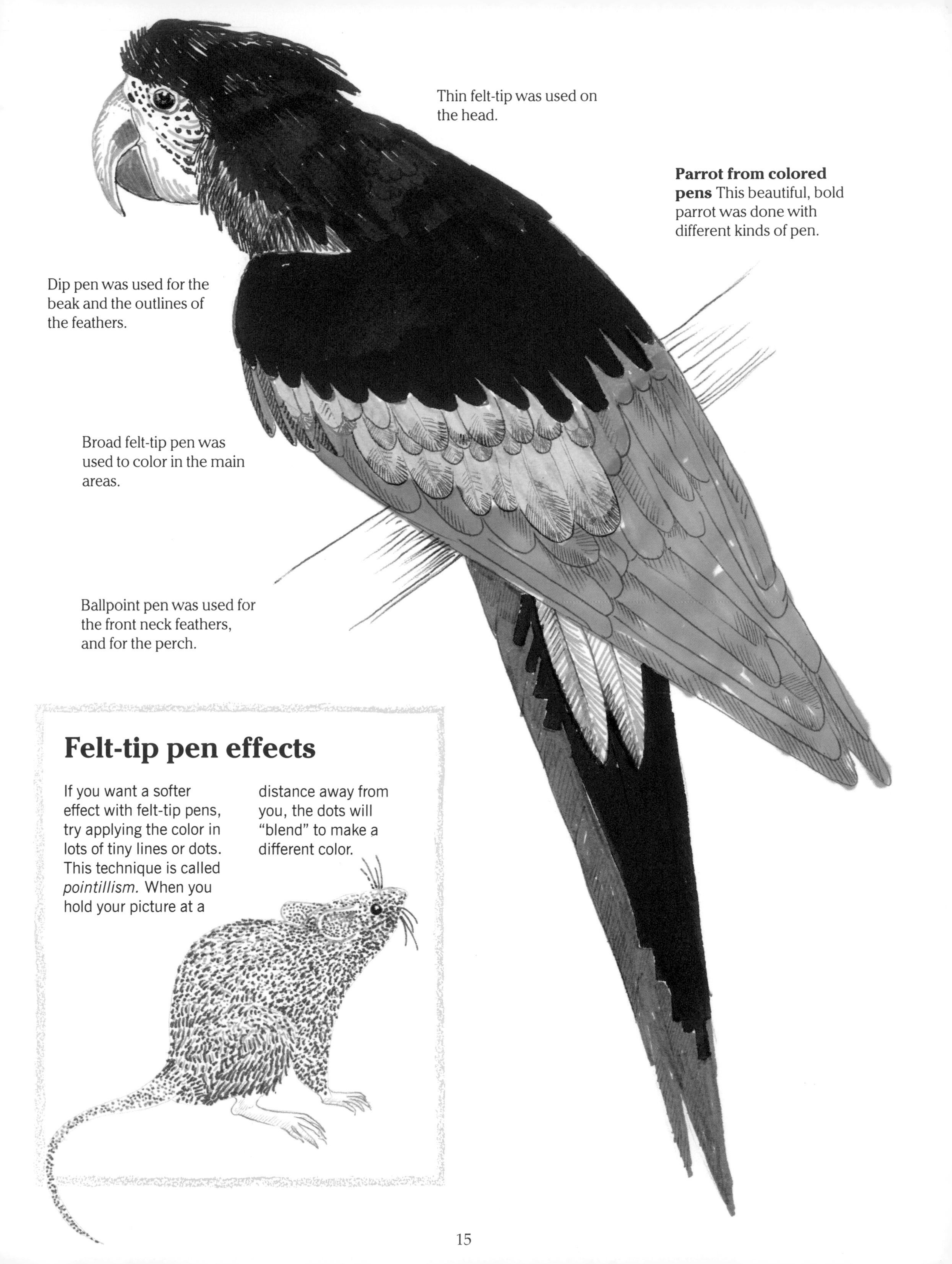

Parrot from colored pens This beautiful, bold parrot was done with different kinds of pen.

Felt-tip pen effects

If you want a softer effect with felt-tip pens, try applying the color in lots of tiny lines or dots. This technique is called *pointillism.* When you hold your picture at a distance away from you, the dots will "blend" to make a different color.

Experimenting with sketches

Sketching does not only mean doing quick pencil drawings in your sketchbook. Experiment with all kinds of drawing materials. See what happens if you paint a watercolor wash over a pencil sketch (a "wash" is a transparent layer of paint which has been mixed with water to make it thinner). Or try drawing with a watercolor pencil and then painting over it with water to make the colors run.

Experiment with wax crayons. What happens if you draw with different colors on top of each other? Wax crayons are greasy, and grease and water don't mix, so what happens if you paint watercolor over your crayon sketch? Is it the same if you paint on the watercolor first?

Make notes about what you have done. Label each sketch with the materials you used, and which you used first. If you think a particular material would be really good for doing, say, an animal's fur, write this down too. For example, smudged gray, black, or orange pastel may really look like fluffy cat's fur.

What other experiments can you think of?

Wax crayon and wash First the outline and main details were drawn with crayon.

Next, some of the fur was colored in using yellow for the light areas and gray and purple for the dark areas.

Last, a watercolor wash was painted over, leaving some areas white to create highlights.

Watercolor pencil was used to draw the outline and main details of this guinea pig.

Some shading was added in the ears and below the body.

Water was painted over to make the pencil run, like paint. See how this has created darker areas.

"Ideas scrapbook"

As well as experimenting with materials, why not also use your sketchbook as an "ideas scrapbook"? Whenever you find a picture of a pet animal you like, cut it out and stick it in your sketchbook. You can simply copy the picture, or use it to develop some ideas of your own.

Here are some of the places you may find pictures of pet animals for your "scrapbook" (but make sure no one else needs them before you cut them up).

- photos
- stamps
- magazine advertisements
- cards
- labels from cans or packages of pet food
- scraps of wrapping paper

Patch says... Why not do drawings of the same animal using different materials? Look at the effect each one has, and compare them to see which one is best for your pet.

Types of fur and feathers Think of all the different kinds of fur animals have – some is short, straight, and smooth, some is long and curly. Experiment in your sketchbook to get the look of different fur. Make studies of the different shapes and textures of feathers in the same way.

Your pet's year

Your sketchbook is one of the most important tools you have. The more you use it, the better your drawing will become, and the more you will have learned about the different materials you have experimented with. But there is another way in which your sketchbook is very useful. As you keep doing drawings of your pet – sleeping, eating, playing, and so on – just think of what a wonderful record you are building up of all the things your pet does.

Why not put all these pictures together to make a really special record of your pet's life, such as an "all-seasons poster" or a calendar of your pet's year. You can either use the sketches you already have, do one specially for each season or month, or do more finished pictures based on your original sketches.

1

All-seasons poster For this you will need four different pictures of your pet, one for each season. For example, you could have your dog with flowers for spring; sleeping in the sun for summer; chasing leaves for fall; and in a cozy basket or by the fire for winter. Paste your pictures on a large piece of paper, writing the name of the season below.

You will need
- 12 pictures of your pet (one for each month)
- 12 pieces of paper
- calendar for next year
- stapler
- glue
- scissors
- paper punch (if available)
- cord or wool for hanging your calendar

Pet calendar On each sheet of paper, paste the picture for that month and the right sheet from the calendar.

2

Staple the sheets together and make two holes at the top with scissors or a paper punch (you may need an adult's help).

3

Thread the cord or wool through the holes and knot it. Then hang up your calendar.

Paints and inks

There are three basic kinds of water-based paint: *gouache*, *watercolor* and *acrylics*. They are called "water-based" because you can mix them with water.

All these paints are made of a colored powder, called *pigment*, mixed with something to bind them together. Watercolors and gouache are mixed with gum, and acrylics are mixed with a chemical binder.

Water paints come in two qualities: students' and artists'. Students' paints are cheaper than artists', but they contain less pigment so the colors are not as strong.

You can also paint pictures with colored inks. Inks and the different paints all have their own special qualities. Which you choose will depend on the kind of picture you want to paint, and how much money you want to spend.

Gouache comes in two forms, poster paint and designers' gouache. It is thicker than watercolor, and it doesn't let the paper show through. It can be watered down easily, but will pick up the color underneath if it is very watery. Work the colors and tones into or over each other.

Watercolor is a thin, watery paint that comes in tubes or blocks, called pans. Because it is transparent, the colors show up best on white paper. It should be used on stretched paper or thick watercolor paper, or card. Build up layers of color and tone, but be careful not to overwork the painting.

Acrylics come in tubes or jars. They can be applied with a dry brush, like the mouse below right, or applied watered down, one color over another in layers.

Stippling with gouache

Stippling is a good technique to use with paint like gouache, which dries to a flat finish. "Stippling" means to apply paint in lots of dots or little lines. It's another way of mixing a color. Instead of mixing it up from other colors and then painting it on, you "mix" it by applying the different colors to the paper.

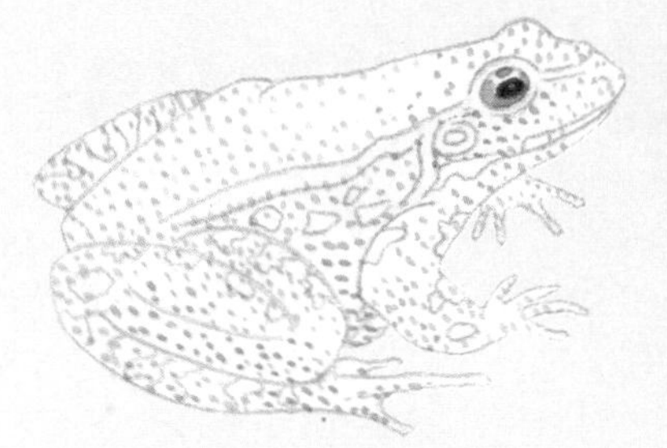

First draw the outline, and brush over a light wash of color, leaving the highlights white. Apply dots of the main color all over.

Individual dots of color combine to create an overall effect of color and tone.

Add dots of lighter and darker colors to create light and dark areas. For the frog, permanent green, sky blue, burnt umber and orange lake light were used.

Patch says... You can lift off watercolor while it is still wet to make highlights. Before the paint dries, quickly brush over it with a dry brush, or take the paint off with a dry tissue or cloth.

A watercolor cat Watercolor can be used to create a soft effect by brushing the color on to wet paper.

1

Lightly draw the animal's outline with pencil.

2

Paint all over the shape with clean water, going slightly beyond the edge. Leave the water to soak in.

3

Apply thin washes of color to the wet paper, stopping before you get to the edge. Use stronger color to build up detail.

Inks come in bottles. They are slightly transparent, but the colors are quite strong. You can mix the colors in the same way as for paints, and water them down if the color is too strong. You can put layers over each other.

Basic animal shapes

One of the main things that makes one kind of animal look different from another is the shape of its body. A clever trick to make drawing an animal easier is first to divide its body up into a few simple shapes, such as circles, triangles, and rectangles.

For example, if you are drawing a cat sitting facing you, you could do a circle for the head and a triangle for the body. If you are drawing a small dog from the side, you could do three rectangles of different sizes for the head, neck, and body.

On these pages we have made it even simpler by using nothing but circles and ovals. Have a look at the drawings to see how to turn these basic shapes into pictures of real animals.

Cats Here is a picture of a cat sitting down, viewed from the side. What shapes can you see in its body?

Here is a drawing of the same cat, broken down into simple shapes. Make sure that the shapes are the right size – for example, the head should not be too big compared to the body.

When you are happy with your rough drawing, draw an outline around the edge. Rub out any lines that you no longer need, but leave important ones such as the line of the chin.

Fill in the silhouette with color, adding details such as eyes and whiskers.

Sitting dog This dog has a fairly long neck, so the circles are some way apart.

Now that the fur has been colored in, the dog looks very realistic.

A dog begging is a little more complicated, but you can still see the circles and

oval shapes. Make sure you get the shapes of the nose and eye right.

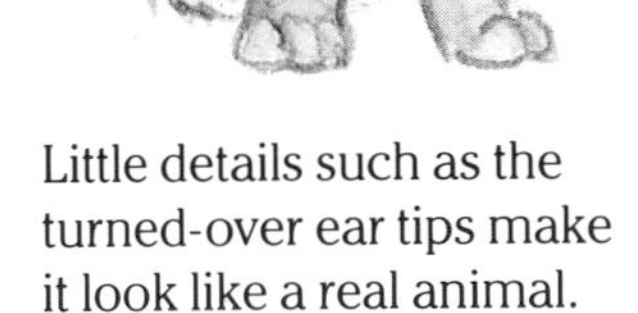

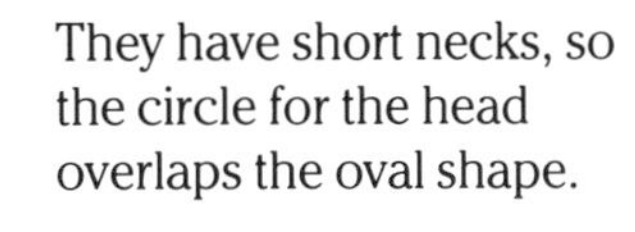

Rabbits (side view)
These are easy to draw because they are made up of lots of simple, rounded shapes.

They have short necks, so the circle for the head overlaps the oval shape.

Rabbits (front view)
Because it's seen from a slight angle, the circle for the head is not quite in the middle of the body.

Little details such as the turned-over ear tips make it look like a real animal.

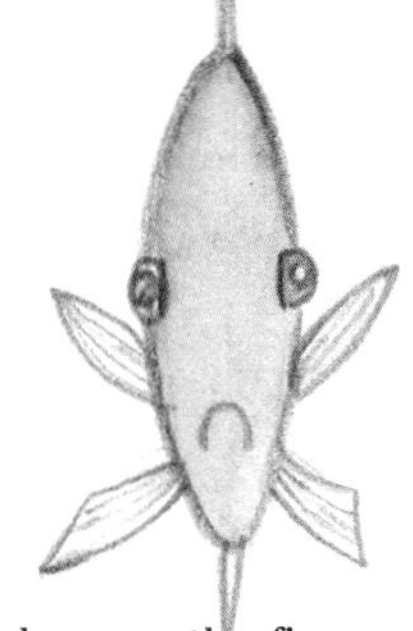

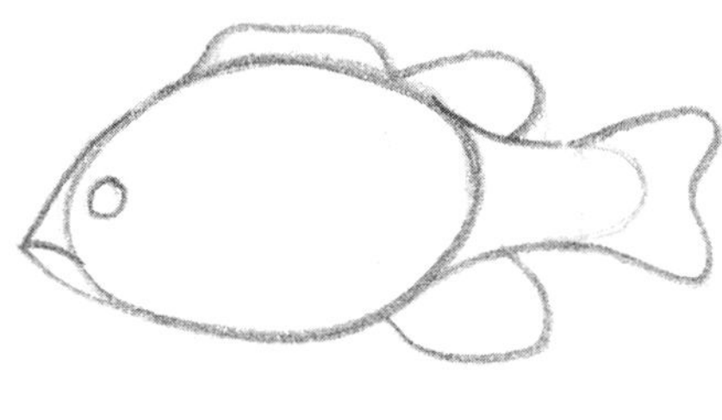

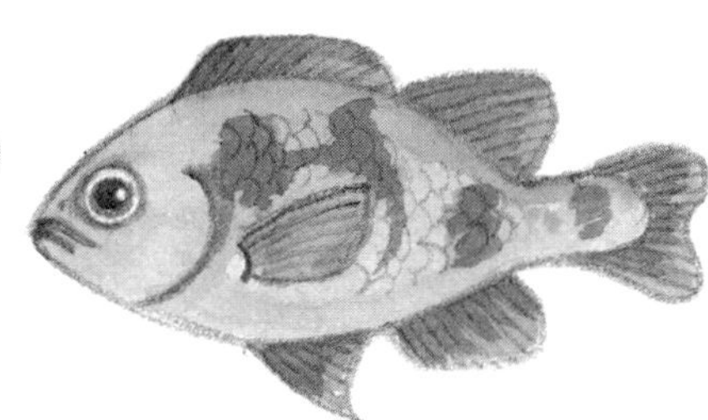

Front view of fish The fish has a very narrow body, so the oval shape is thin.

Make sure the fins are even, or the fish will look lopsided.

Fish from the side makes a bigger, wider oval.

You don't have to draw every single scale to make the fish look real.

Budgerigars are tricky, but they still fit into circles and ovals.

Don't try to paint every feather or you will get into a muddle.

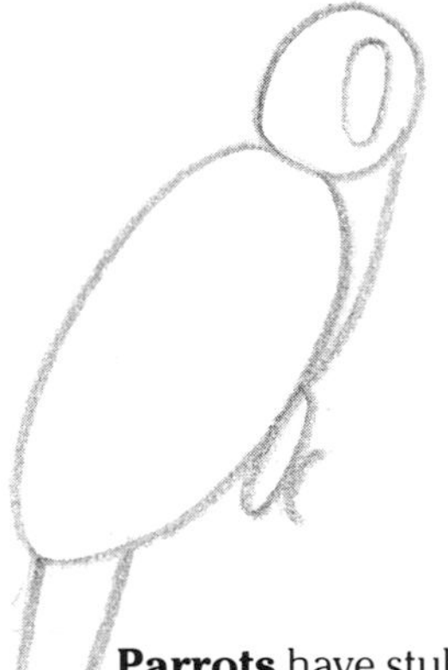

Parrots have stubby tails, and are larger than budgerigars.

Like all birds, parrots have beady eyes.

Lizards have long bodies, so the oval shape is very stretched out.

They don't stay still for long, so you will have to watch carefully to see the main shapes.

Lizard from the front
The head is a circle with a triangle below.

The body looks round because it's seen from the front. This is called foreshortening.

For the side view of a pony, start like this.

Then color it in.

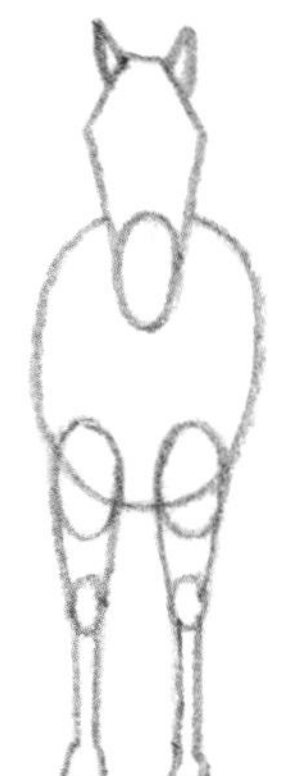

Pony (front view) The front view makes even easier shapes.

Don't forget the forelock when you color in.

Pony's head from side A pony's head is a little more difficult.

You will have to use triangles as well as ovals.

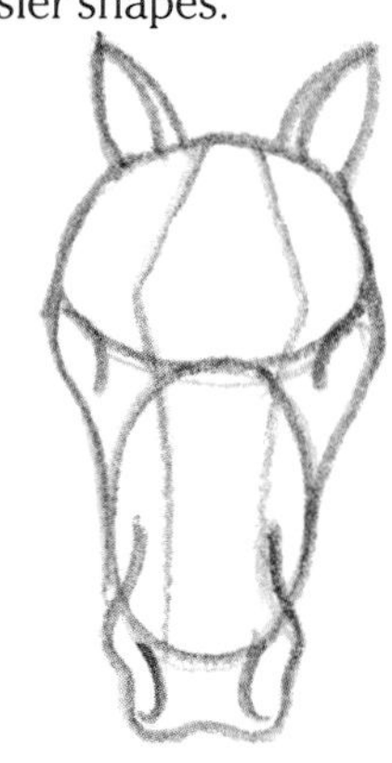

Pony's head from front A pony's head is fairly long, and broad at the top.

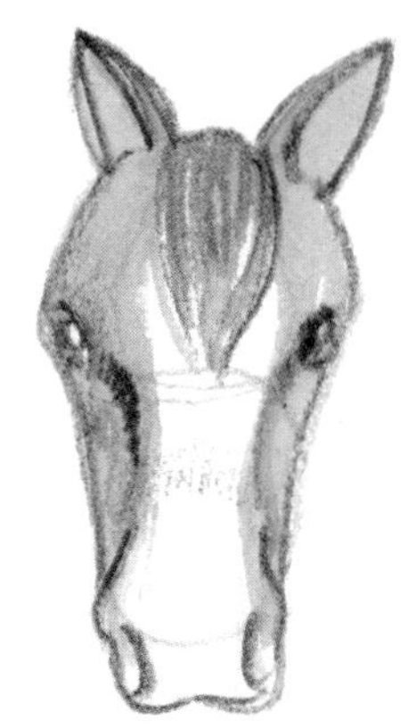

The eyes bulge out slightly, and the ears are pointed.

Guinea pig (front view) Use round shapes; the ears are half circles.

It's best to draw the shapes before you put in the fur.

Guinea pig (side view) From the side, you can see how big guinea pigs' heads are.

Does your guinea pig have long hair or short hair?

Turtle from front Turtles have big oval-shaped shells...

...and scaly, rectangular legs.

Turtle from side Turtles' necks look fairly long.

They have lovely patterns on their shells.

Mouse from side Mice are easy to draw...

...they have round ears and pointed heads.

Mouse from front The body makes two ovals...

...and a long, thin tail with no fur on it.

Rabbit (side view)
Rabbits have oval-shaped bodies and heads.

Rabbits can be long- or shorthaired. Which type are you trying to draw?

Rabbit (front view)
Rabbits are made up of overlapping circles.

When drawing a rabbit from the front you cannot see its tail.

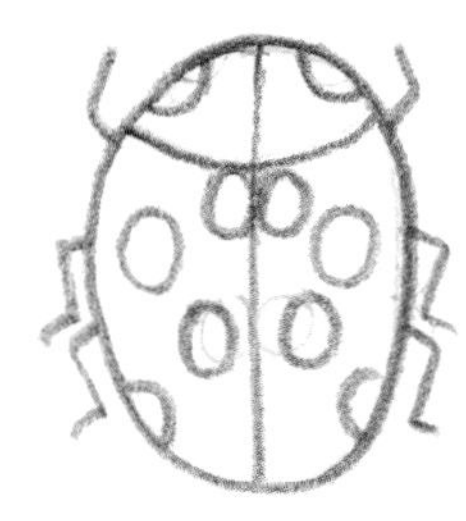

Ladybug Ladybugs are really easy. Just draw an oval...

...then color it in, adding six legs.

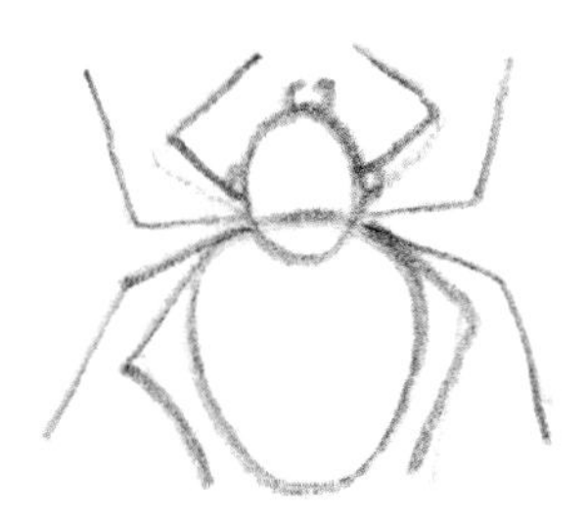

Spiders Spiders are made up of two circles.

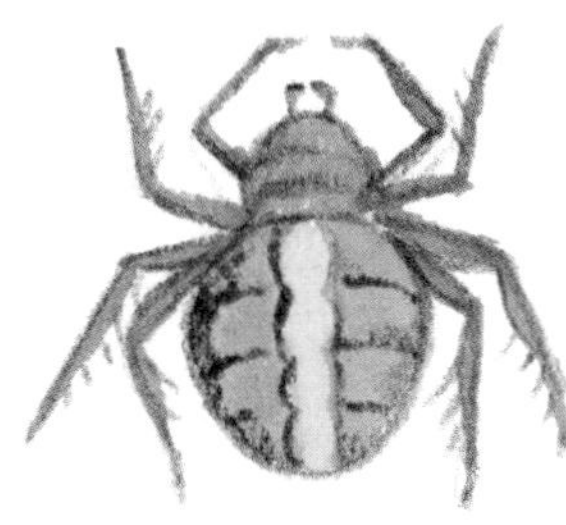

Notice where the legs join the body.

Grasshoppers
Grasshoppers are flat on top, and curved underneath.

Look carefully at the shape of the legs.

Butterflies Butterflies' wings are like two triangles.

Have fun coloring or painting in the beautiful markings.

Beetles Beetles' bodies are made of two ovals.

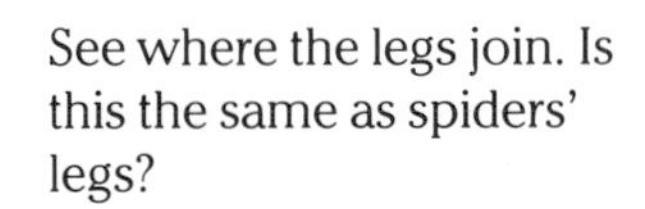

See where the legs join. Is this the same as spiders' legs?

Patch says... Remember that the same animal's body will be made up of different shapes depending on whether you are seeing it from the front, the side, or from above.

Stencils and templates

Stencils and templates are really two versions of the same idea. They are both cut-out shapes you use to make a picture. With a stencil, you use the shape you have cut out *inside* your cardboard or paper; with a template, you draw around the *outside* of the shape. Both stencils and templates can be used again and again, either in the same picture, or to make other pictures.

If you use them carefully, stencils and templates give a very neat outline, so they are ideal for any pets that have a sleek silhouette – such as shorthaired cats or dogs, or goldfish, for example. Remember to keep the shape simple so that it is easier to cut out and work with.

You will need

- thin cardboard or thick paper
- pencil
- eraser
- scissors
- paper (for your picture)
- paints
- stiff brush (or special stencil brush)

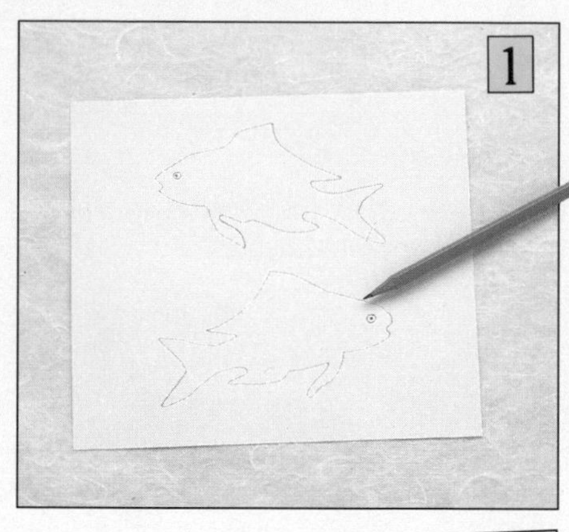

1

For a stencil, draw your pet on the cardboard, leaving a wide border around the edge.

2

Carefully cut away the *inside* of the shape you have drawn. If you have drawn an awkward shape, ask for help cutting it out.

3

Hold your stencil firmly down on the paper, and paint inside.

Lift the stencil off carefully, then add any other details you want (below).

4

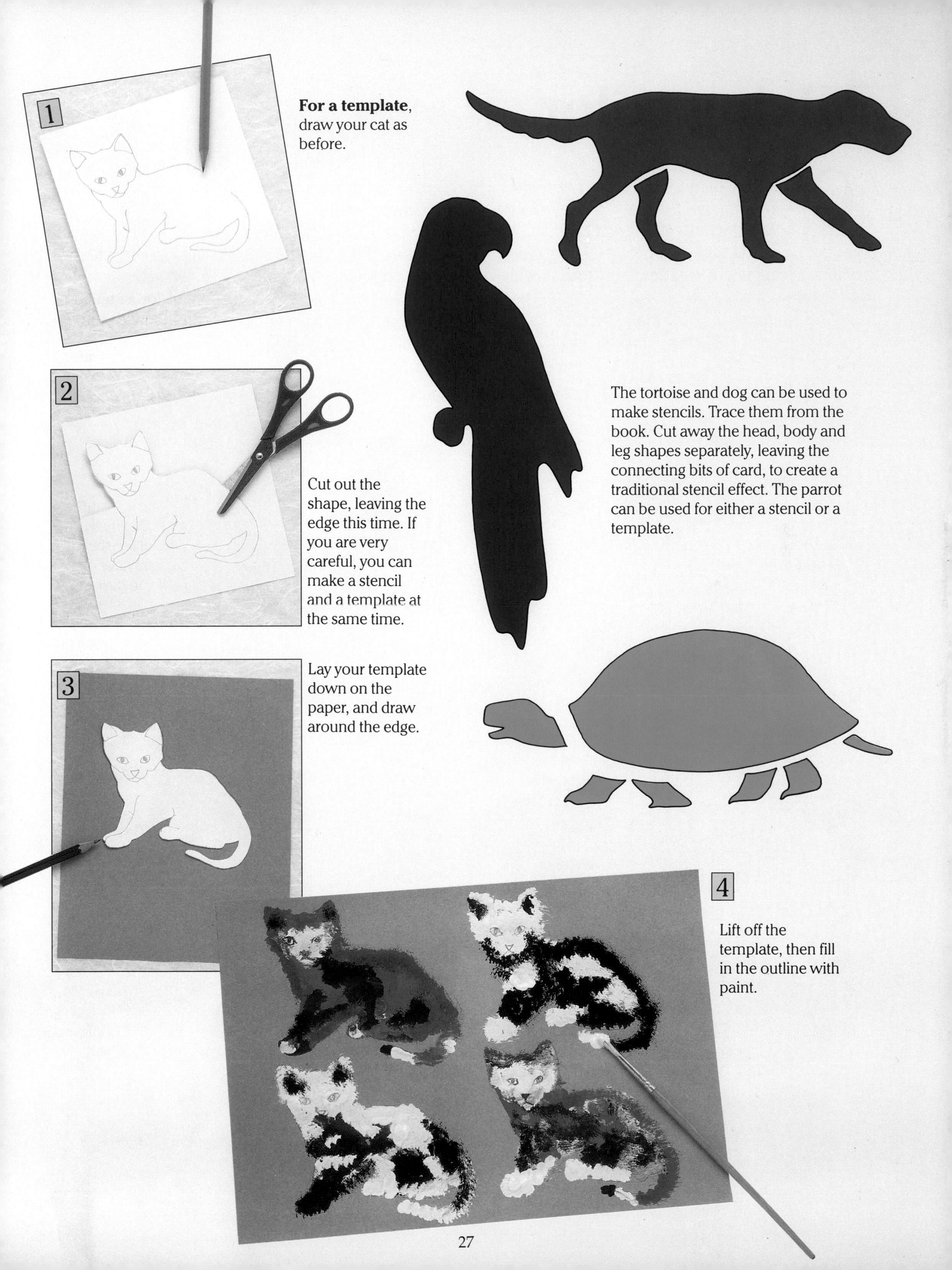

For a template, draw your cat as before.

Cut out the shape, leaving the edge this time. If you are very careful, you can make a stencil and a template at the same time.

Lay your template down on the paper, and draw around the edge.

Lift off the template, then fill in the outline with paint.

The tortoise and dog can be used to make stencils. Trace them from the book. Cut away the head, body and leg shapes separately, leaving the connecting bits of card, to create a traditional stencil effect. The parrot can be used for either a stencil or a template.

Mixing color

Colors are divided into three groups – *primary, secondary,* and *tertiary* (pronounced "ter-shary"). The *primary colors* are red, yellow, and blue, and they cannot be mixed from other colors. But all other colors, except white, can be made from mixtures of these three.

Secondary colors are made from two primary colors. Green is made from blue and yellow, orange from red and yellow, and violet from red and blue. *Tertiary colors* are made from one primary and one secondary color.

Look carefully at colors you see around you and compare them. There is more than just one blue, for example. Some blues have more red in them and look like purple; others have more yellow and look like green. Practice mixing colors to figure out what you need to add to change one color into another.

Yellow is the base color of this labrador.

Red is the color of ladybugs.

Blue feathers come from budgies or parrots.

Orange can be used for "ginger" cats.

Violet is one of the colors on some tropical fish.

Green is the color of some lizards.

Blue-brown is the "cool" brown of this mouse.

Red-brown is the "warm" color of this rich brown horse.

Yellow-brown is the base color of this rabbit.

A color wheel

This wheel is divided into three circles. In the middle there are the three primary colors, red, yellow and blue. Next there are the secondary colors made from mixing the two primaries next to them. You can see that yellow and blue make green, red and blue make purple, and red and yellow make orange. The outside circle shows the tertiary colors, made by mixing the secondary colors that are next to each other. If you count up the colors in the wheel, you will see that there are nine in all – starting from just three primaries.

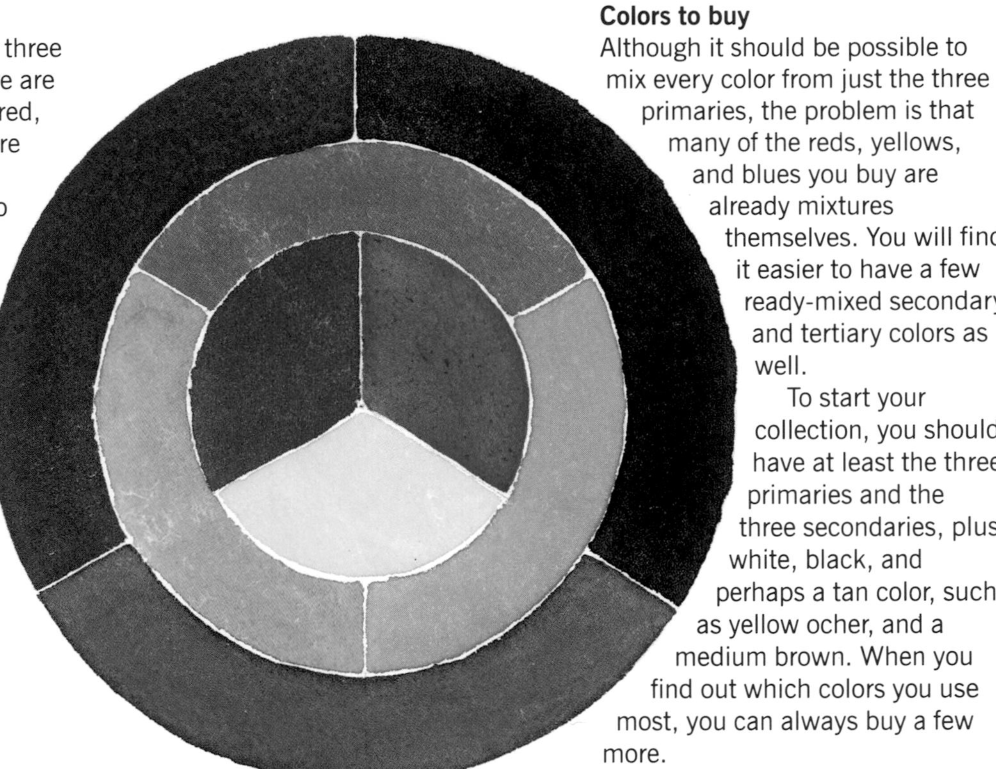

Colors to buy
Although it should be possible to mix every color from just the three primaries, the problem is that many of the reds, yellows, and blues you buy are already mixtures themselves. You will find it easier to have a few ready-mixed secondary and tertiary colors as well.

To start your collection, you should have at least the three primaries and the three secondaries, plus white, black, and perhaps a tan color, such as yellow ocher, and a medium brown. When you find out which colors you use most, you can always buy a few more.

Warm and cool colors
Have you ever thought of colors being "warm" or "cool"? Red and orange – the colors of fire – are warm colors, blue and green – the colors of water – are cool colors. Browns and grays can also be warm or cool, depending on how much red or blue they contain.

warm red-brown

Patch says... If you are painting with gouache or poster paint and you want to make a color paler, add a little white. But if you do this with watercolor, it will only make the paint go dull and muddy-looking. To make watercolor paler, just add a little water to thin the paint.

If you want to make a color darker, add some black, but not too much.

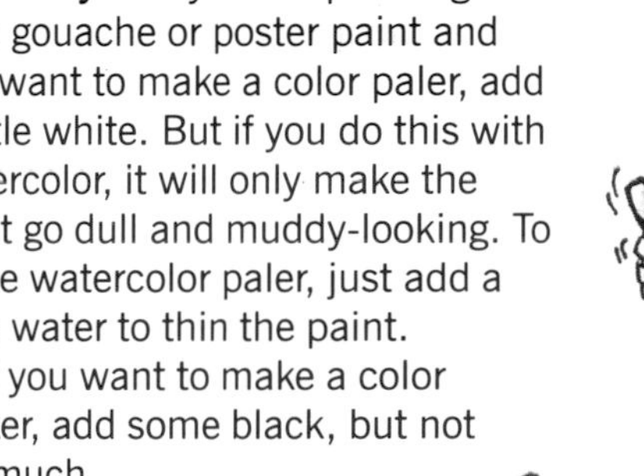

Mixing browns

"My dog's brown," says a friend. Well, most mammals are brown, so it doesn't tell you much about your friend's dog. You'd want to know if it's dark brown, light brown, a reddish brown, a sandy-colored brown, an orangey tea brown or a chocolate brown. In other words, there are many different browns, and you will need to mix the right one if you want a realistic painting of your pet.

Try mixing some of the browns below and then experiment by adding a little more of one of the colors to the wet paint and see how it changes the resulting color.

This pale, sandy-colored-turtle brown is made from mainly the yellow and the orange, with a little gray and a tiny spot of green. The green and the gray stop the brown from being too reddish.

The pale brown on this cat was made with more yellow than gray paint. The darker brown used more gray than yellow. The artist also used pink on the ears and nose.

The dark brown patches on this dog were made by mixing equal parts of red, yellow, and blue paint. Look at the difference between this and the hamster, which was also done with the same colors in pencil.

This reddish-brown is made of blue and red, which you might think would make a purple horse! In fact, very little blue was used, and the red paint is actually an orange-red, which means it's already fairly close to brown.

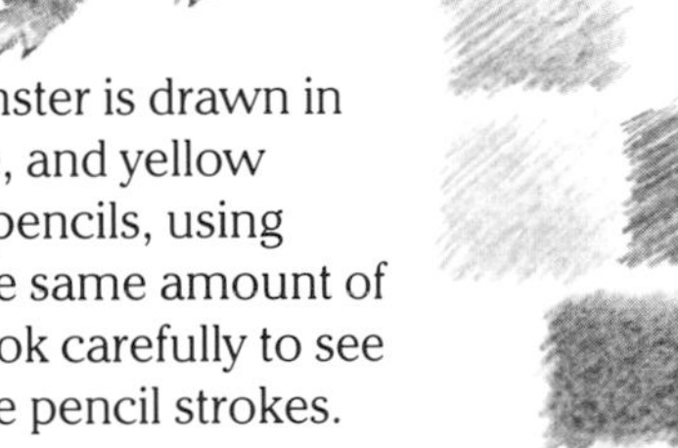

This hamster is drawn in red, blue, and yellow colored pencils, using about the same amount of each. Look carefully to see the single pencil strokes.

This is a painting of two dogs. Or is it? Look carefully, and you'll find some other animals hidden in the picture. The picture has been done in nothing but browns, and the artist has used a mixture of watercolor paints, colored pencils, colored felt-tips, and chalk pastel crayons. **Watercolor** is good for quickly brushing over large areas of solid color where you want to cover the white paper completely and don't need any detail. You can thin it out to make very pale colors. **Colored pencils** are good for detail but can also be used to cover quite large areas. Depending on how hard you press, you can make a color light or dark. As you can see on the dogs' hair, you can get interesting, uneven mixes of color with pencils. **Felt-tips** are excellent for adding strong-colored detail such as outlines and eyes. **Chalk pastel crayons** are fairly thick and are good for covering large areas. Pastels can give strong colors. Add them last because they smudge.

Special effects with paint

There are many different ways of using paint other than just painting it on with a brush. Keep experimenting with ways of applying it – not only will your paintings look much more interesting, but you will also enjoy doing them even more.

Here are just a few ideas to get you started.

Adding detail This beetle was painted in two greens. The shine on its back was left unpainted, and black pastel was used for detail.

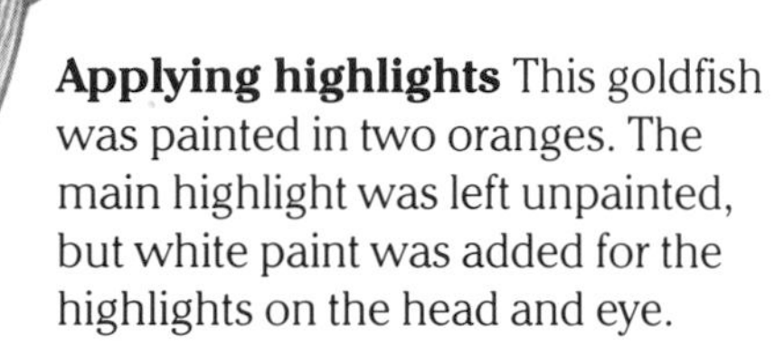

Applying highlights This goldfish was painted in two oranges. The main highlight was left unpainted, but white paint was added for the highlights on the head and eye.

Pale washes These lovebirds were first painted in very pale washes. The feathers and other details were then built up with colored pencil.

Blending colors A pale, pinky-brown wash was first painted on this cat. A darker brown was then added while the wash was still wet so that the colors blended.

Creating soft effects The spots on this rabbit were added while the paint underneath was still wet. This made them spread and look soft and "splotchy."

Using a thin brush A thin brush was used to paint lines for the hair on this pinky-brown mouse. Notice how the lines follow the shape of the body.

Overpainting with bands of color Bands of black and orange were first painted on this guinea pig. Then thinner lines were painted on top to look like hair.

Using different colors Six different colors were used on this little bird. Can you see which they are? See how well the blue shadow on the chest works.

Mixing paint and pastel The only paint on this horse is the light brown wash on its head. The rest was finished with black and brown pastel.

Using different shades of the same color This dog was first painted in brown and an orangey-pink. A darker brown was painted under the stomach and on the neck and head. Thin white lines were added for highlights.

Making fur realistic Notice the different colors on this rat: the head is yellower than the body. See how the artist has painted brush lines for the hair.

Mixing washes These two hamsters were painted in an orangey-brown wash. A darker wash was then added for shadow, and the hair and eyes drawn with lead pencil.

Mixing paint and colored pencil This lizard is a mixture of paint and colored pencil. The green stripes and spots were painted first; then the picture was finished with colored pencil.

Painting quickly The colors on this butterfly were painted quickly so that they blended softly together while the paint was still wet.

Cats

Cats can bend and stretch their bodies into all sorts of interesting shapes, so they are wonderful animals to draw or paint.

Although there aren't as many types of cat as there are dogs, cats do vary in shape. There are roughly three kinds of shape. Some cats are long and thin, with pointed faces, big ears, and long, elegant legs. Others have such long fur that they look like big, round balls of fluff, although underneath all that fur, their bodies are quite skinny. Somewhere in between these two is the shape that most ordinary cats have – a fairly round body with a head and legs that aren't too long. Is this the shape of your cat?

long, curved body

stretched up at back, tail curled forward

wide body, short legs

Look at all these different silhouettes of cats. Notice how the length of a cat's fur affects its shape. Which of these silhouettes looks most like your cat? Choose that one to copy, starting by drawing the inner shapes first (see page 24).

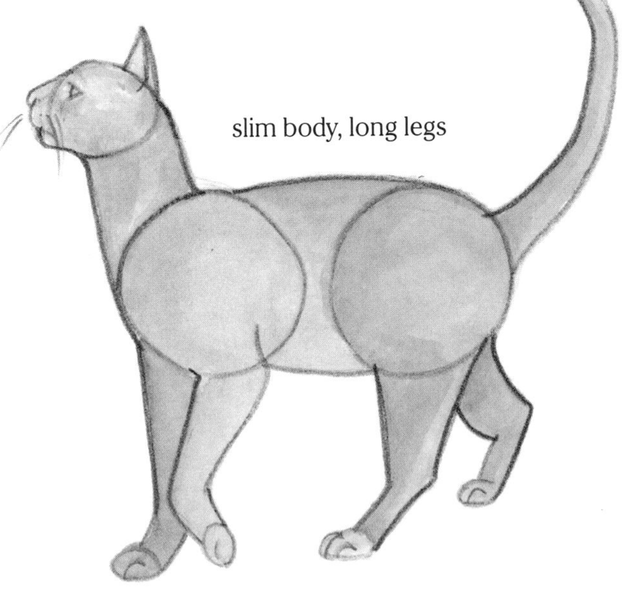

slim body, long legs

arched back, head lowered

triangle-shaped seated cat

oval shape, legs folded
under, big ears
wide back, tail
stretched out
short legs, wide body and
tail, small ears
narrow body, big ears
long legs, tail tucked in
long, lean body,
pointed head
square head, wide
body, short legs
high at front sloping
down to tail
big ears, narrow head,
long legs

Close-up on cats

How would you start to draw a cat's head? Would you draw a circle for the face and two triangles for the ears? That would probably be fine for most cats, but have you ever compared the shape of different cats' heads? Just as different kinds of cat have different-shaped bodies, so they have different-shaped heads.

Long, thin cats tend to have long, narrow, pointed faces, with big, pointed ears. Very fluffy cats have round, flat faces with what appear to be very small ears because their ears are hidden by their long fur. Most cats' heads are a mixture of these two types. Look at the pictures below to see the difference.

To draw a cat's face, begin as you would for its body: draw the inner shapes first, then draw the outline around them.

Types of head

A fluffy Persian type.
Round, flat face, small ears.

A smooth Siamese.
Narrow, pointed face, big ears.

An ordinary ginger tomcat.
Round face, medium-sized ears.

1

Cats' heads are easy. Start with two circles, then add triangles for the ears and a little triangle for the nose.

2

Draw circles for the eyes and below the nostrils, and add a line inside the ears to show the fold in the ear.

3

Draw another circle for the pupil of the eye (the black part). Make some dots for the whisker ends.

4

Draw the whiskers and sketch in a few hairs around the nose and ears. Shade in the drawing.

Cats' eyes

The pupil in a cat's eye changes depending on how much light there is. If it is bright and sunny, the pupil will be just a narrow slit, like this.

If it is dark, the pupil will be large and round, with just a sliver of the iris (the colored part) showing.

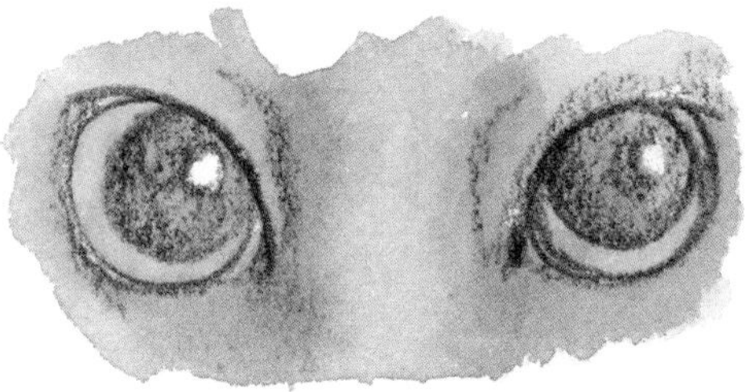

Patch says . . .
Don't forget to add a flash of white for the "glint" in a cat's eye!

Tails

Cats' tails are easy to draw – just start with a line . . .

. . . up in the air

. . . stretched out on the floor

. . . curled around the cat's body

Paws

Cats have five toes on their paws but they are not easy to see because they are covered with fur.

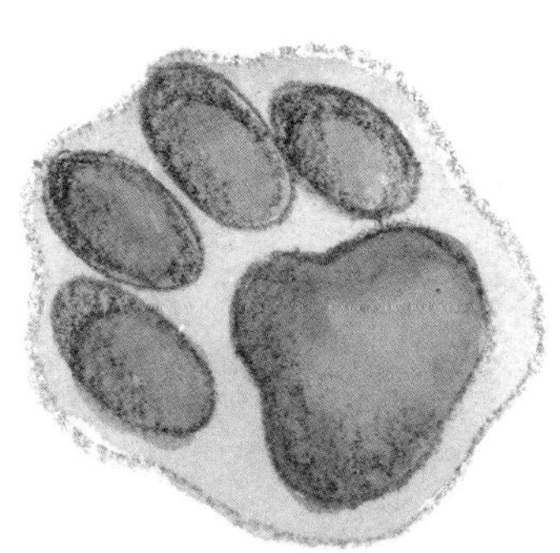

You can see the toes most clearly from underneath.

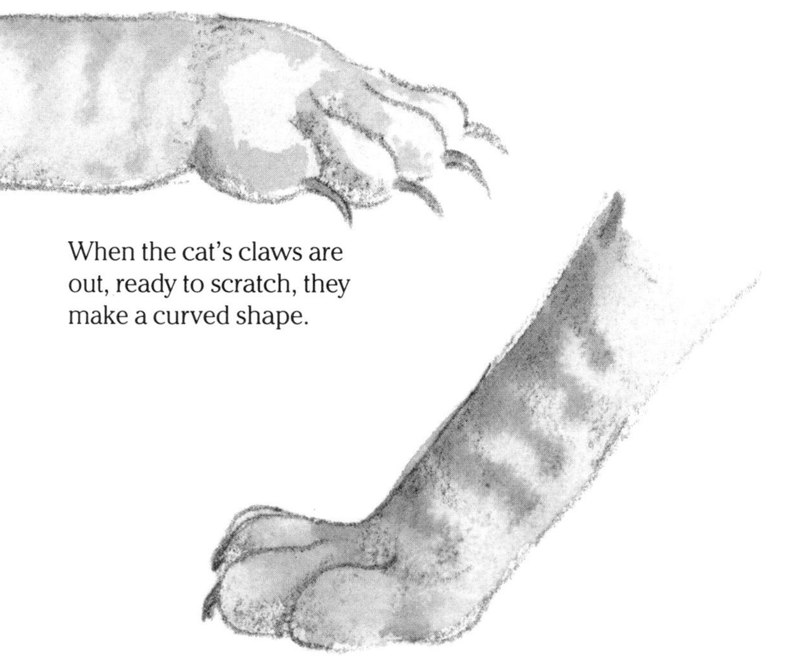

When the cat's claws are out, ready to scratch, they make a curved shape.

Midnight cat

Here is a really dramatic way to do a "night-time" picture of your pet, using just wax crayons and black ink.

When drawing and coloring in with the wax crayons, don't be tempted to use them too much. The finished picture should contain more black areas than color. After all, it is supposed to be nighttime, and the only thing that should really stand out is your pet! In the picture of the "midnight cat" opposite, the less important details such as the houses in the background are shown with just a simple crayon outline. The only details that have been heavily colored in, to make them stand out, are the moon and the cat's eyes. Too much color would have made a much less dramatic picture.

A wax crayon cat Draw and color your pet in wax crayons, using different marks for different parts. Lots of short lines could show fur, for example.

You will need
- a sheet of white paper
- wax crayons
- black writing ink (not waterproof)
- soft paintbrush

Brush ink right over your picture. The ink will not stick to the greasy crayon, so the picture shows through.

3

The finished picture looks completely different once you've added the black ink – it's really quite spooky now! You can see from this picture of the midnight cat that paler colors stand out much more than darker ones. It's worth remembering this when you want to make special effects or to make certain parts of your pet's body stand out more than others.

This turtle has been done using watercolor paint instead of ink. The turtle and grass were drawn in, and white wax crayon was used for the clouds. Blue watercolor paint was then brushed over the whole picture. Watercolor paint is best used quite watery on wax drawings, because if it is too thick it will cover the wax crayon.

Dogs

Dogs come in many different sizes, colors, and shapes. When you start a picture of your dog, the first thing you must do is get the overall shape right; adding eyes, ears, nose, and tail can come later.

On pages 24 to 27, you saw how it helps to divide an animal's body into several simple shapes, such as circles and ovals. Look carefully at your dog and you will probably notice some triangles and rectangles as well as round shapes. For example, a long, thin dog with a body that gets narrower toward the back is similar to a triangle, and a wide, stocky body is shaped very much like a rectangle. Does your dog's back slope down toward the back legs, or is it straight? Are the legs long or short, and have you ever noticed how the back legs are shaped differently from the front legs?

Noticing all these small differences is important because these are what give each kind of dog its own special look.

When you think you have got the overall shape right, turn to the next page to see how to draw details like the eyes and ears.

Here are some silhouettes of different dogs. Do you see how the length of a dog's coat can affect its shape? Some small dogs with really long coats look as if they have no legs at all! Copy the silhouette that looks most like your own dog.

long, low
rectangle shape
muscular body, square jaw
pointed tail,
square face
legs almost hidden
by coat
big head, huge ears
very long legs
long,
floppy
ears
straight line
from head
to tail
short legs, fleshy neck
rounded shapes,
pompom tail
droopy face,
long tail
tapering head, stocky body
square head,
pointed tail

Close-up on dogs

Dogs come in all shapes and sizes, which makes them more difficult to draw than other animals because you cannot use the same basic shapes for all of them. But fortunately, some of the details, such as eyes and noses, are much the same for all dogs. Dogs' heads do vary, but the main difference is in the shape of the noses. There are basically two nose shapes – long and pointed, like an ice cream cone, or tube-shaped and flat at the end.

Ears also have two shapes – triangular or oval. Which of these drawings looks most like your dog?

Tip for long-haired dogs

Always use the basic shapes as your guide, even if your dog has very long hair.

Dog with tube-shaped nose Draw a circle for the head, a tube for the nose and an oval for the ear.

Put on the basic color and make the ear a little less symmetrical.

Add the details, such as nose and eyes, and do a little more shading if necessary.

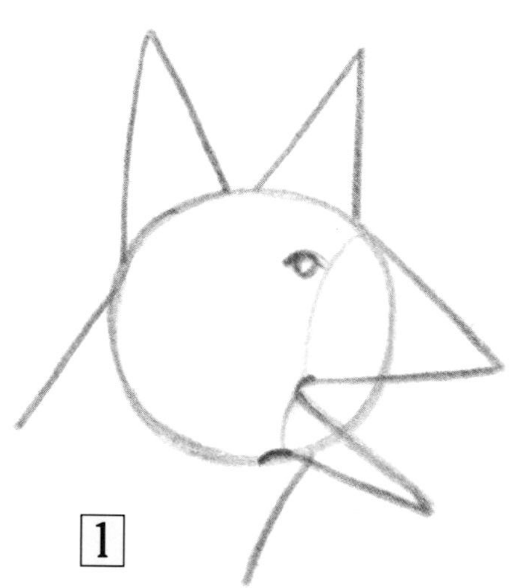

Dog with cone-shaped nose Draw a circle for the head and triangles for ears, nose, and jaw.

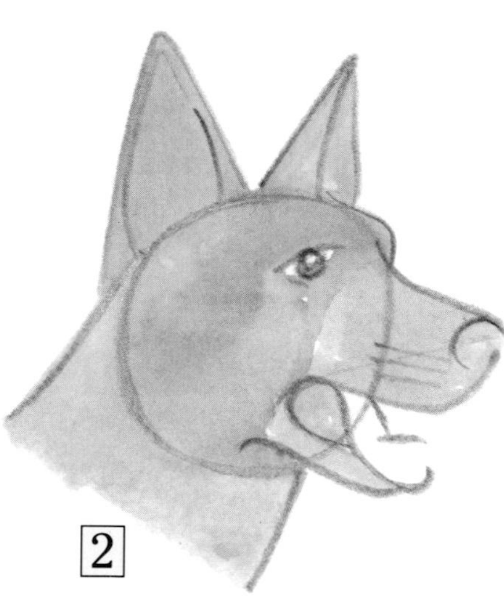

Now draw the curve from the tip of the nose into the mouth. Draw the tongue.

Color in the head. The little white speck (highlight) in the eye makes the dog look alert.

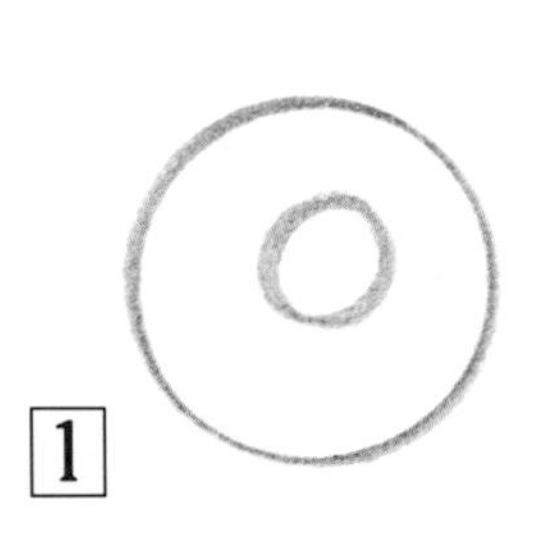

1

Eyes Dogs' eyes are easy. Just start with a circle and then put in another one if you want to have a highlight.

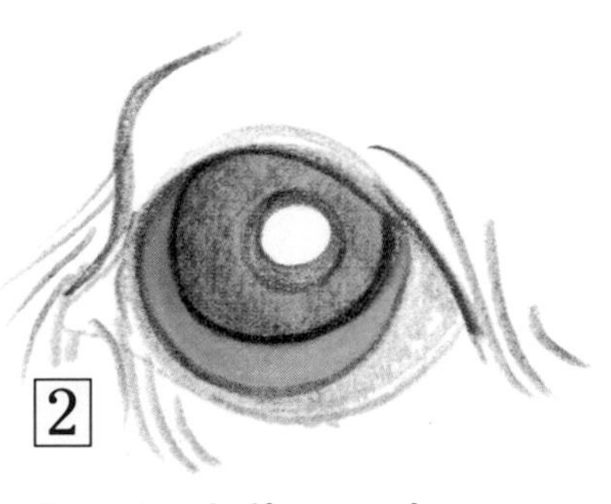

2

Color in a half-moon shape for the brown part of the eye. Use a dark color for the pupil (the black center part) and leave a white highlight.

fifth toe at side

paw print

Paws Here are some pictures of dogs' paws from different angles. Practice copying them.

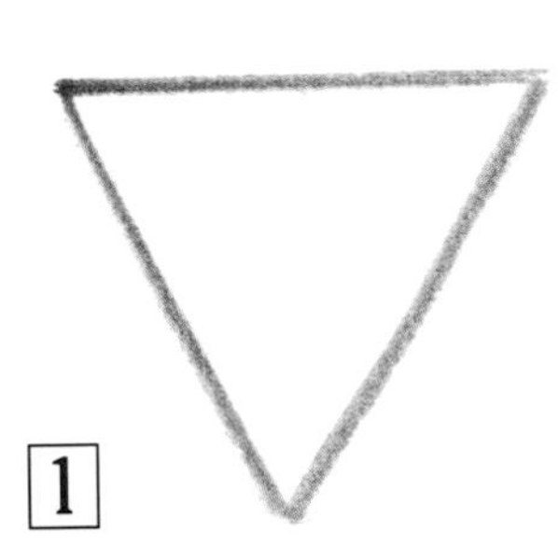

1

Noses Because the nostrils are fairly complicated shapes, noses look harder than they are. As long as you start with a triangle you will find it quite easy.

2

The curly edges of the nostrils fit neatly into the triangle. The dark insides make two shapes like commas – or polliwogs.

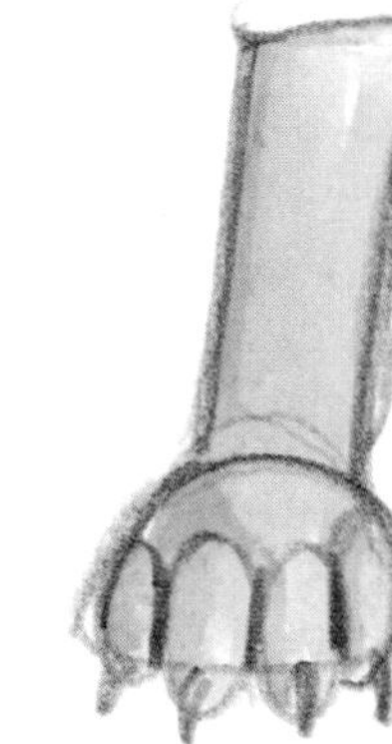

four toes

toes hidden by long hair

Tails Which of these tails looks most like your dog's?

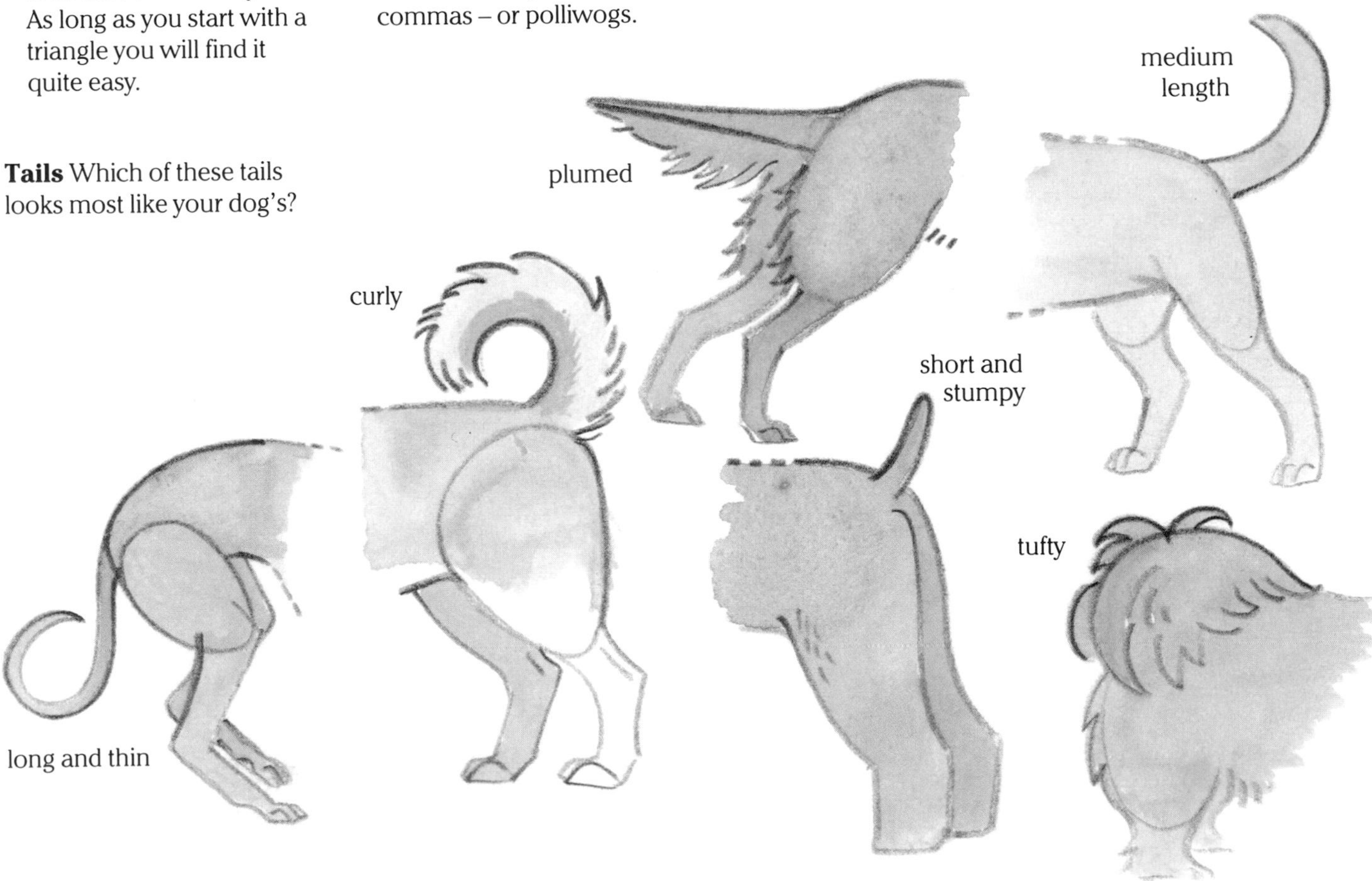

Spotty dog

Brushes are not the only tools you can use to apply paint – almost anything will do as long as it can make a paint mark on the paper. You could use your fingers, knives (not sharp ones!), forks, or combs, for example, or you could spread the paint across your picture with a piece of cardboard. Each of these tools will make a different kind of mark, and you should remember this when choosing which ones to use.

Dabbing paint on with your finger will give you blobs of color, which could be good for the spots on a dog's coat, like those on the dog in the picture opposite. Applying the paint with a cotton ball will give softer, bigger patches of color like the markings on a guinea pig.

Before you start your final picture, experiment with paint and various tools first, to see what kinds of marks you can make. What do the different marks remind you of?

Spotty finger dog Lightly draw the outline of your dog on the paper, changing any parts you don't like until the drawing is the way you want it.

Now fill in the outline with paint, using a finger, fork, comb, or whatever tool you choose. Remember to wash your finger if you change colors!

3

You will need
- thick paint (such as poster paint)
- tools to apply paint
- paper
- pencil
- eraser

Your pet's portrait is finished. Doesn't he look proud and spotty!

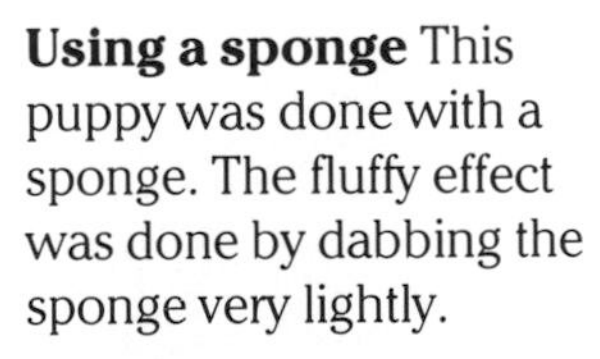

Using a sponge This puppy was done with a sponge. The fluffy effect was done by dabbing the sponge very lightly.

Using a flexible knife This cheerful spotted dog was done with paint on the end of a bendy knife. The spots were added with fingertips.

Using cotton swabs This thoughtful dog was done with cotton swabs (often used for eye makeup). Because they are so small, you can dab paint exactly where you want it.

Hamsters, rabbits, and gerbils

Do you have a rabbit or a hamster, or some other similar pet? If you do, you have probably noticed how your pet looks like a small, round cushion when it is sitting down, with its legs and feet tucked up neatly by its side. But have you seen how much its shape changes when it is doing other things? When a rabbit is sitting up on its hind legs, for example, it becomes longer and flatter. Hamsters and mice can make themselves much longer and thinner so that they can squeeze through small spaces.

Practice drawing the different shapes these animals make, with details like eyes, nose, and feet.

Feet

Draw the basic shapes of the foot, then add the toes. Always check that you are drawing the right number of toes.

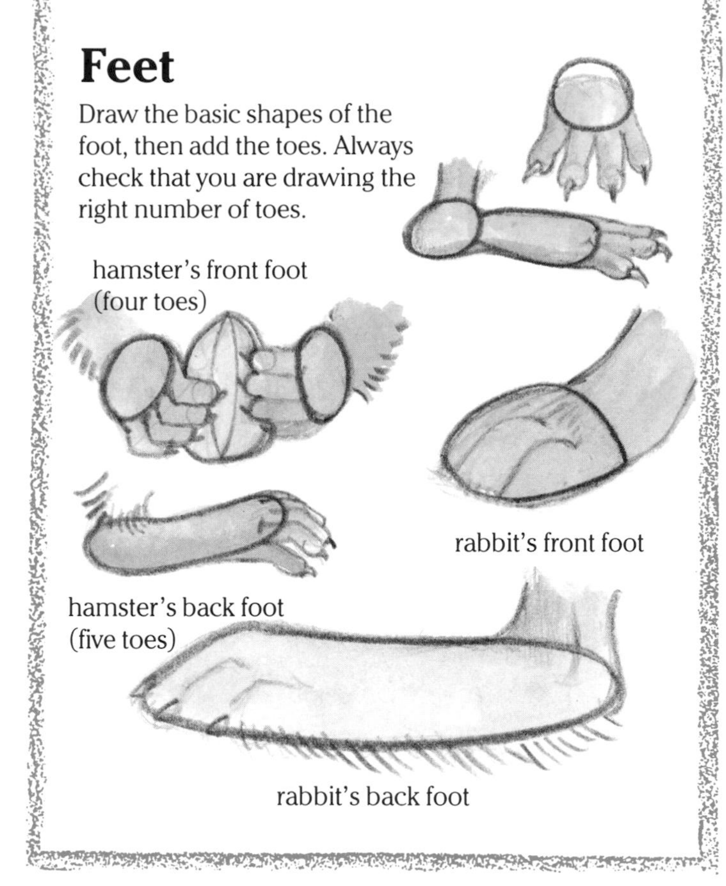

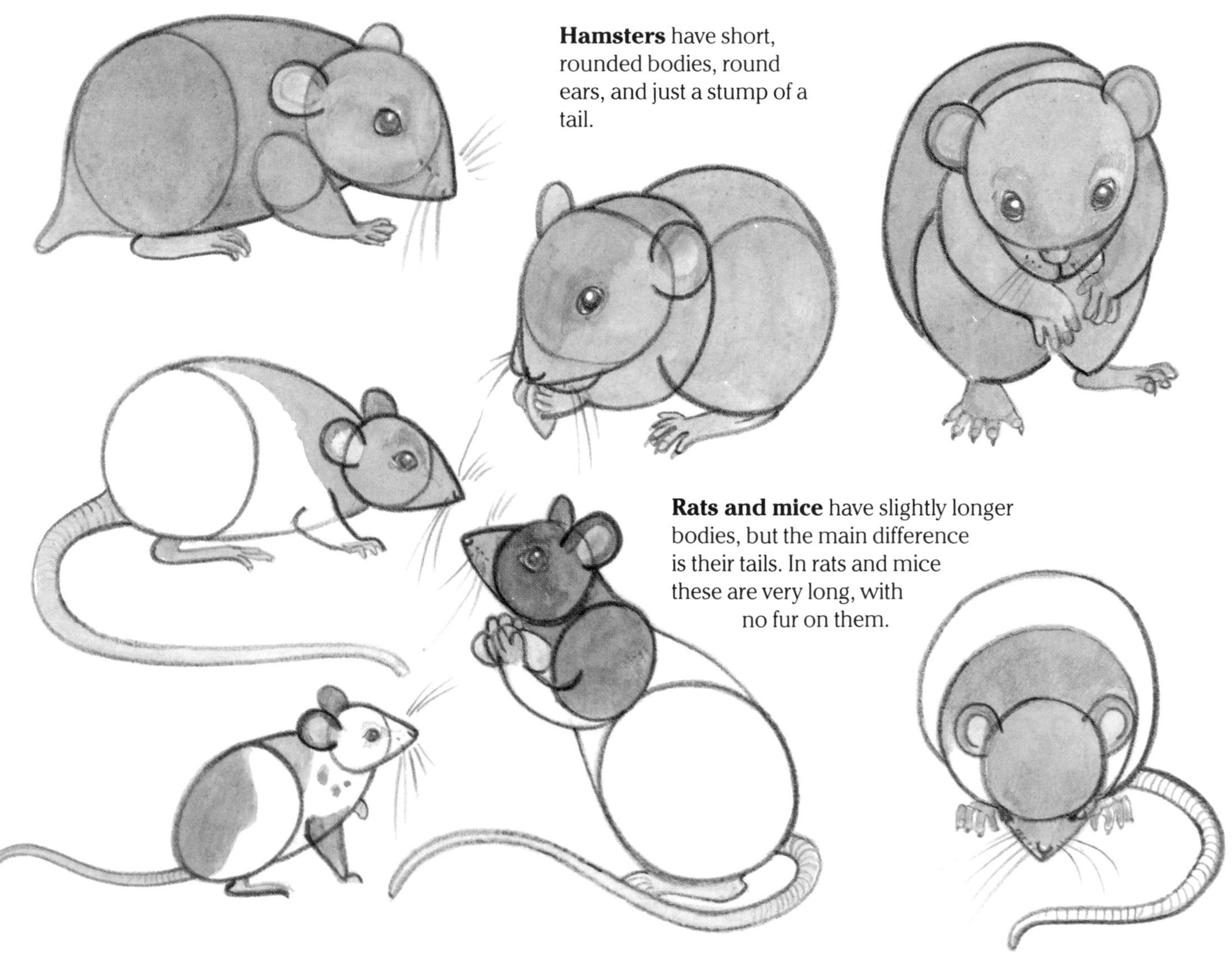

Hamsters have short, rounded bodies, round ears, and just a stump of a tail.

Rats and mice have slightly longer bodies, but the main difference is their tails. In rats and mice these are very long, with no fur on them.

Rabbits have long bodies, which you can see best when they are moving or sitting up. Their ears are long too, and when seen from the side, their heads make an oval shape.

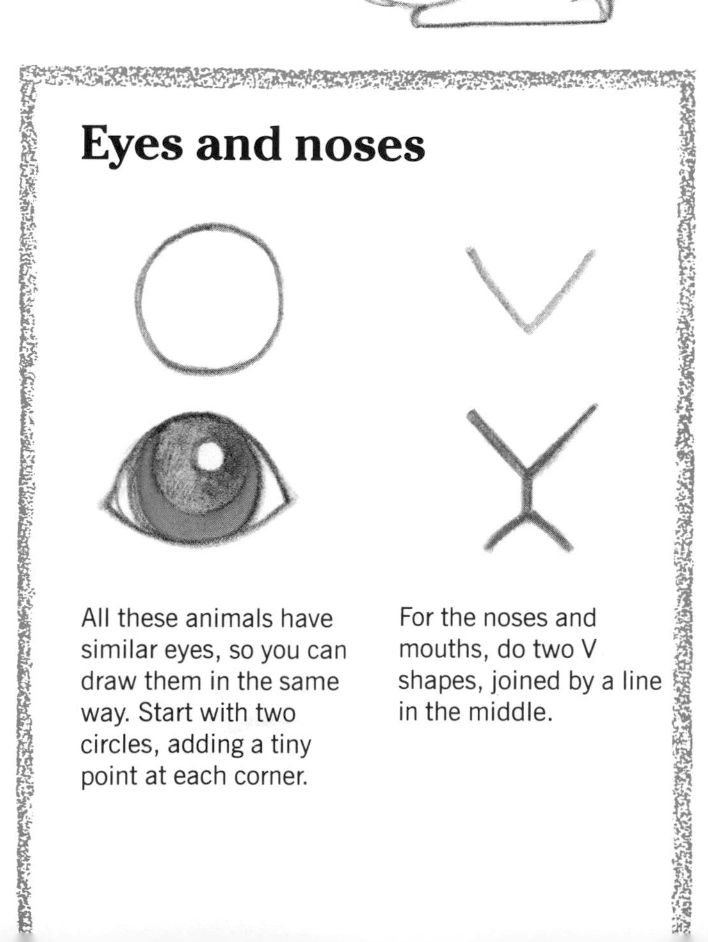

Eyes and noses

All these animals have similar eyes, so you can draw them in the same way. Start with two circles, adding a tiny point at each corner.

For the noses and mouths, do two V shapes, joined by a line in the middle.

Guinea pigs have short bodies and very large heads. They come in a variety of colors, and some have long hair.

Monoprints

Monoprints are exciting because you never know exactly how your finished picture will turn out! A monoprint is like a "backwards" painting. In a painting, you add paint to the paper to make a picture. In a monoprint, you scrape paint away, and instead of working directly on paper, you first make a picture on a metal tray.

You can think of the paint you scrape away on a monoprint in the same way as lines you would add with a brush to an ordinary painting. The green print here was made in this way by scraping an outline in paint on the back of a kitchen tray. But you can get interesting effects if you use scraped lines as highlights, and the paint that's left as shadows.

Try different scrapers for interesting effects. An old toothbrush (not the one you use to clean your teeth!) can make feathery marks and a toothpick or used matchstick is good for details. Use a piece of cardboard to scrape large areas. Try different paper colors also.

Before you do your final print, try some small prints on the corner of the tray until you get the paint thickness right – too much paint will make blobs and spoil your picture.

You will need

- an old metal tea tray or flat baking sheet
- PVA paint mixed with a few drops of dishwashing detergent to slow drying
- a large paintbrush
- paper
- cloth
- different scrapers (such as toothpicks, *used* matchsticks, or pieces of cardboard)

1

A monoprint. Make sure the back of your tray is clean (wash and dry it if it isn't), then paint all over it – the paint washes off easily after printing.

2

Scrape the outlines of your picture using different scrapers for different parts to give your monoprint lots of interesting textures.

When you're ready, lay the paper carefully on the tray and *very* gently rub all over it with a cloth. Don't let the paper move or you may smudge the lines on your picture.

Carefully lift up a little of each corner to see if the print is ready. If it's not dark enough, rub over the paper a little more. Then peel the paper off.

Birds

Birds cannot bend and stretch and change their shape in the way cats do, and there are only a few kinds of pet bird – unlike dogs that come in so many different varieties. But this does not mean that they aren't worth drawing or painting – what makes birds really interesting is their beautiful colors.

Because birds have fairly simple shapes, they are one of the easiest pets to draw. All you need to do is a circle for the head, an oval for the body, and a long, pointed tail. You can use these same basic shapes whether you are looking at your bird from the front or from the side.

The only time you can see a bird's wings properly is when it is flying. At other times, it keeps them neatly folded back by its sides.

The most popular pet birds are budgerigars, but some people have larger birds such as parakeets or cockatoos.

Bird shapes Budgerigars can be yellow, green, blue, or gray, or a mixture of these colors. Canaries are smaller, and a lovely yellow all over. Parrots are similar in shape to budgies, but they are much bigger and their colors are brighter. Cockatoos have a wonderful crest of feathers on top of their heads. Finches are smaller than any of the others, and the zebra finch has a jaunty patch of red on its face.

Legs and Feet

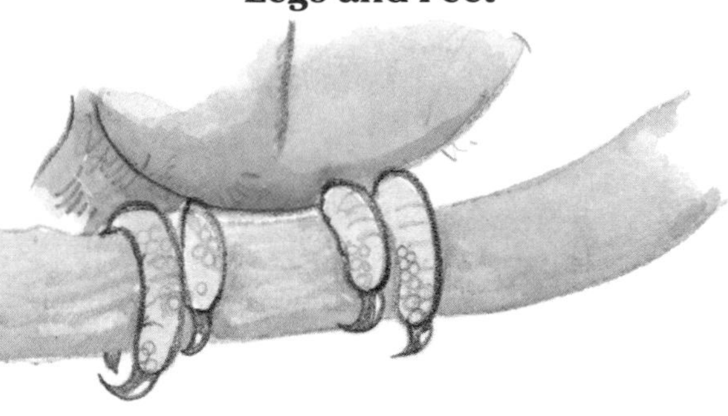

When a bird sits on its perch, it tucks its legs under its body, and curls its claws around the perch to hold on.

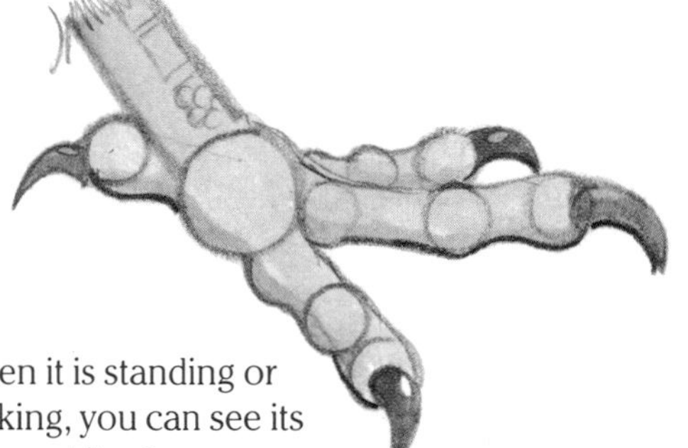

When it is standing or walking, you can see its legs, and its claws are stretched out flat.

Notice how the legs join on to either side of the body.

Beaks and Eyes

The beaks of budgies, parakeets, and cockatoos are shaped like short triangles. Notice how the top is rounded, and how the end curls over.

Birds' eyes are dark and round, and placed on either side of the head.

The beaks of other pet birds such as canaries or finches come to a straight point at the end.

Feathers

The feathers on the chest and head are short. The feathers on the wings and tail are longer.

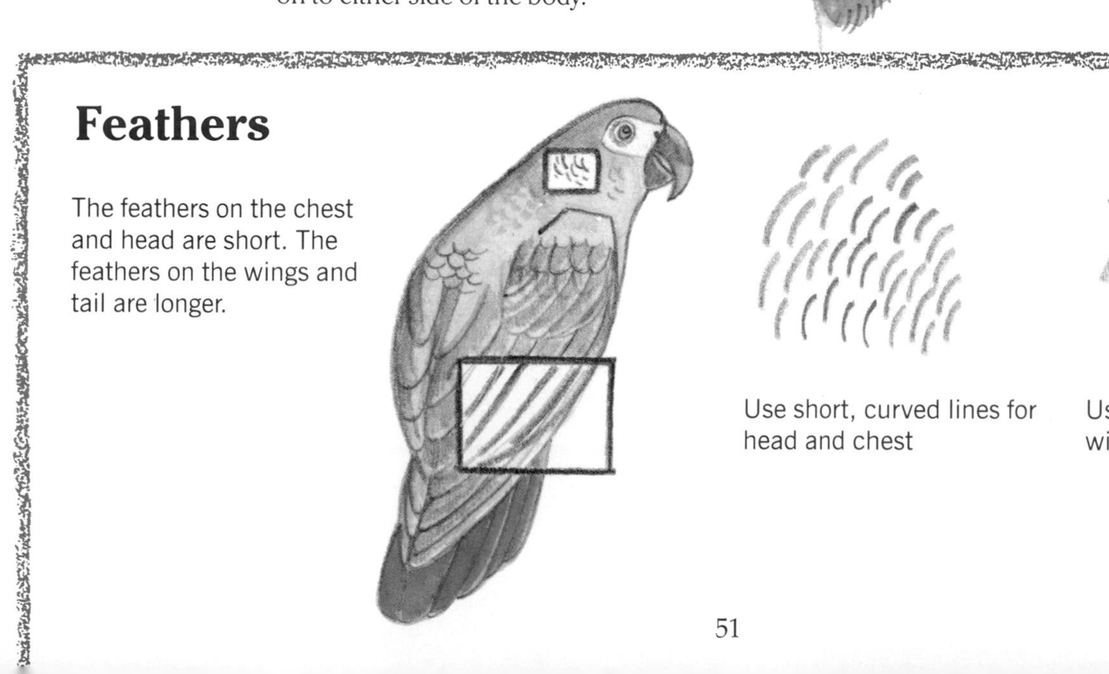

Use short, curved lines for head and chest

Use long, straight lines for wings and tail

Paper collage

A collage is a picture made up of pieces of paper, fabric, or other small objects – such as string, beads, dried peas, or corn – all glued onto background paper or cardboard.

If you are making a paper collage, you can use any paper you like: plain-colored paper, patterned wrapping paper, wallpaper, shiny silver or gold candy wrappers, white or colored tissue paper, newspaper, corrugated cardboard, or things made from paper, like straws.

It doesn't matter if the pieces of paper are small, or old and crumpled: just smooth them out and you can still use them. Why not save any pieces of paper you particularly like and build up a collection of scraps especially for your collages?

The paper can be cut into shapes, or you can tear it. Move the pieces around on the background sheet until they look just right, changing any pieces you don't like before you finally stick them down. You can paste the pieces alongside each other, like fitting a jigsaw puzzle together, or you can overlap them.

Lindsey made this parrot collage from paper she colored with crayons. She cut the paper into thin strips and curved each piece by rolling it tightly round a pencil. Finally, she carefully arranged and glued the curved strips in the shape of a parrot.

You will need
- background paper or cardboard
- scraps to paste
- glue
- scissors
- pencil
- eraser

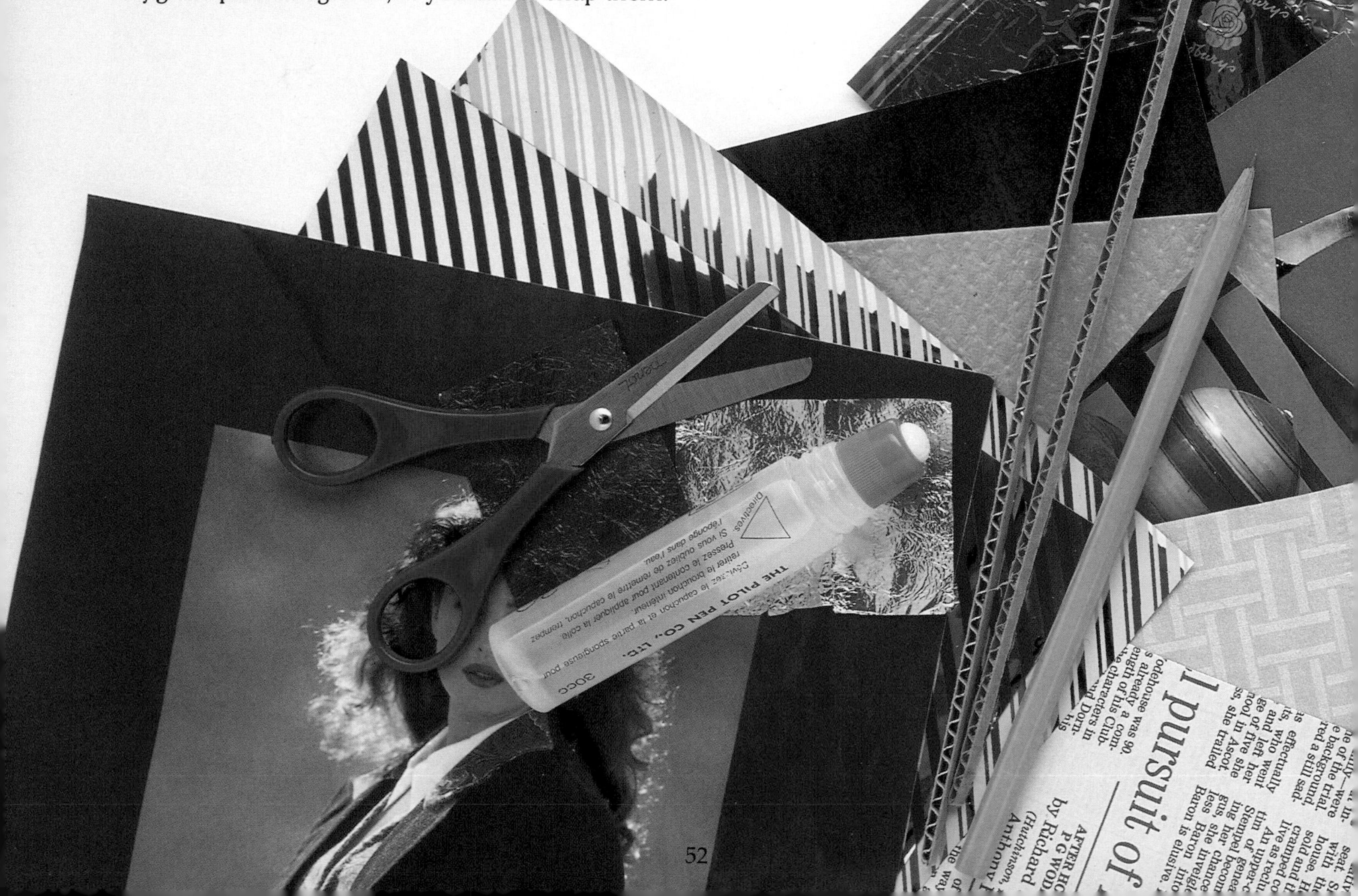

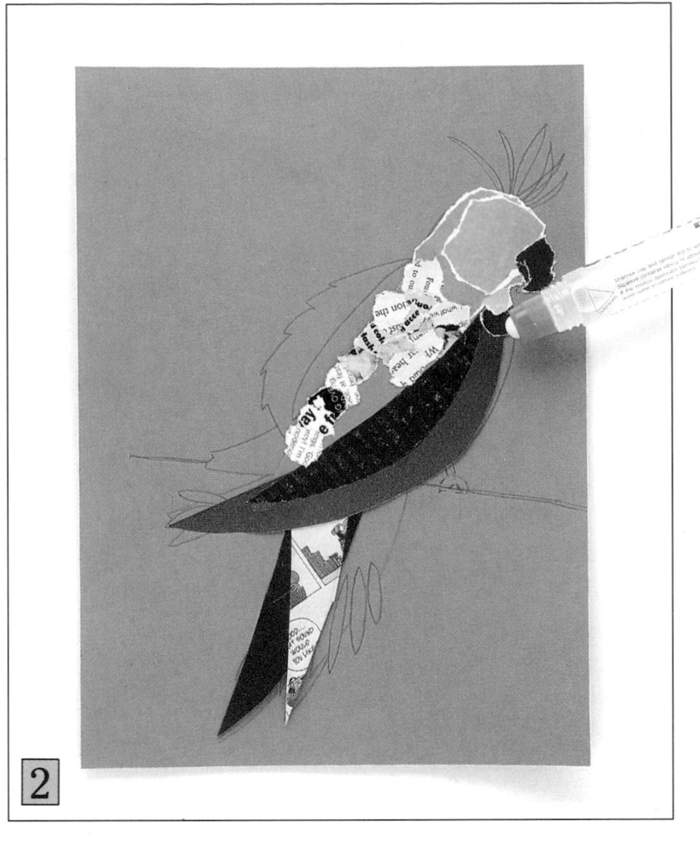

Paper parrot Draw your pet's outline on background paper. Cut or tear paper into shapes for different parts. For example, circles and strips make this wing.

Glue down the pieces. To overlap shapes, do the bottom layers first. For example, the long feathers here were stuck first and the small ones added later.

As well as using different paper colors and textures, try using transparent colored paper – its color will mix with what shows below to make new colors.

A few leaves will finish your collage and give it a jungle feel. Mount backing paper on cardboard.

Fish

It's fascinating to watch fish swimming about in the underwater world of their tank, darting backward and forward, their tails gently waving in the water.

Fish, like birds, have quite simple shapes that make them easy to draw. All you need to do is one shape for the body, and then add the fins and the tail, and other details like the eyes and mouth.

Goldfish are the commonest pet fish – of course, they aren't really golden, they are a kind of orange color. There are other kinds of pet fish, too, such as tropical fish. Some of these have very beautiful colors and may be striped or spotted. Look carefully to get the colors right. At first glance, you may think that your fish is all one color, but if you look more closely, you may notice delicate changes – some parts may be lighter or darker, or perhaps a little more yellow or silver.

Tips for showing scales

Fish are covered with little scales. Can you think how to show these? Perhaps you could do lots of little curved lines, or zigzag lines going across the body. Stop when you get to the head – the head should look quite smooth. For fin and tail bones, you could do straight lines, fanning out toward the edge.

Fish shapes Fish come in lots of different shapes and sizes. Some have long, torpedo-shaped bodies and small fins; others have almost circular bodies and triangular fins. Notice how different a fish's shape is when you see it from the front.

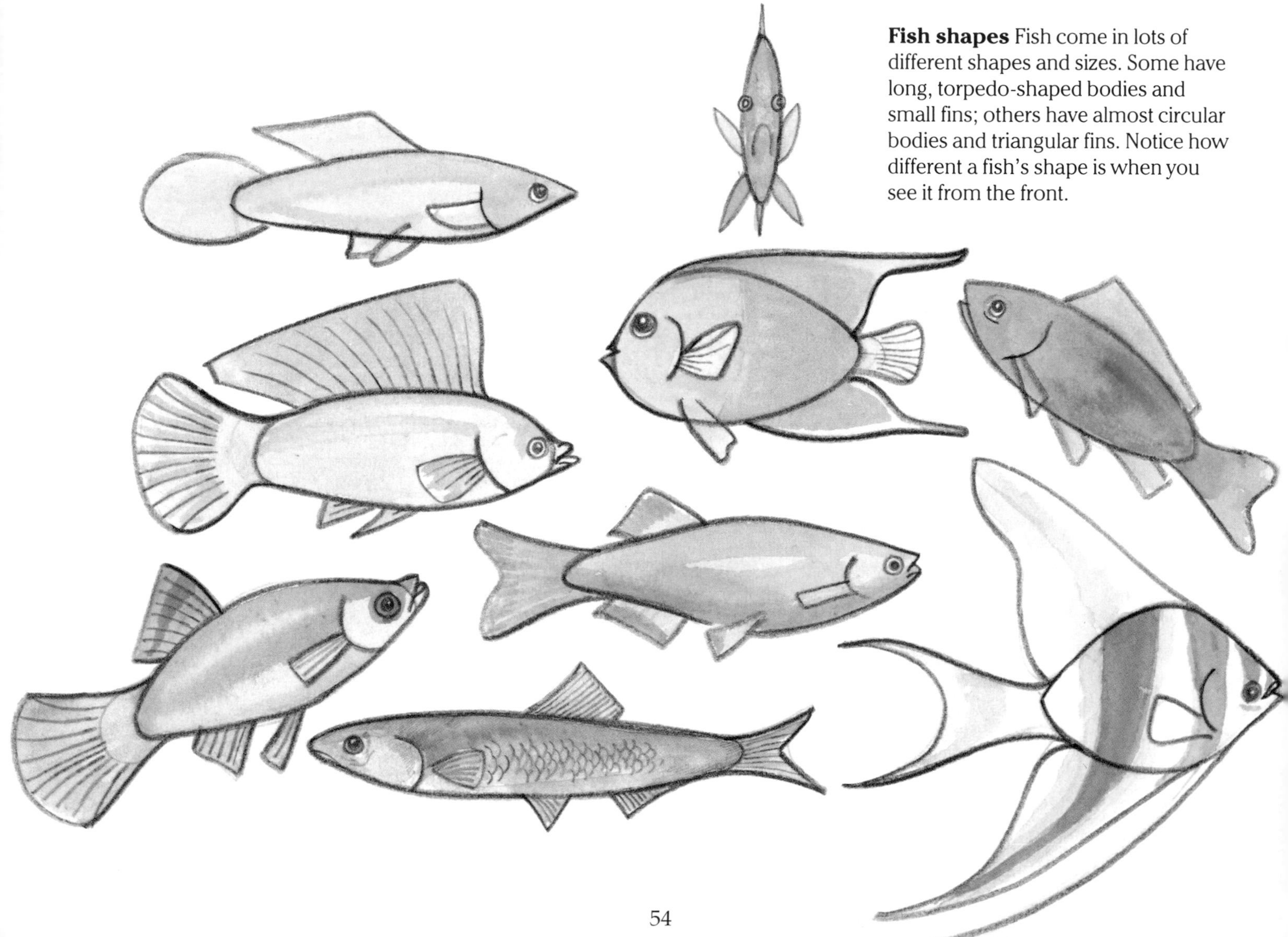

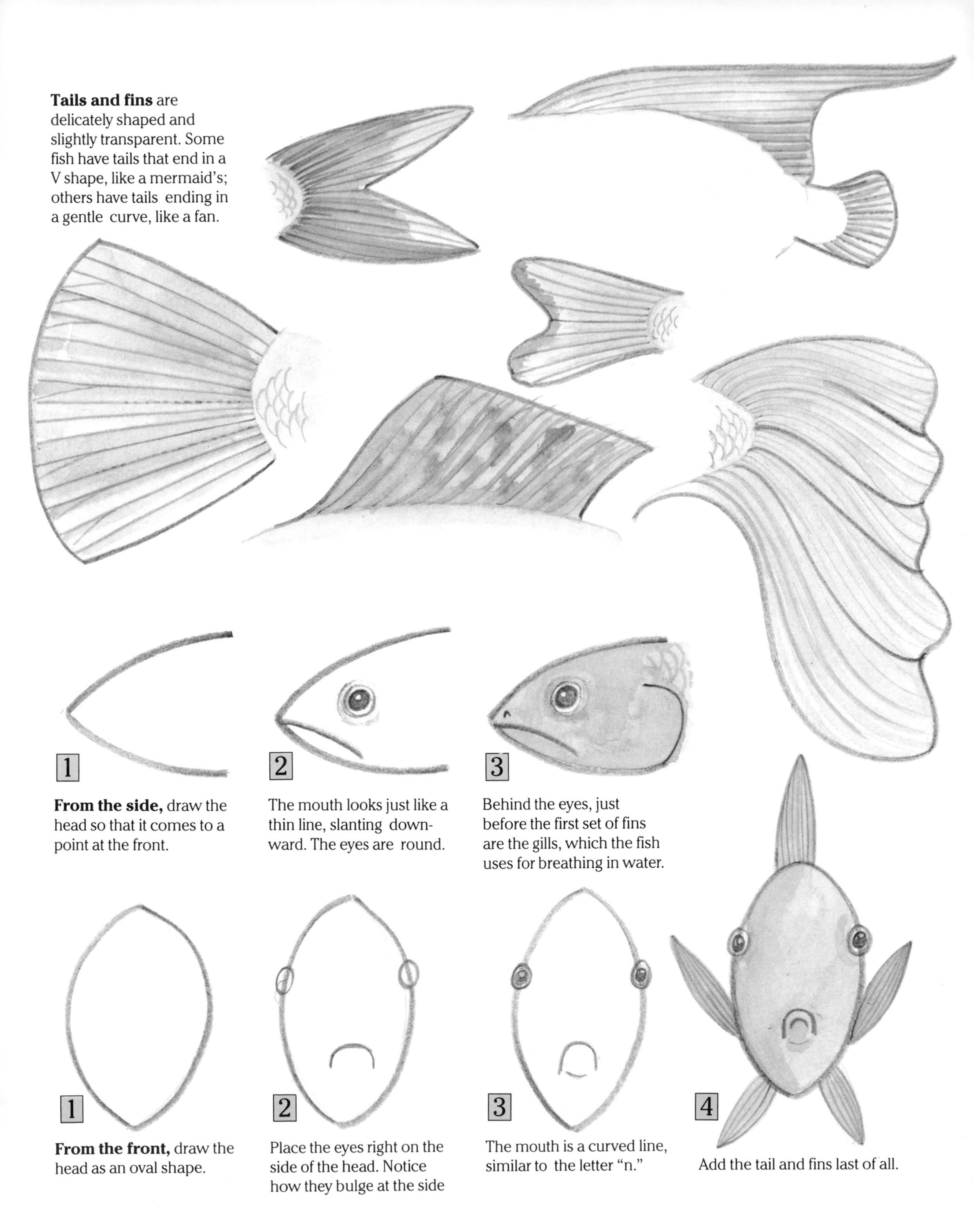

Tails and fins are delicately shaped and slightly transparent. Some fish have tails that end in a V shape, like a mermaid's; others have tails ending in a gentle curve, like a fan.

1 **From the side,** draw the head so that it comes to a point at the front.

2 The mouth looks just like a thin line, slanting downward. The eyes are round.

3 Behind the eyes, just before the first set of fins are the gills, which the fish uses for breathing in water.

1 **From the front,** draw the head as an oval shape.

2 Place the eyes right on the side of the head. Notice how they bulge at the side

3 The mouth is a curved line, similar to the letter "n."

4 Add the tail and fins last of all.

Wash-off pictures

Wash-off pictures are fun because you don't know exactly how a finished picture will look. To do one, paint your shapes on cardboard, using paint you mix with water. When the paint is dry, cover the cardboard with waterproof ink. When the ink's dry, wash away the painted shapes, leaving pale silhouettes (the paint stains the cardboard so some color stays). The waterproof ink does not wash off.

You can do just one animal, but wash-off pictures look best if you do lots of the same kind of pet, such as dogs or a tankful of fish, for example.

When you choose colors, think how they will look next to each other in the finished picture.

You will need
- a piece of cardboard
- pencil
- eraser
- thick water-based paint (poster color is ideal)
- waterproof ink
- paintbrush

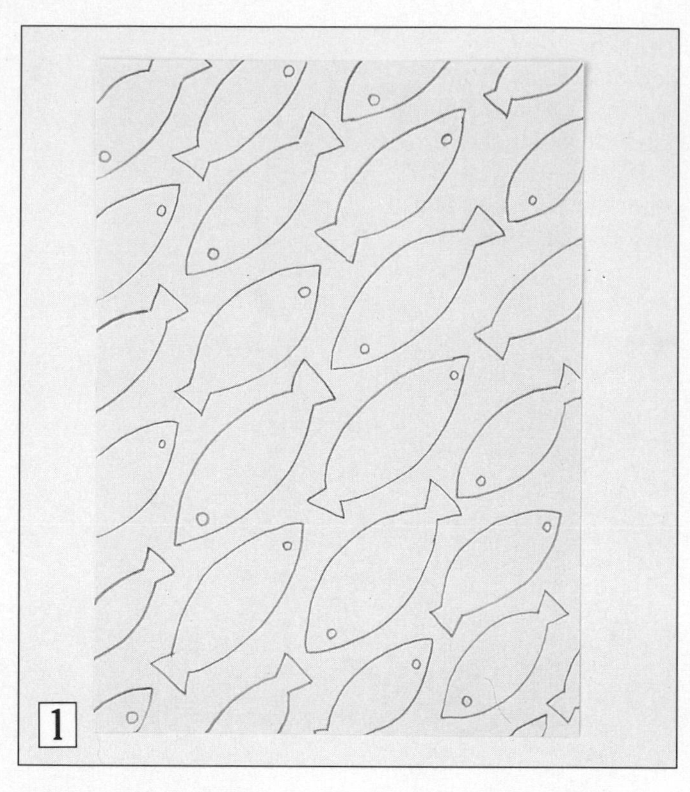

1

A shoal of fish Draw your animal shapes on the cardboard, rubbing out to correct if necessary. It's best to keep the shapes very simple, so don't add lots of detail. Repeated shapes will look very effective.

2

Fill in the shapes with the thick paint. You could leave "holes" for the eyes or other details, such as the spots on a spotty dog – the ink you use next will fill in the holes. Let the paint dry completely.

When you're sure the paint is dry, brush all over the cardboard with waterproof ink – if you do this before the paint is dry, the ink will mix with the paint and blur the shapes and colors and spoil the picture.

As you wash off the ink, support the cardboard with both hands so that there is no danger of tearing it. As if by magic, ghostly silhouettes of the fish will start to appear.

Hold the cardboard under some warm water and gently wash off the ink. Hold the cardboard downward so that the inky water runs down into the sink and not all over you!

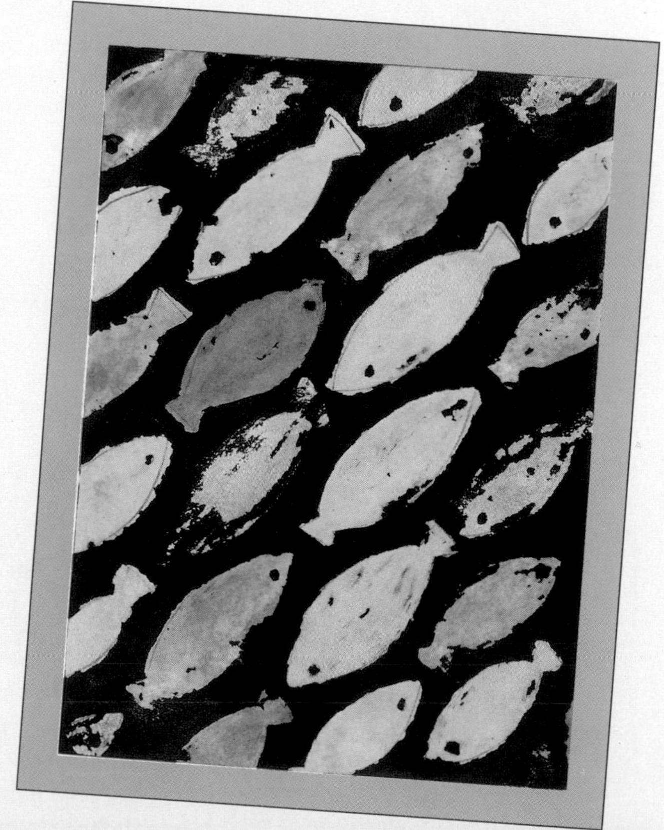

6

Don't your finished fish stand out well against the dark ink! Why not try some different ink colors?

Reptiles

Snakes are more unusual pets than cats, dogs, or rabbits, and they are not everyone's choice. They are certainly wonderful to draw and paint, since they have lovely colors and markings. They also stay still for quite long periods so that you can study them, and when they move, they make marvelous curling shapes.

Quite a lot of people keep lizards as pets, and they are fascinating to watch, darting about, and flicking their tongues in and out. They never stop moving for long, though, so if you want to draw and paint them you will have to observe them carefully.

The best of all "artist's models" are turtles, because they move so slowly that you have plenty of time to copy them! Turtles' bodies are mostly hidden away under their shells so that all you can see are their heads and legs. The shells are shaped like hemispheres – similar to an open umbrella – curling upward slightly at the edges where the head and legs come out.

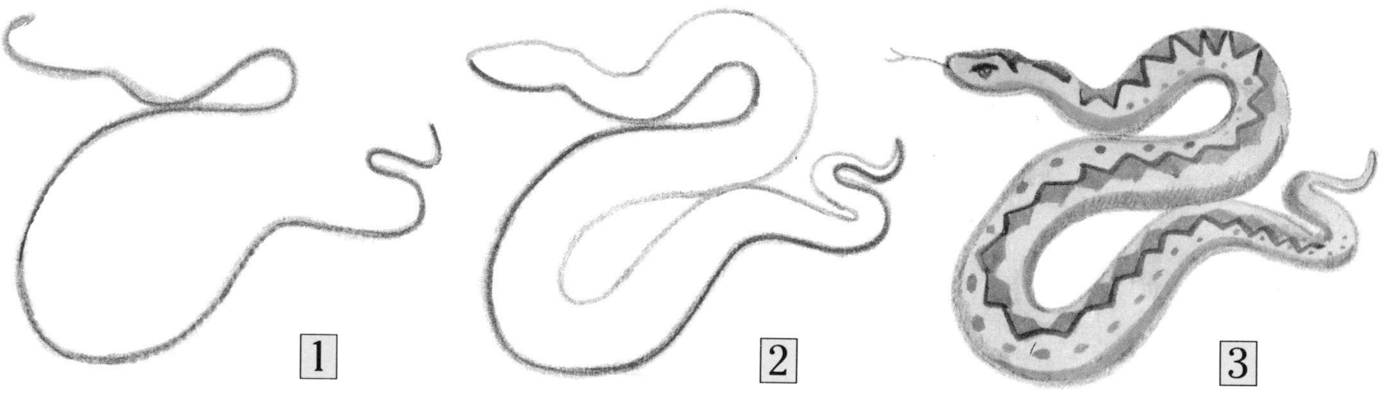

Snakes are the easiest of all pets to draw. Start with a simple line to show the shape.

Notice whether your snake's body is wider than its head. Some snakes have quite thick bodies.

Now color in the markings. You'll enjoy this, particularly if your snake is a colorful one.

Painting scales

Begin by sketching in the pattern in pencil. Notice how the scales overlap one another.

Put on a flat color all over the snake's body.

Now color in the scales in paint or crayon.

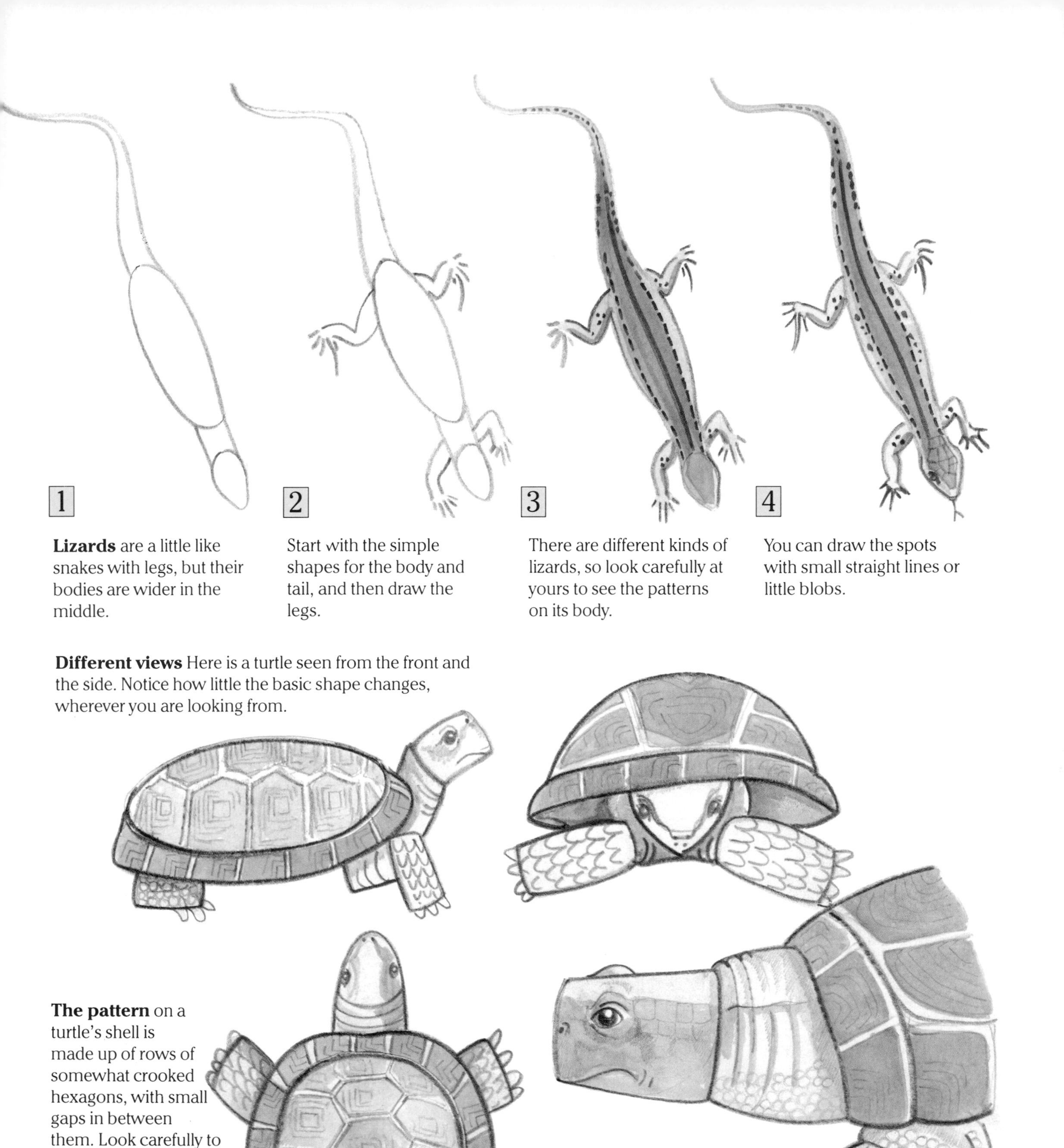

Lizards are a little like snakes with legs, but their bodies are wider in the middle.

Start with the simple shapes for the body and tail, and then draw the legs.

There are different kinds of lizards, so look carefully at yours to see the patterns on its body.

You can draw the spots with small straight lines or little blobs.

Different views Here is a turtle seen from the front and the side. Notice how little the basic shape changes, wherever you are looking from.

The pattern on a turtle's shell is made up of rows of somewhat crooked hexagons, with small gaps in between them. Look carefully to see how they make up the pattern. You could either draw the hexagons themselves or the spaces between them.

Head Have you ever noticed that your turtle's head looks similar to a snake's? In fact, turtles come from the same family of animals as snakes, and have the same kind of scaly skin on their heads and legs.

Stained-glass windows

Have you ever been inside a church on a sunny day? If you have, you probably saw some beautiful colored lights on the walls made by sunlight shining in through the stained-glass windows. You can easily make your own stained-glass picture of a favorite animal.

You'll need some thick paper or thin cardboard that light will not show through, and some see-through colored tissue or candy wrappers. It's best to use dark-colored cardboard or paper so that the tissue shows up well. Cutting holes in the cardboard or paper and sticking tissue over them will let light shine through to make your picture. If you are very careful, you can use a craft knife to cut out the holes. Besides being careful not to cut your own fingers, don't leave a sharp knife lying around where someone else might cut themselves on it! Or you can use scissors instead.

You will need

- colored tissue paper or clear colored candy wrappers
- thick colored paper or cardboard
- scissors or a craft knife
- pencil
- eraser
- glue
- tape

Using a craft knife to make a stained-glass snake Draw a snake in simple, strong lines on tracing paper. Add shapes for cut-out holes for the tissue paper. Leave wide enough strips between each hole onto which to glue the tissue.

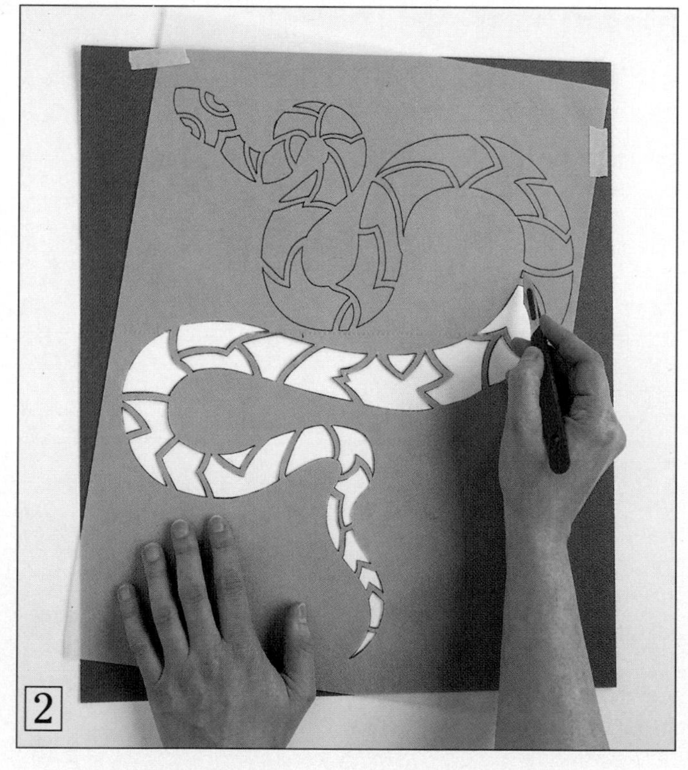

Tape the tracing paper on a piece of cardboard so it won't slip when you cut the holes. Lay the cardboard on something that doesn't matter if it gets cut – don't use the dining table! Cut out the shapes with a craft knife – *it's very sharp, so take care!*

Patch says ...
you can color plain tracing paper with felt-tip pens, crayons, or pencils instead of using tissue paper, as in the turtle and snail here.

3

4

When you have cut the holes, lay colored tissue under the cardboard and trace around the holes onto the tissue. Cut the tissue with scissors, leaving a little extra all round the pencil line for gluing. Spread a little glue round the hole and fix on the tissue.

When you finish your stained-glass picture, tape it to a window that gets lots of strong sunlight. If you like, add a nice frame to your snake, just like a real church window. (Use a ruler to draw and cut straight lines.)

Insects

Stick insects have a very clever disguise to fool other creatures that might want to eat them – they look exactly like sticks or twigs, and this is how they got their name. To make the disguise even better, they are a beautiful green color, just like the stems and leaves they live on – sometimes it's almost impossible to see them.

Other insects you might keep as "pets" for a short time are ladybugs and ants. Perhaps you have an ant or ladybug colony in a shoebox, full of soil and leaves and twigs. Although it is fascinating to watch these little creatures, it's best not to keep ants and ladybugs indoors for too long before you put them back outside.

Stick insects, ladybugs, and ants all have three pairs of legs, but their body shapes are quite different.

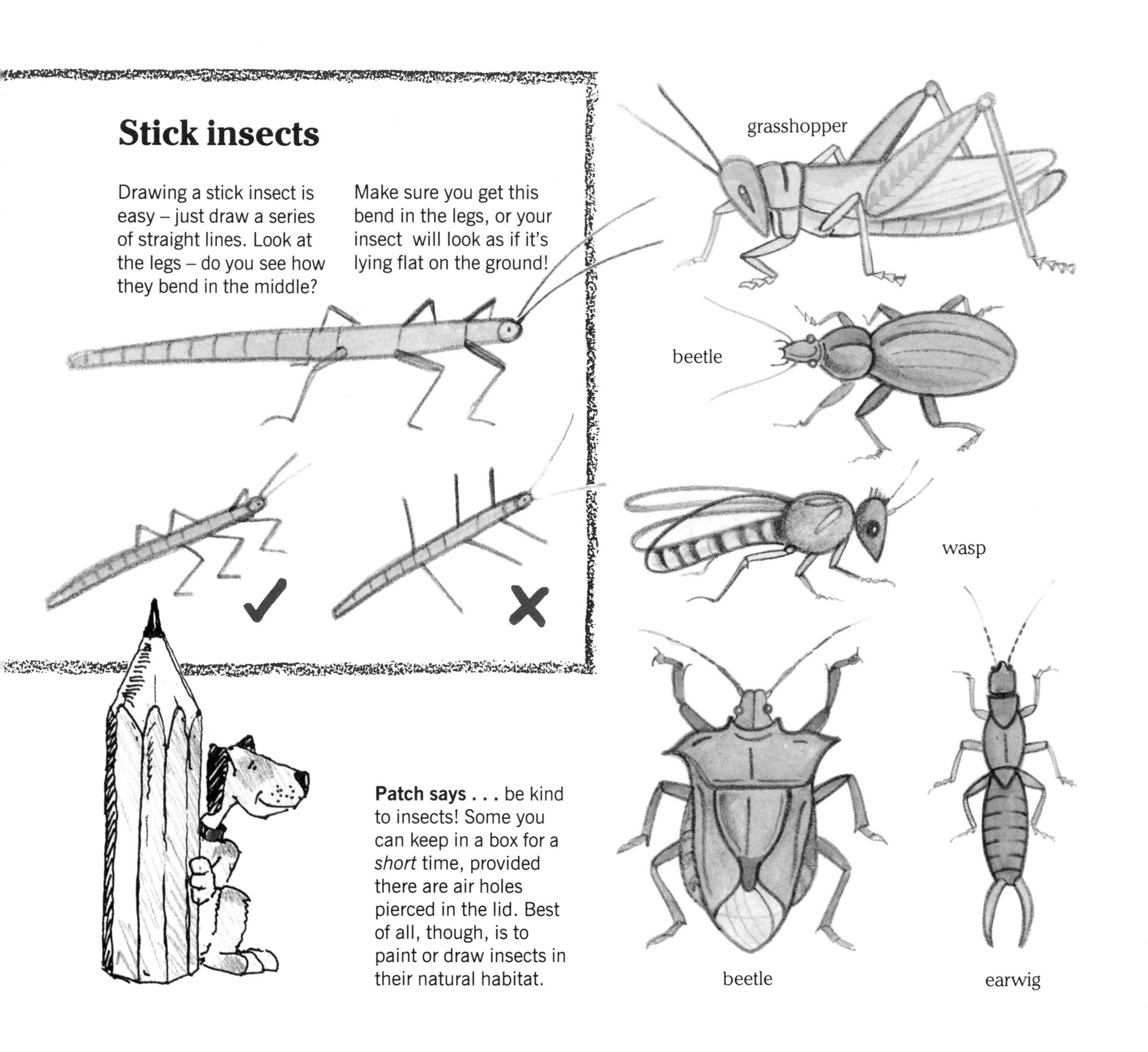

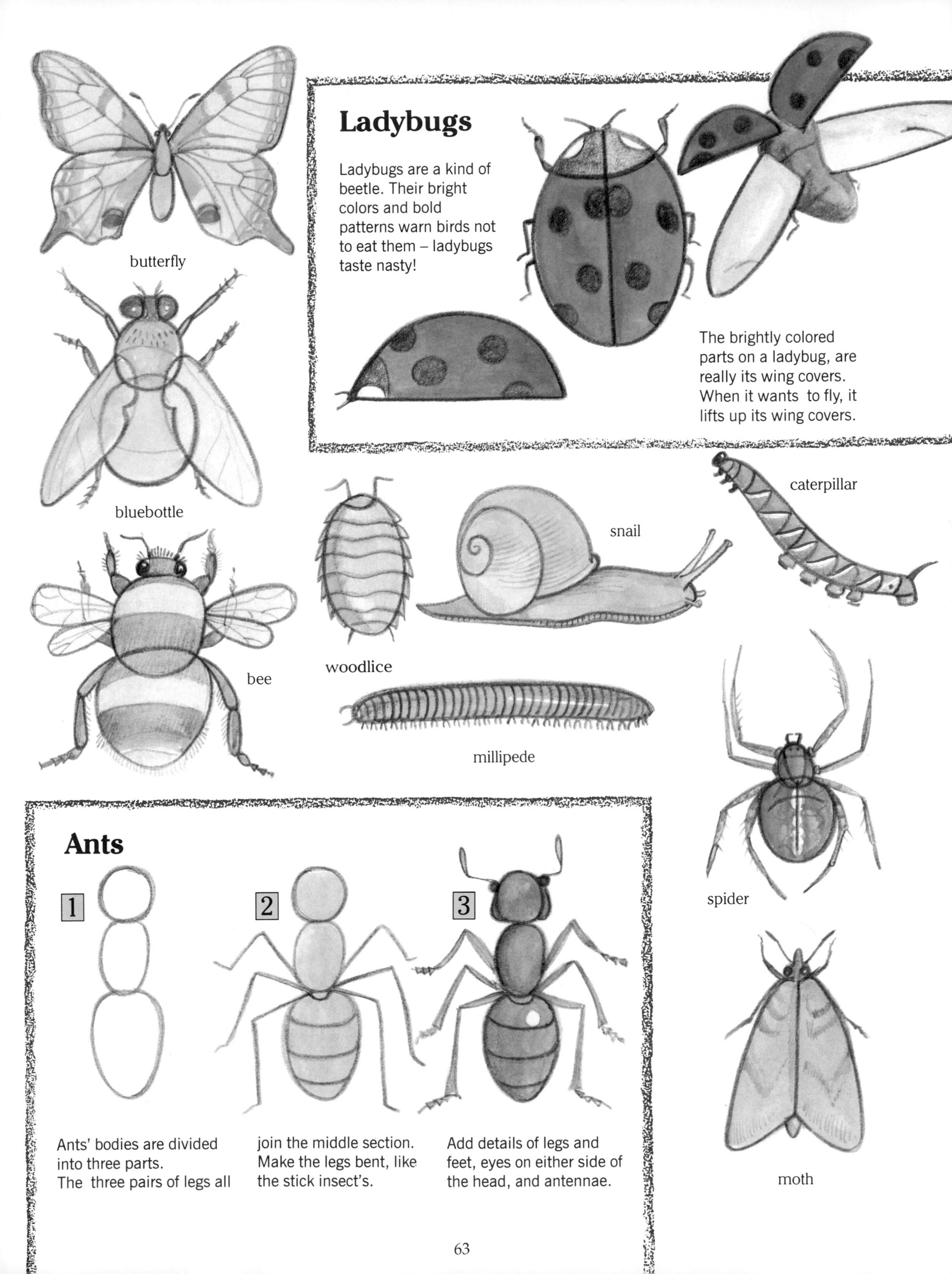

Ladybugs

Ladybugs are a kind of beetle. Their bright colors and bold patterns warn birds not to eat them – ladybugs taste nasty!

The brightly colored parts on a ladybug, are really its wing covers. When it wants to fly, it lifts up its wing covers.

Ants

Ants' bodies are divided into three parts. The three pairs of legs all join the middle section. Make the legs bent, like the stick insect's.

Add details of legs and feet, eyes on either side of the head, and antennae.

Scratch pictures

Have you ever done a scratchboard picture, where you scratch through the top layer to show the color below? You can buy scratchboards in stores, but it's much cheaper and more fun to make your own. Most bought scratchboards are white underneath, so you get white drawings on black backgrounds (there are a few other colors, too, such as bronze or silver). One of the best things about making your own scratchboards is that you can have any color you want and as many of them as you like.

It's best to use light, bright colors on the base, otherwise they won't contrast enough with the black and your drawing won't show up very well. You can use colors similar to your pet's, such as orange, yellow, or brown, or you can make a "rainbow" effect with, say, green, red, and blue, which would be good for brightly colored tropical fish or birds.

When you paint black over the colors, it's hard to know where colors begin and end, but you'll have a rough idea. For example, if you want your dog sitting on the grass, you can color the bottom of the board green, so when you scratch that area, green will show through.

You can use all sorts of things for scratching. Pins, nails, forks, coins, or your fingernails are just a few ideas. A mixture of different lines – thick or thin, straight or wavy – will add interest to your picture, so use different tools to draw different parts of your pet. A fork, for example, could make wavy lines that look like fur.

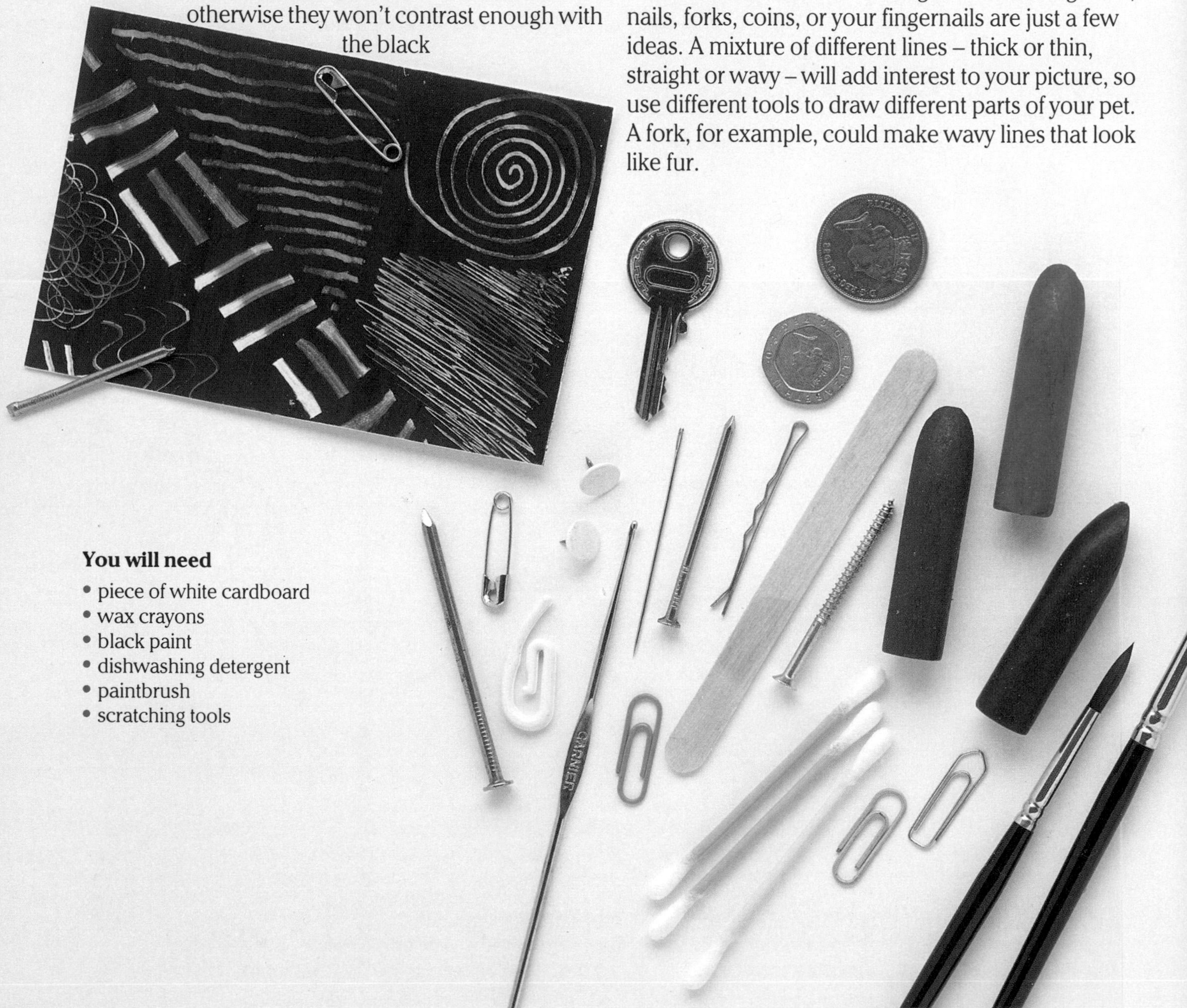

You will need

- piece of white cardboard
- wax crayons
- black paint
- dishwashing detergent
- paintbrush
- scratching tools

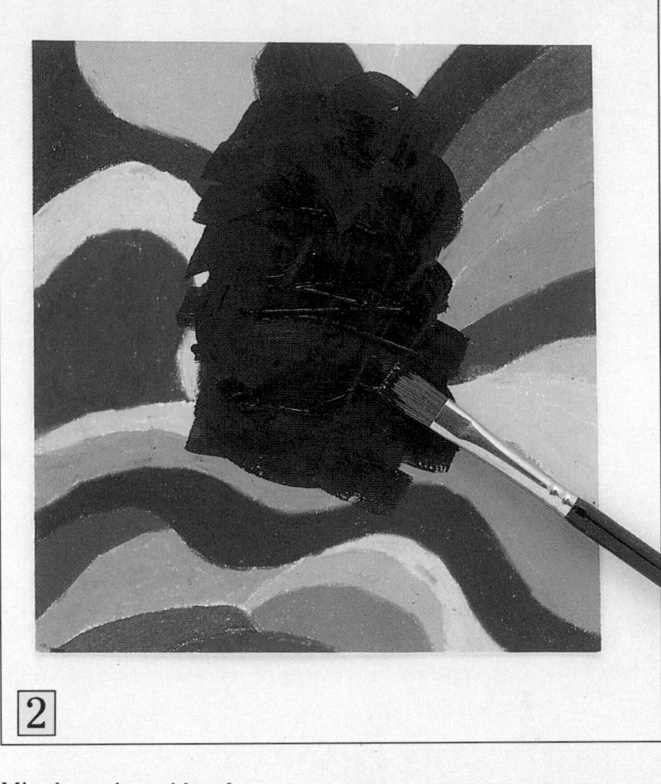

Rainbow scratch bugs and butterflies color the cardboard with the crayons, thinking about where you want each color to be in your finished picture.

Mix the paint with a few drops of dishwashing detergent. This will give it the right thickness, which should be like thick cream. Brush over the cardboard.

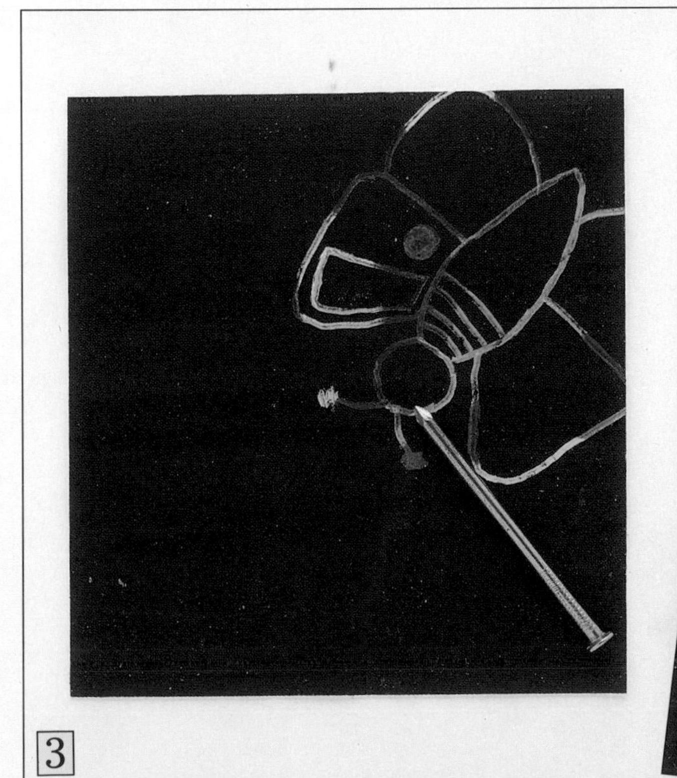

Wait until the paint is completely dry before you start using your scratchboard. Scratch out a picture and watch the colors appear.

The colors underneath are revealed, producing multi-colored insects.

Horses and ponies

People who enjoy riding often like horse pictures to remind them of their "four-legged friends." Horses and ponies can be quite difficult to draw because they have a more complicated shape than many other animals, but if you begin by copying the ones on these two pages, you should be able to get quite a good likeness.

Notice how many shapes go to make up the silhouette of a pony. Compare the front and back legs – they really look quite different. The front legs are straight and more or less the same width all the way up; the back legs are very wide at the top and almost come to a point in the middle.

Pony and rider

Why not do a picture of yourself on your pony? Draw the pony first, then use the "stick person" guide here to help you draw yourself. Finally, fill in the colors.

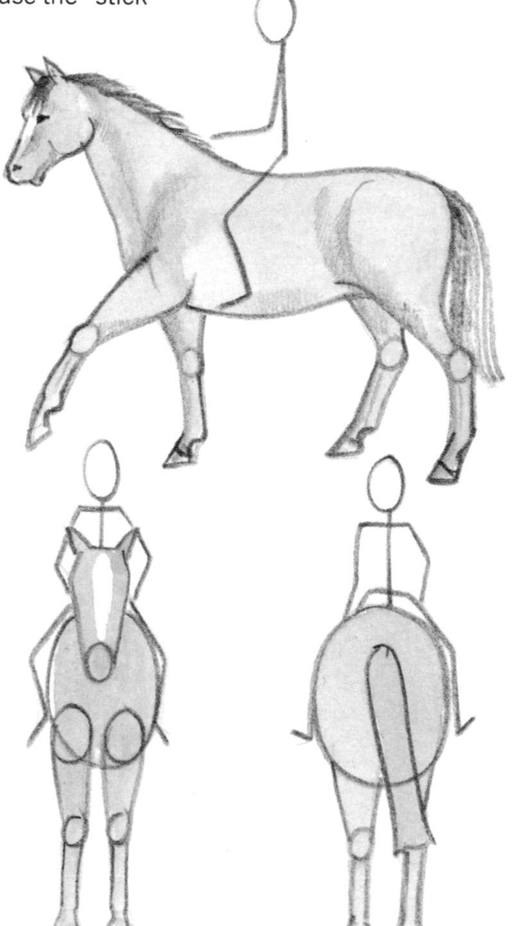

Drawing from the side

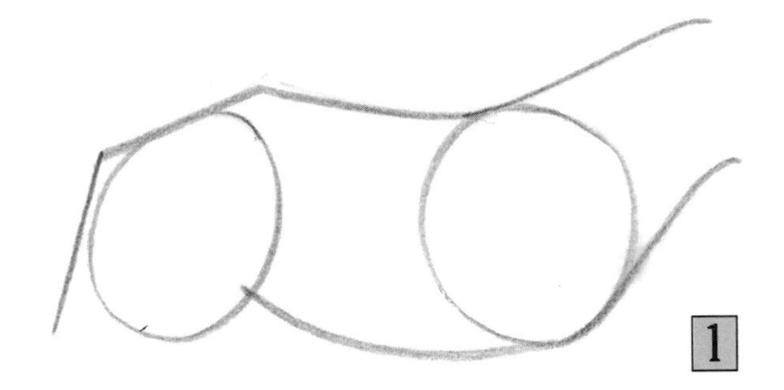

Ponies' bodies are mostly made up of circles and ovals.

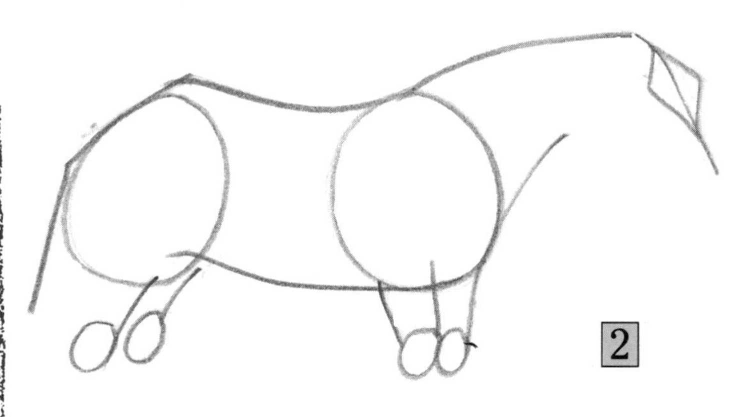

Draw the circles for the body and then the smaller ones for the knees.

When you have finished the outline, color in the body and put in some shading to make it look nice and round.

Drawing from the front

Start with two circles and pointed ovals for the ears. Then draw the shape for the nose.

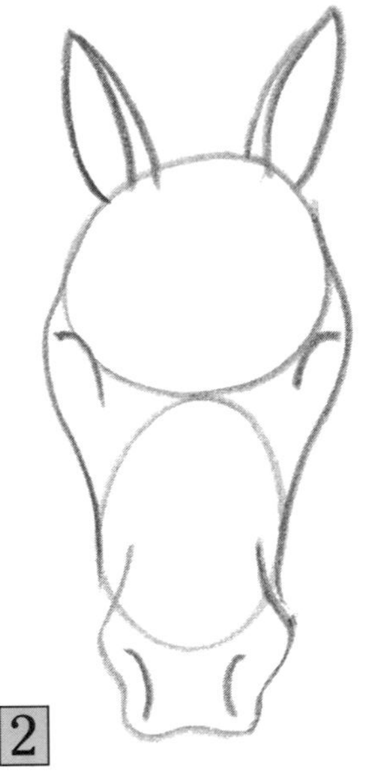

Draw curves for the top eyelid, and the same curves the other way around for the nostrils.

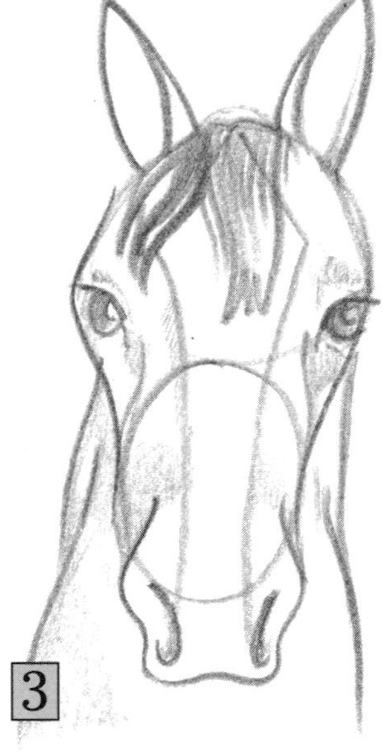

Draw lines down to the nose for the sharp bone that gives the face its shape. Finish off by shading in the eyes and forelock.

Types of horse and pony Look at the difference in size and proportion between different types of horses and ponies.

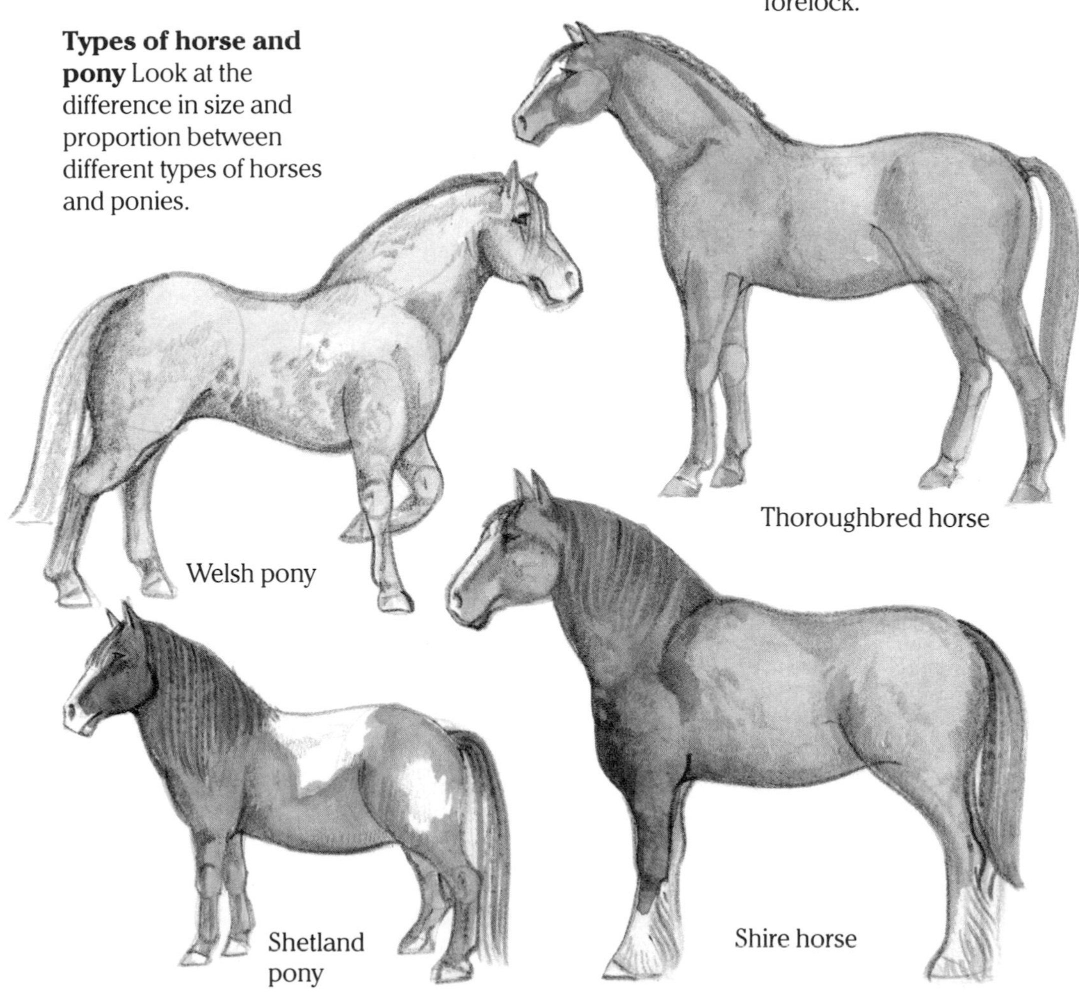

pony with correct proportions.

pony with legs too short.

pony with legs too long.

pony with head too big.

Getting the proportions right Try to get the "proportions" of your pony right. This means getting the parts the right size for each other. If you make the legs too short, the body will look too heavy and fat; if you make them too long, your pony will look too skinny!

Close-up on horses

When you have got the general shape of your pony or horse right, you can begin to fill in the details. These drawings show you how to do them.

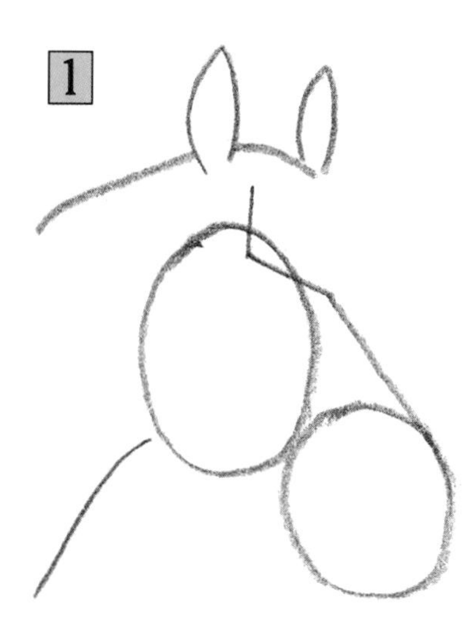

Horses' heads are made up of circles joined by straight lines. Start with these.

Put in the eye near the top of the big circle. It fits just under the brow bone, which makes a triangle shape.

Put in the nostrils, mouth, and forelock, and shade in the drawing.

Ears Horses' and ponies' ears are shaped like triangles.

Eyes They have soft, gentle eyes, placed on either side of the head. Notice how the eyelids bulge out above the eyes.

Nostrils Their nostrils are large, and slant down toward the front of the nose.

Donkeys

Donkeys have much longer ears than horses and ponies, and their manes and forelocks stand up like brushes.

Techniques for heads and manes

Heads
Start with a drawing in light pencil, and then use paint or crayons to fill in the ponies' main color. If your pony has a white blaze like this one, go around the edges carefully. Color in the forelock, mane, and eyes last.

Manes
Horse's manes flop down between their ears, and down the sides of the neck. You can draw them with wavy lines or paint them with a thin brush. Manes and tails are usually darker than their coats.

Legs and hoofs

Horses' legs are a lovely knobby shape. Notice how the front leg goes in and out above and below the knee.

Hoofs Horses wear "shoes" to protect their hoofs. They are made to fit around the underneath of the hoof.

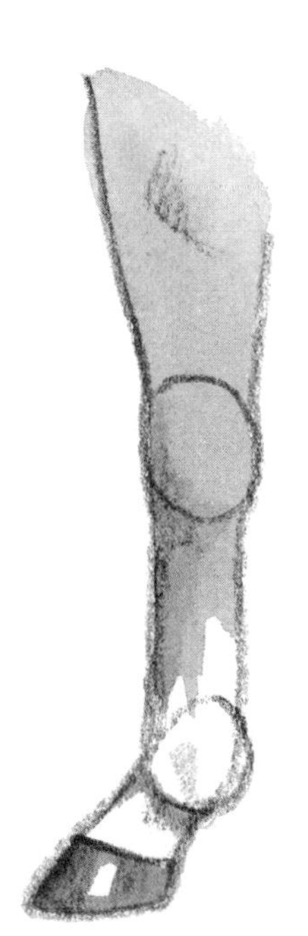

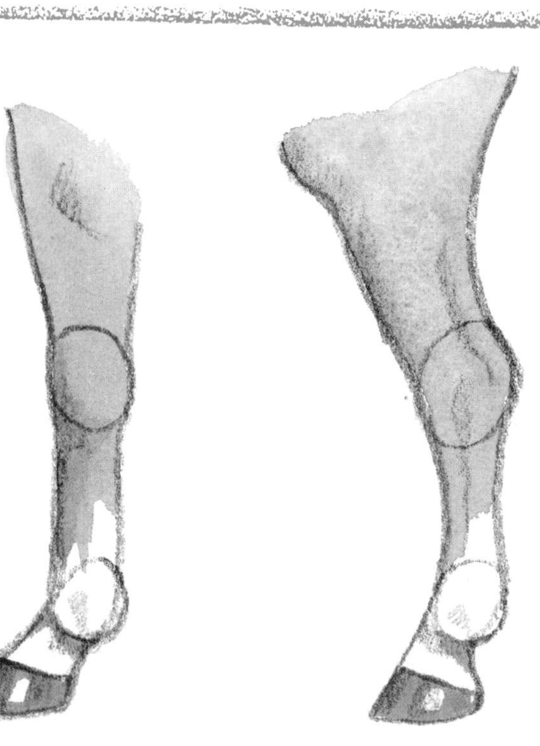

The back leg is much thicker at the top than the front one. When you're drawing horses' and ponies' legs don't forget to put in the little knob just above the hoof, at the back of the leg – it is one of the most distinctive features of a horse's leg.

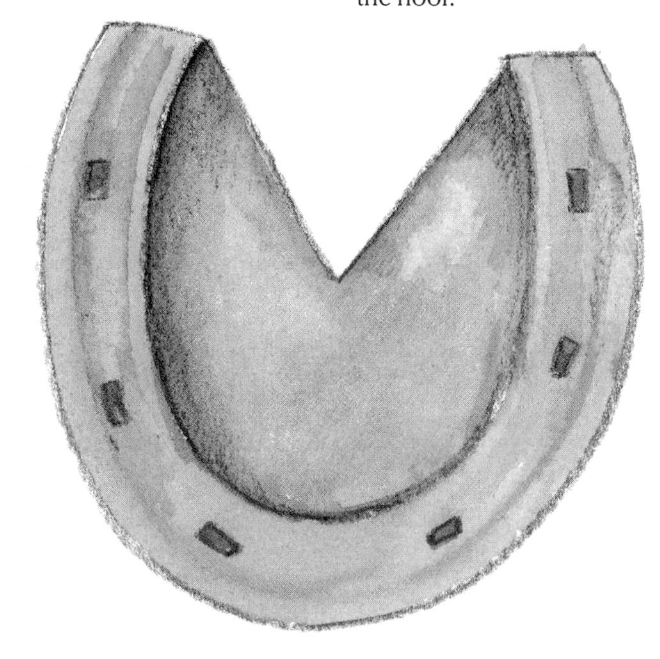

Allsorts collage

You can make a collage from almost anything as long as you can paste it down on cardboard or paper. If you like doing collage, it's a good idea to build up a collection of materials you could use, such as scraps of paper, fabric, wool or string, buttons, paper clips, seeds, pieces of pasta, toothpicks, and so on.

When it comes to making your collage, choose suitable items from your collection according to the color, pattern, or texture of the subject they are representing.

You will need

- thick paper or cardboard
- all-purpose glue
- pencil or ballpoint pen
- eraser
- light and dark brown felt
- pieces of wool
- string
- toothpicks
- colored tissue paper
- foil paper
- green fabric
- poppy seeds
- pearl barley

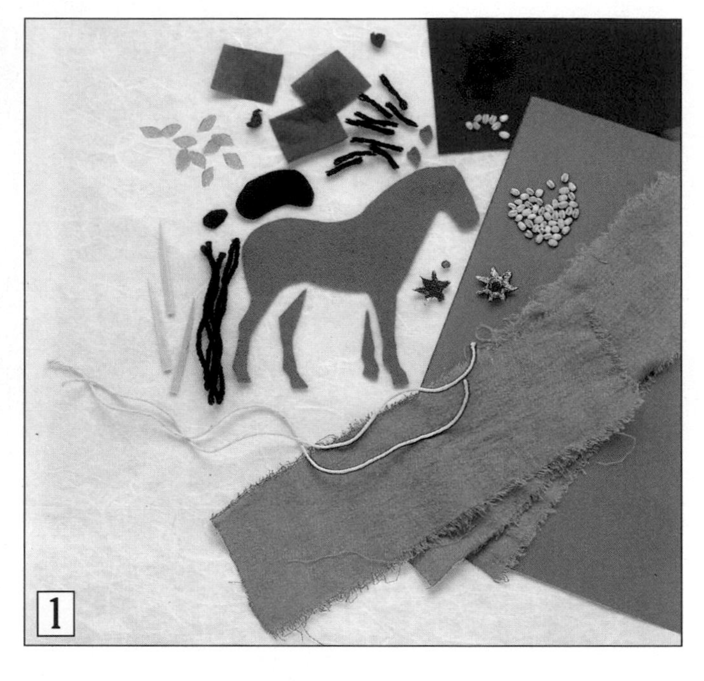

1 Cut out the main shapes for your collage. If necessary, draw them first with a pencil, or a pen if you are drawing on fabric. Cut out the shapes just inside the outline so that it won't show.

Arrange the shapes on the cardboard the way you like them, then glue them in place. Finally add the smaller details like eyes or ears.

3

Patch says... Think about what you are trying to show, and use the item that looks most like it. For example, what could you use for whiskers – toothpicks, silver paper, string, or nylon line? Dried peas, buttons, or seeds could be good for eyes, and so on. The picture shows a few of the items you can add to your collection.

Different colored patches of felt and paper were used for the rabbit's coat, and rough, woolly fabric was used to create the effect of the cat's fur. Pieces of fabric in different colors and patterns were used to create the rainbow fish.

Cartoons

Cartoon animals are not meant to look like real-life animals, but they can do all sorts of things that real animals cannot do, such as smiling, frowning, walking about on two legs, and so on.

Some of the most famous cartoon characters are animals. How many can you think of? There are Mickey and Minnie Mouse, Donald Duck, Bugs Bunny, Tom and Jerry, Snoopy, and the Teenage Mutant Turtles. Can you think of any others?

Cartoon animals have exaggerated shapes – they may have extra big heads, noses, or feet, for example. The other difference from real-life animals is that cartoon animals look a lot more "human" and can have the same expressions on their faces as people. So, if you want to do a picture showing how your pet is feeling, why not do a cartoon?

Have a look at your pet. What is it doing at this moment? Perhaps it is going to sleep, or playing. Try to imagine what its feelings are – do you think it feels sad, or happy, or tired? Here are some hints to help you to get the right expression on your pet's face.

How to draw a cartoon pet Start drawing your cartoon animal in the same way as other animals, with circles and other basic shapes.

Now add smaller details, such as the chin and the feet. Here, small circles are used for feet, eyes, and chin.

Last of all, rub out any lines you don't want, and color your picture in, adding tiny details like whiskers and claws.

Sleepy Lidded eyes and open mouth, yawning, look sleepy

Sad Eyes drooping down at the corner look sad

Startled Round eyes, raised eyebrows, and round mouth look scared

Angry V-shaped eyebrows and mouth turned down at corners look angry

Patch says... Felt pen is good for cartoons because it gives a simple, bold outline. The colors in cartoons are usually quite strong, too, so felt pen is also good for filling in.

Scared cat: round, popping eyes, drops of sweat

Frightened horse: round eyes, sweat drops

Wriggling lizard: little lines around feet and tail show movement

Goody-goody parrot: with halo above head

Thinking mouse: round eyes, straight mouth, tapping fingers

Dizzy cat: ring of stars, heavy lids, silly smile

Worried fish: round eyes, mouth turned down

Watching monkey: pupils in corner of eyes, small smile

Greedy mouse: tongue licking lips

Moving animals

Drawing moving animals is very hard, but the more you practice, the easier it will get. Because it is so difficult to tell what is happening by watching a live animal move, you need to learn about movement by studying and copying pictures of moving animals. Look in magazines, newspapers, or books. If you can take photographs of a cat or dog running, a rabbit hopping, or a budgie flying, that would be even better.

On these pages are pictures of all kinds of creatures moving, which you can copy. Each sequence is broken down into separate stages to show the movement. You can add your own pet's features and colors afterward.

When you have learned more about how an animal's body works, you can try drawing from life. If there are parts you are not sure about, you can always check back to the pictures you looked at and copied. Remember that it is easier to draw your pet from the side than from the front.

You will need to draw very quickly, so choose a drawing material that covers the paper quickly. Pencil is rather slow, but charcoal, soft chalk, or wax crayon would be good. Using the side to draw with, rather than the tip, is even quicker.

Dogs If your dog is well trained, you may be able to get it to do the same movement again and again so that you can study it.

Cats Study the sequence of movements of the cat's legs as you copy these pictures.

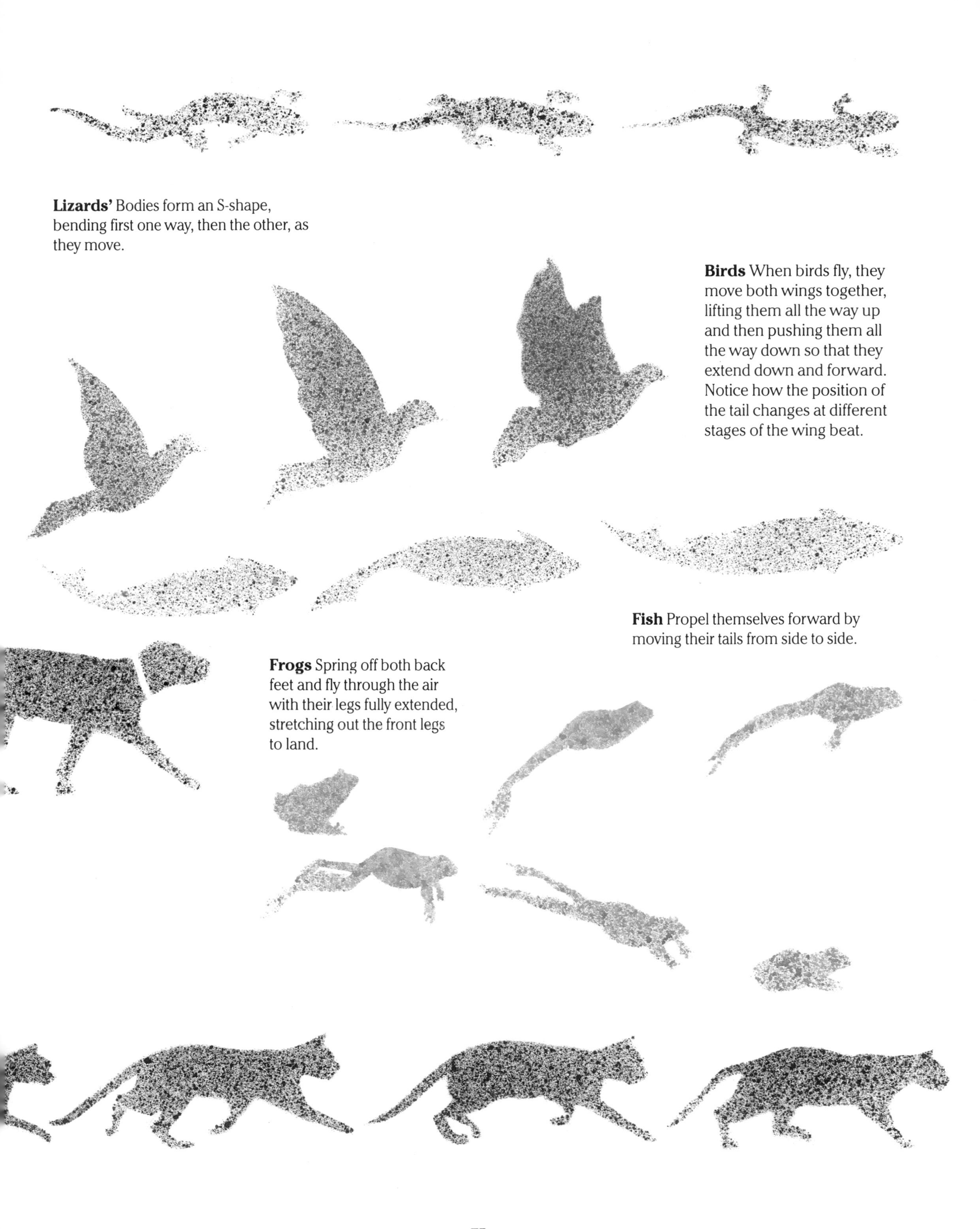

Lizards' Bodies form an S-shape, bending first one way, then the other, as they move.

Birds When birds fly, they move both wings together, lifting them all the way up and then pushing them all the way down so that they extend down and forward. Notice how the position of the tail changes at different stages of the wing beat.

Fish Propel themselves forward by moving their tails from side to side.

Frogs Spring off both back feet and fly through the air with their legs fully extended, stretching out the front legs to land.

Horses See how the horse picks up one foot at a time as it walks. A horse moves differently when it is trotting, cantering, and galloping. When it jumps, it takes off from both hind feet together, but it lands on one front foot followed by the other.

Dog running At the start of the stride, with its feet gathered under it, its body is compressed. In the middle of the stride it is at full stretch.

Cat running Even at full speed, the cat always has one foot on the ground.

Flicker book

When you see a movie or cartoon, it seems as if you are watching one long moving picture. In fact, movies and cartoons just trick you into thinking this. They are actually a sequence of lots and lots of *separate* pictures that flash past your eyes so fast that they seem to blend into one movement.

Although it takes a very long time to make a movie or cartoon, you can still use the same basic idea, in a much simpler way, to make a *flicker book* of your pet. When you flick through the book, you will see your pet "move."

Choose some simple activity, such as your horse jumping a fence, or your budgie landing on its perch. Think of all the different movements that go into doing this one thing. Do some rough sketches first to try out your idea.

You could look back to pages 76 to 79, which are all about moving animals.

You will need
- sheets of paper
- something to draw with (pen, pencil, etc)
- stapler, or needle and thread
- scissors

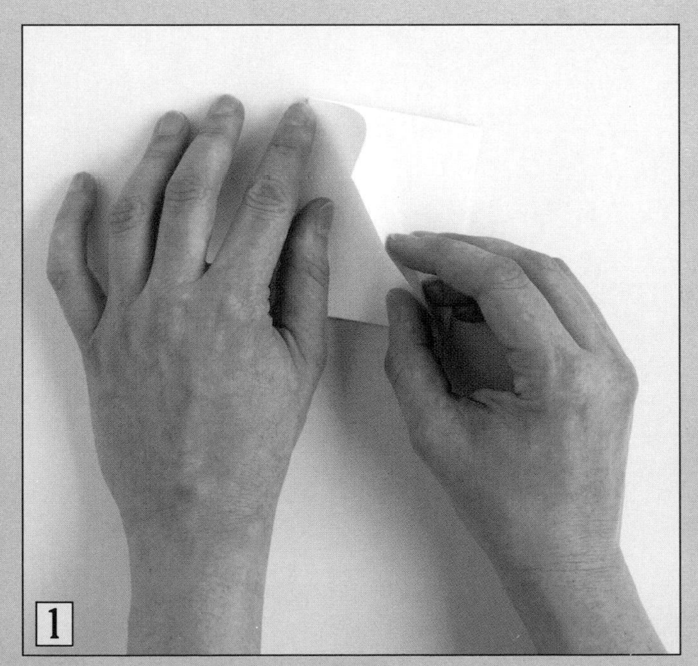

Cut out some strips of paper, all the same size (you can always cut out more later if you find you haven't enough). Fold them in half down the middle.

Here are some flicker-book ideas based on the sequences of moving animals on pages 76 to 79.

An animal can be made to look as if it is moving by changing its position in relation to another object.

If there is too much of a difference between one picture and the next, it will create a "jump" in the sequence, making it seem jerky when you flick through it. You will need to add some extra pictures between the ones where the sequence jumps.

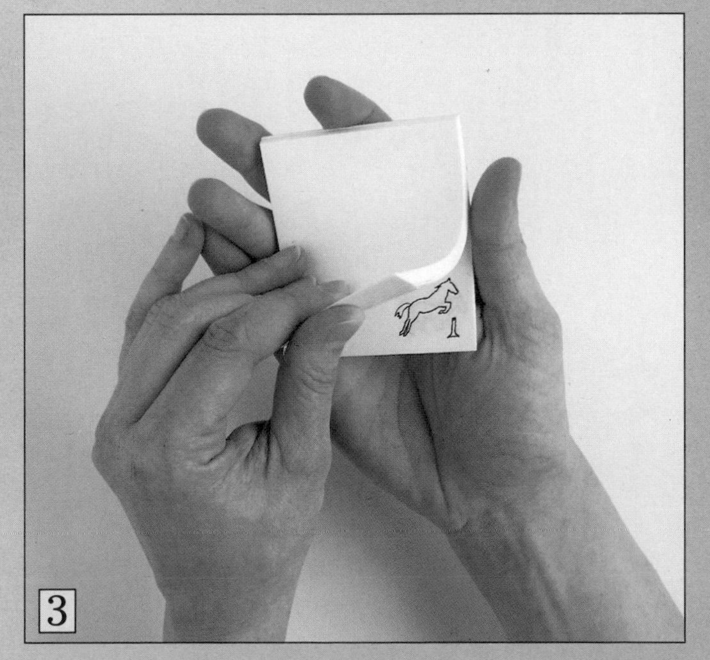

Staple or sew the strips together to make a book.

Start at the back of the book. On the right-hand side of each strip of paper,

do a drawing of each movement in your sequence.

Flick through the book, from back to front, and watch your pet "move."

Texture

Texture is the name for how something feels when you touch it. Texture is an important part of how your pet looks – for example, a cat with a short, sleek coat will look different from a cat with long, soft, fluffy fur. They are both cats but the texture of their coats makes them look different.

Showing the texture of your pet's coat will add something extra to your picture, and make it look more lifelike. You can show different textures by using different materials. For example, smudged pastel or charcoal would be good for a fluffy cat, and smooth, even paint or felt pen could be used for the sleek, shorthaired cat. The examples shown here will give you some more ideas, but try thinking up some of your own, too. Think also about how to do different parts of your pet – would you use the same material for all of them? For example, would you do a smooth, wet nose in the same way as a rough, shaggy coat?

Always be sensitive to texture. It's as important a part of your picture as getting your pet's shape right.

Fluffy cat Colored pastels in four different browns have been smudged together here to give a soft, fluffy look.

Scaly lizard Beautiful paint colors have been worked over with criss-cross pen lines to show the scaly "feel" of this lizard's skin.

Shiny fish The smooth, shiny skin of this fish has been painted a smooth, even orange, with touches of white paint added for highlights.

Shaggy mouse Colored pen lines look like coarse hair on this mouse. Its smooth ears and tail have been painted.

Velvety rabbit Soft black and brown oil pastel give this rabbit its velvety-smooth coat.

Feathery bird Lots of colored pencil lines give the soft look of feathers.

Shaggy dog Scribbled colored pencil in black and gray shows this dog's rough, curly coat.

Pictures from rubbings

Have you ever done a pencil or crayon rubbing? Perhaps you have done one using a coin, and watched the pattern of the coin begin to appear on the paper.

To do any rubbing, you need something with a rough surface that you can feel with your fingers, such as corrugated cardboard, sandpaper, or even wood. If the surface is too smooth, you will just get a solid area of color, without any pattern.

The ladybug rubbing shown here uses the same template over and over again. This kind of rubbing is good if you have a lot of pets of one kind – a tankful of goldfish or a box of ladybugs. Instead of drawing or painting each one separately, you simply cut out a template and move it around under your paper, taking a rubbing each time.

You can fix the shape in place to stop it moving. And remember not to use thick paper, or you won't be able to "pick up" the shape underneath.

You will need

- drawing paper or thin cardboard for cutting out the ladybug shape
- pencil
- eraser
- scissors
- paper punch
- paper
- crayons

Rubbings using a template Draw the shape of your pet, keeping it simple. Simple silhouettes work best, and are easier to cut out. For the ladybugs just draw the body shape – details like legs can be added later.

Cut out the shape you have drawn. For spots or eyes, cut holes in the shape, or punch them out with a paper punch.

Lay the shape on a tray or board, sticking it in position if you like. Lay the paper over the top. Rub over the shape with

Experimenting with rubbings

You can take rubbings from all kinds of things, but for a picture of your pet you need to use something that will give the right kind of texture – so try out different things first. Corrugated cardboard was used for the dog's shaggy coat (below); for the snail (right) a wicker tablemat was used; and the parrot was made by rubbing crayon on paper laid over a tablemat and textured wallpaper.

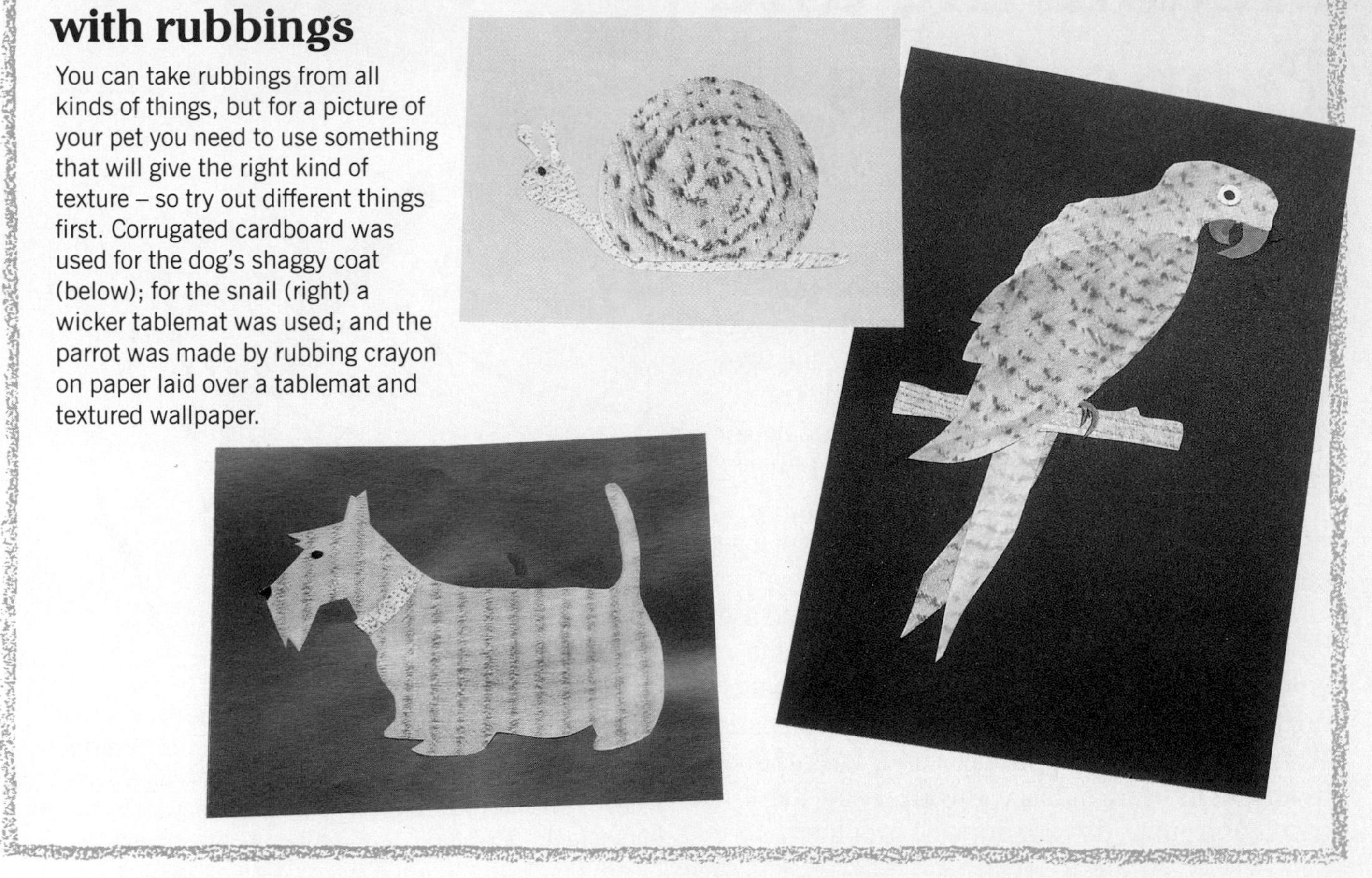

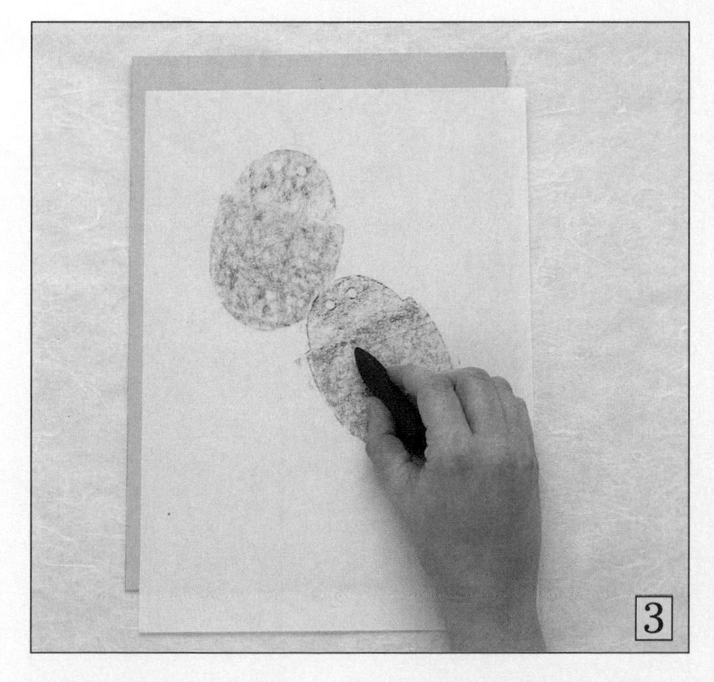

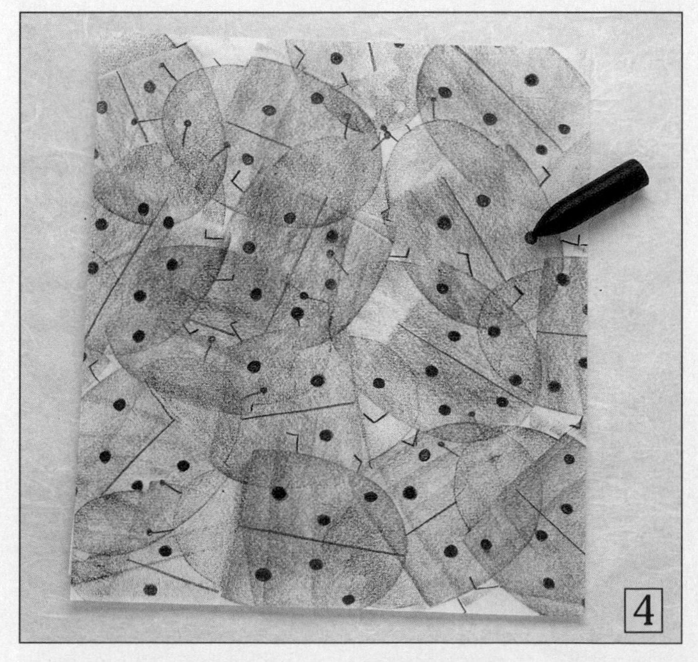

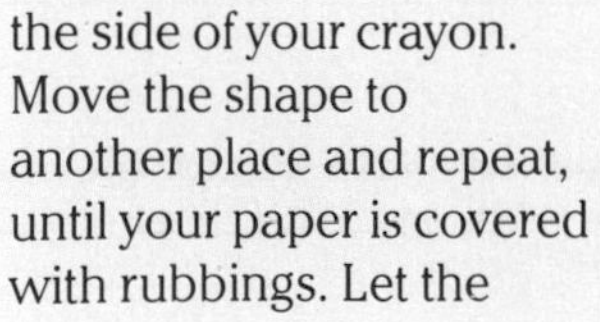

the side of your crayon. Move the shape to another place and repeat, until your paper is covered with rubbings. Let the rubbings overlap – it will make the picture more interesting.

Now use your crayons to add any details you want, such as spots, antennae, and legs, or any extra colors. This is a good way to produce a really busy design.

Measuring and Proportions

Often, people draw things the size they imagine they are, rather than looking very carefully and drawing them the size they actually look. If you want to do a really good picture of your pet, it's very important to get the *proportions* right – this means getting the sizes of the different parts right for each other. It's no good drawing a beautiful head for your budgie, for example, if it's too big or too small for the body.

A good way to get proportions right is by measuring. You may find it difficult at first, but it gets easier with practice.

Hold your pencil up in front of your pet, and use your thumb to measure the different parts of the animal, as in the picture below. Then make marks on the paper to show how long or wide each part is. You may discover that your pet's body is three times as long as its head, or twice as wide. Using these marks as a guide, do your drawing over them.

Enlarging a picture
It is possible to make a copy larger (or smaller) than the original picture or photograph. Trace the outline of the picture on to tracing paper. Now divide the tracing evenly into squares, using a ruler to measure the squares.

To measure your pet, hold your pencil up, the top level with the top of its head, and "mark" its chin with your thumb.

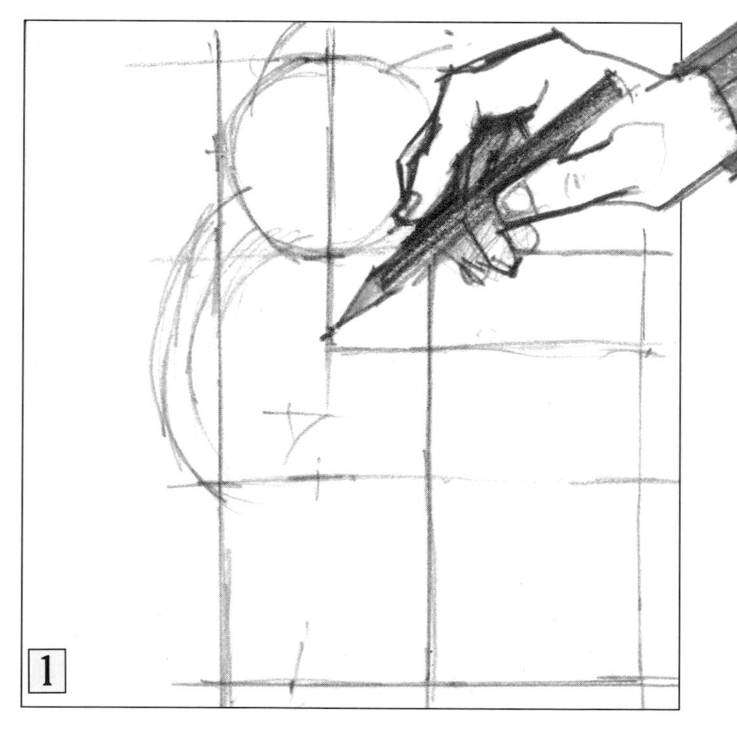

Measure down the body to see how many head-sizes you can fit in. Make marks down the paper to show how many "heads" you measured. Work out the width in the same way.

On your paper, mark the size you want your copy to be, then divide it into the same number of squares as on the tracing. Copy the little bit of outline that appears in each square, joining up the lines as you go so that you get a complete outline.

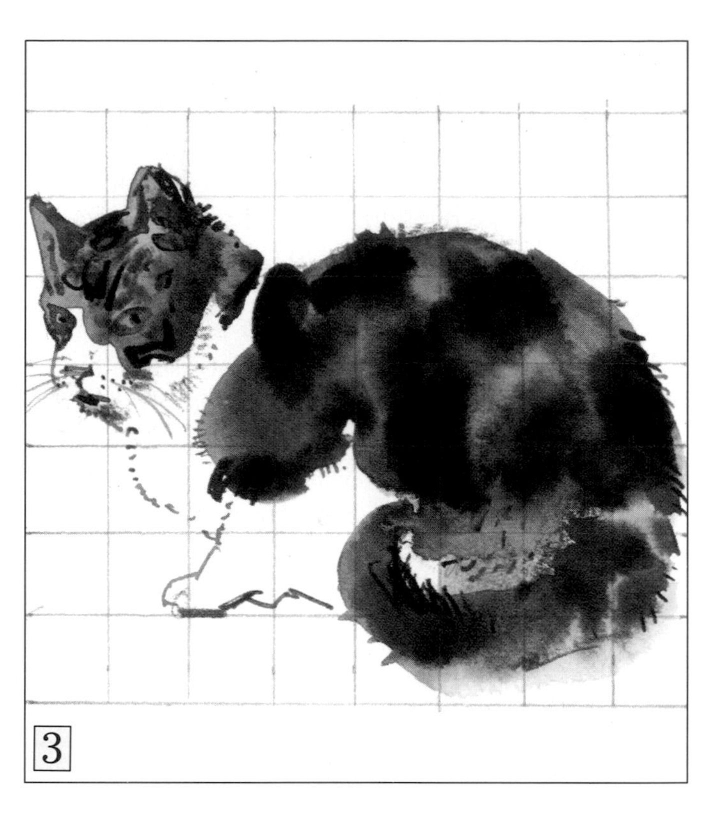

Now you can fill in all the smaller details, such as the whiskers. Using the original picture as your guide, paint or color in your outline. And don't forget to rub out the little squares!

Using the measurements you have made on the paper to guide you, start drawing in the outline of your pet. When you are happy with the outline, rub out the measurements, and fill in the details.

Here is the finished picture.

Making the picture work

Composition is the name for how you arrange the things in your picture. Here are some hints on how to create a good composition.

One of the basic rules of composition is to have something in the "foreground" (front), something in the "middle ground" (middle), and something in the "background" (back). This will give your picture depth, and make it seem as if you are looking right into the scene in front of you. Think of it as being like one of those puppet theaters made of cardboard: the characters stand at the front, the wings on to the stage are behind them, and the painted scenery is right at the back.

Besides thinking about where to place the objects in your picture, you can make your composition work even better by careful choice of size and color. The picture opposite shows how important these are.

Inventing a framework Imagine your picture divided up by a framework of lines, with each of the important things in the picture placed along one of the lines. You could even draw the lines on your paper, but don't place them across the center – your composition will look much better if the lines are above or below the middle, or to one side of center.

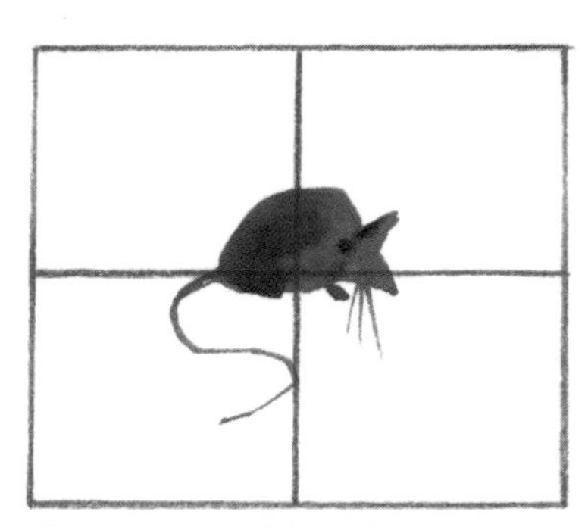

Poor composition: lines cut across center.

Good composition: lines to one side of center.

Choosing a shape for your picture

There are two basic shapes for pictures: "portrait," which is tall and high, and "horizontal," which is long and wide. The picture above is a horizontal shape, and the picture on the left is a portrait shape. In the horizontal picture above, you can see all of the horse's head, but a portrait shape "matches" the shape of his head better.

To show all of the snake in the picture above, a long, horizontal shape has been chosen. But sometimes leaving out part of the animal can make a more dramatic picture. In the portrait-shaped picture on the left, the artist was only interested in the snake's head. The portrait shape also suits the L-shaped outline of the snake.

your composition will look better if you arrange things in groups, rather than place them on their own
objects look larger in the front, and gradually become smaller as they get farther away
more detail also makes things look closer; the farther away they are, the less detail you can see
overlapping parts of your drawing gives depth
warm, strong colors, such as reds or deep browns, make things look closer;
paler, cool colors look farther away

Rabbit in a hutch

Why not make a picture of your pet in its home? This picture of a rabbit in its hutch uses a variety of materials and involves painting a picture of the rabbit, cutting out the hutch in cardboard, and then gluing the hutch over the picture of the rabbit. String is used to make the hutch door.

See what other ways you can think of for painting pets in the places where they live. For example, you could do a pony in its stable by cutting out the stable in cardboard, and then cutting the top half of the door around three sides so that it opens. Make a painting of the pony's head and stick it to the back of the stable so that the pony's head is in the open door. The pictures opposite should also help to give you some ideas.

You will need

- sheet of paper
- piece of thin, colored cardboard
- paints
- pencil
- brush
- scissors
- glue
- tape
- string

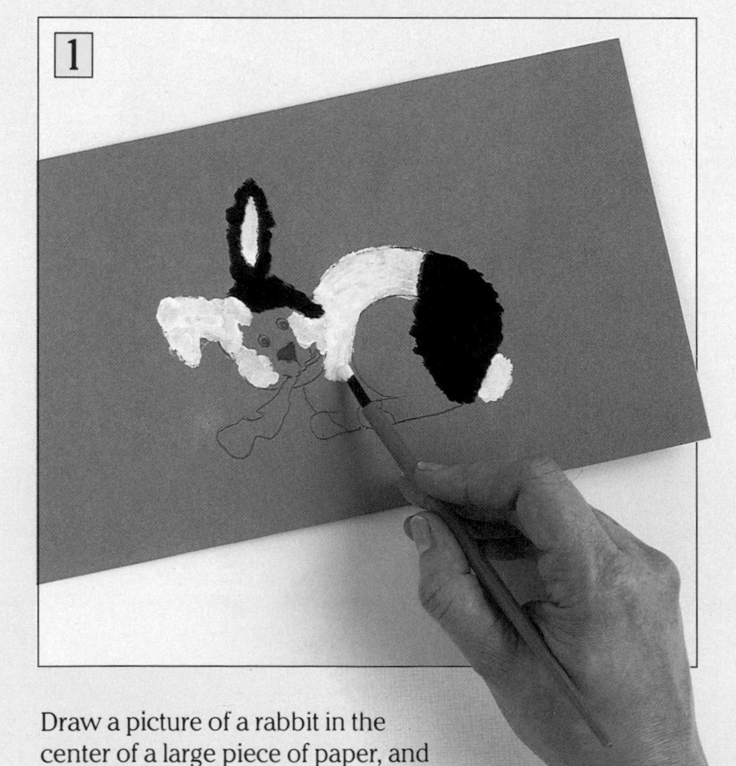

Draw a picture of a rabbit in the center of a large piece of paper, and paint it in.

Cut out the hutch shape in thin cardboard, and cut out the door in the front of the hutch. The hutch must be the right size for your rabbit.

For a picture of goldfish in their bowl, you could cut out a frame in the shape of the bowl, and stick clear plastic wrap across the back of the frame to give an impression of glass. Then stick the frame down over the picture of the fish. The fish, plants and rocks have been colored with felt-tip pen, and the water lightly shaded in with blue crayon.

When painting a bird in its cage, remember that the bars need to be drawn over the top of the bird to give the idea that it is in its cage. The cage bars were drawn in with light grey felt-tip pen.

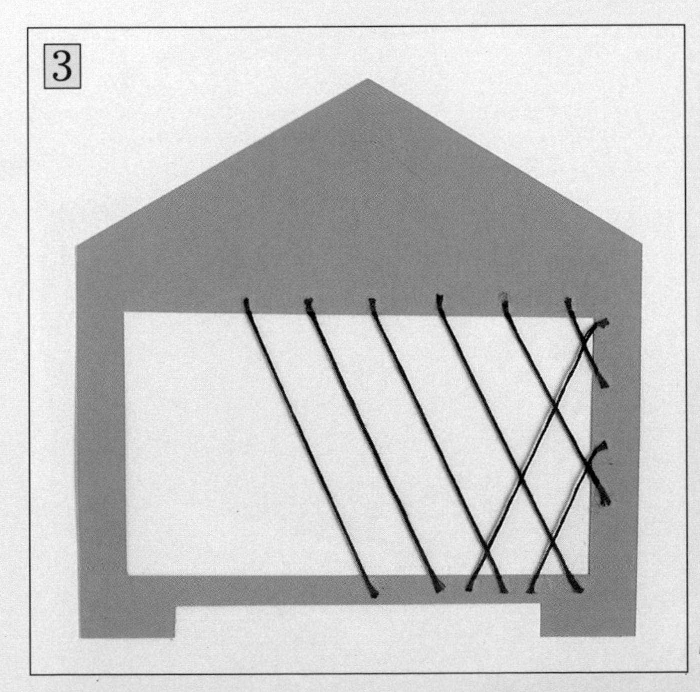

Glue or tape pieces of string on the back of the hutch in a diagonal pattern across the hutch door.

Cover the back of the hutch with glue and stick it down over your picture of the rabbit.

Out and about

Most animals like to go outside and enjoy the sunshine and fresh air. Does your pet have a favorite spot outdoors? Perhaps it likes to keep cool in the shade of a tree, or does it prefer to bask in the sun on the doorstep or window sill? All dogs love going for walks – in the park, in the fields, or in the woods, depending on where you live. If they get the chance, they also love to play about in water, at the beach or by the river.

Think about what your pet likes to do best when it is outside, and do a picture of it, using whatever materials you like. You could draw your pet close up, or farther away as part of a more general scene.

When you are doing this kind of picture, it will be helpful to look back at some of the other pages earlier in the book. For example, you may need to check back to see how to draw moving animals, on pages 76 to 79. Getting a good composition (pages 88 to 89) is also important here.

Making a viewfinder When you are looking at a scene in front of you, it can be difficult to decide which parts of it to include in your picture, and what to put where. Should your pet be big or small, for example, and should it be at the top, bottom, or side of the picture? This is where a *viewfinder* can help.

You can make one yourself out of cardboard. Cut a square or rectangle out of a piece of cardboard (or a circle if you want a round picture). The cut-out shape should be the same shape as your finished picture, but need not be the same size.

Hold the viewfinder up in front of you to "frame" what you see. Move it about until you find what looks best. If you want your pet to be big, go closer to it; if you want it to be smaller, go further away.

And now – before you forget – quickly sketch the view you have chosen on paper.

By cropping the picture on the left of the dog, a strong composition has been achieved in which the dog and the wood pile balance each other.

Patch says... When you are doing a picture of an outdoor scene, mix your colors carefully. The colors in nature are much softer and subtler than those that come straight from a tube or jar!

"Close-up" pictures The dog in the picture on the opposite page is out in the country, and is seen from quite a distance. If you are doing a picture of your pet at home, it will probably be much closer to you – lying on a wall in the sun, or hiding in a bed of flowers.

To make your pet look "close-up," you should let it take up more of the space in the picture. In this picture, the cat almost fills the area, and the things around it are not important. In the opposite picture, the dog is part of the whole landscape.

Collage cat If you are doing a picture of your pet outdoors, you don't need to stick just to paint or pencils. Why not use collage as well? It could save you a lot of work. Instead of having to paint each flower or leaf, or even the bricks in a brick wall, you could just cut out and paste down pictures of them. Experiment with making your own collage bits and pieces. A collage of pasted leaf shapes, cut from tracing paper scribbled with green pencil, can look very effective.

Face Painting

From cowboys to clowns, pirates to princesses, 40 amazingly original designs for the perfect children's party

LYNSY PINSENT

CONTENTS

Face Painting

How to Draw and Paint The Outdoors

Introduction

Body decoration has been used for over 40,000 years all over the world and for many different purposes. In the Western world it may be used to make a statement, for example by a punk rocker who wants to challenge society, to follow fashion or enhance looks, by performers in the theatre or circus, or simply for fun.

In other societies, the way in which a body is decorated instantly distinguishes between race, tribe, class and age. In all parts of the world, those who do not conform to the norm risk rejection by society. However, the more "primitive" cultures use pattern and paint for rituals and celebrations and to symbolize their physical and spiritual being.

ABOVE: Red is a significant colour for many tribes. It is mostly connected with blood, life, energy, success and well being. Upon marriage, women of many Asian and Middle Eastern countries, for example Bahrein, tint their hands and feet with red henna to invite success and good health to the home.

ABOVE: Nadia Strahan making up as Bombalurina in Andrew Lloyd Webber's musical Cats.

RIGHT: Before going to war, some North American Indians painted red around their eyes and ears to invoke good luck in hearing and vision. They wanted to frighten their enemies and receive protection from the spirit world. In contrast, a modern soldier's "war paint" is designed to keep him from view.

ABOVE: *For the Mount Hagen people of Papua New Guinea, body decoration is a vital element of their culture. They are a fiercely competitive society and try to ensure their decorations meet the approval of their elders. The picture shows a tribesman decorated for the pig festival.*

ABOVE: *The Japanese Kabuki theatre and Chinese Opera (shown here) are not simply forms of entertainment, they also follow ancient rituals and traditions within the performances, costumes and make-up. The dramas performed are based on traditional legends. Specific colours and designs are assigned to particular types of characters.*

Equipment

For the designs in this book you will need the following:

EQUIPMENT

- Aqua-Colours (water-based paints in a range of colours)
- Black eye pencil
- Bran flakes or cornflakes
- Brushes
- Cotton buds
- Derma Wax (or "nose putty")
- Fake blood
- Glitter gel for skin
- Grey eye pencil
- Hair brush & comb
- Hair clips/hair band
- Hair gel
- Hairspray
- Lead pencil
- Mirror
- Palette knife/spatula
- Soap
- Sponges
- Tissues
- Toothpick/orange stick
- Towel
- Tracing paper (or greaseproof paper)
- Water
- Water jar

Note: All the paints recommended in this book are professional Aqua-Colours. These are specially formulated for use on skin, are non-toxic and have been carefully tested. However, if you suspect that your model might have sensitive skin, test the paint on the inside of the model's wrist before you begin. If there is no reaction after an hour or two you should be safe to proceed.

Aqua-Colours

The main advantages of using professional Aqua-Colours are that they cover the skin well, yet only need a thin layer of paint to do so. They are available in a huge range of colours that can be mixed easily and dry very quickly on the skin, enabling other colours to be added almost immediately.

Because Aqua-Colours are water based they are easily removed by washing with ordinary soap and water, and can also be used on the hair for the same reason.

Aqua-Colours are inexpensive and can be bought individually or in palettes of 6 or 12 colours. Fluorescent colours are also available. A list of suppliers can be found on page 96.

Brushes and Sponges

Special make-up sponges can be bought from most chemist shops, but an ordinary bath sponge will do the job just as well, if not better sometimes.

A professional "stipple" sponge is good for applying beard stubble, but a plastic pan scourer will produce the same effect.

A selection of quality brushes are essential for a good make-up. The most useful are: No. 2 for eye-lining and fine detail; No. 6 for lips and eyes; 6mm (¼in) domed for highlights and blending; 12mm (½in) domed for painting large areas and for blending.

The best type of brushes are sable, although other, cheaper types can be used instead. Sable brushes

ABOVE: Equipment for achieving special effects.

are worth the extra initial expense because they are versatile and long lasting. Look after them carefully by washing them gently with soap and water after each session, then lubricating the hairs with a touch of cold cream. Your local art shop will be a good source of brushes.

Preparation Tips

☞ Set out all your materials and equipment in front of you so that you can see at a glance what you need.

☞ Lay out a towel or cloth to protect the table or work surface.

☞ Keep a waste bin or carrier bag handy to hold dirty tissues etc. and keep the work area clear.

☞ Try to ensure that your model sits on a seat that is high enough for you to work comfortably without straining your back.

☞ Have a mirror close at hand, preferably standing in front of you, so that you can check that your make-up design is balanced and the colours are evenly applied.

☞ Before you start, wrap a towel round your model's shoulders to protect the clothes.

☞ Keep the model's hair off the face with hair clips or a hair band.

☞ Have a good supply of cotton buds handy for blending colours and erasing any smudges.

☞ Most important of all, work out your designs beforehand using a copy of the make-up chart on page 15. It is much better to make your mistakes on paper rather than a model's face! The chart will also be a useful record for future use.

Application Tips

☞ Always begin with a clean, dry face.

☞ For some designs you might find it helpful to sketch the outline onto the face first using grey eye pencil.

☞ When a full white base is required, try to apply it as thinly as possible while still achieving good coverage – this will avoid muddiness when other colours are added.

☞ Do not apply glitter too close to the eyes.

☞ When using Derma Wax (or nose putty) don't handle it for too long or it will become too sticky to use.

☞ Fake blood can be darkened by adding a little instant coffee, and can be made less orange or pink by adding a touch of green.

☞ Fake blood can stain clothing – take great care with it.

☞ When painting animal faces, it often helps to keep a photograph of the animal nearby. This will inspire you to imitate the real thing as accurately as possible.

☞ Keep each sponge for one colour only – washing sponges between colours takes up too much time.

☞ Change the water often.

☞ Always apply the lightest colours first, then progress to the darker ones.

☞ Wait until the previous colour is dry before applying the next one.

☞ Blend colours with a clean, damp brush or by stippling with a barely damp sponge.

☞ Take extra care when working near the eyes. If possible, ask the model to keep their eyes closed until you have finished.

☞ Always apply make-up with as much care as possible. Do not rush – the features will become ill-defined and uneven. Symmetrical shapes and neat lines are the essence of a good make-up. Practice makes perfect!

Basic Techniques

Applying a Base

TIP: Use a damp sponge to apply a full-face base. It is much quicker and gives a smoother finish than a brush. To avoid streaks or patchiness, make sure the sponge is not too wet.

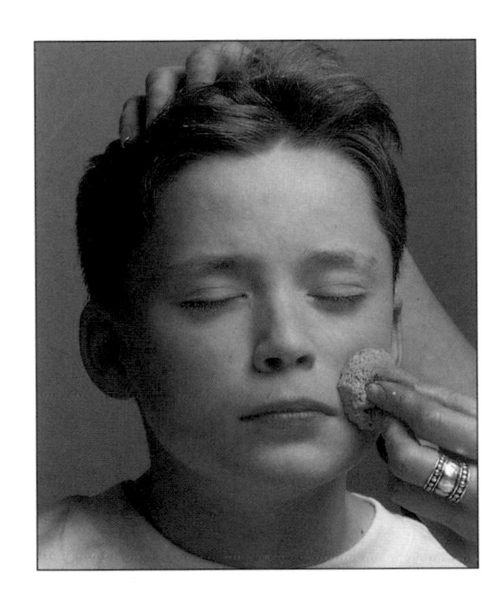

1 If you want a duotone base, always apply the lightest colour first – yellow in this case.

2 The yellow base reaches almost to the hairline.

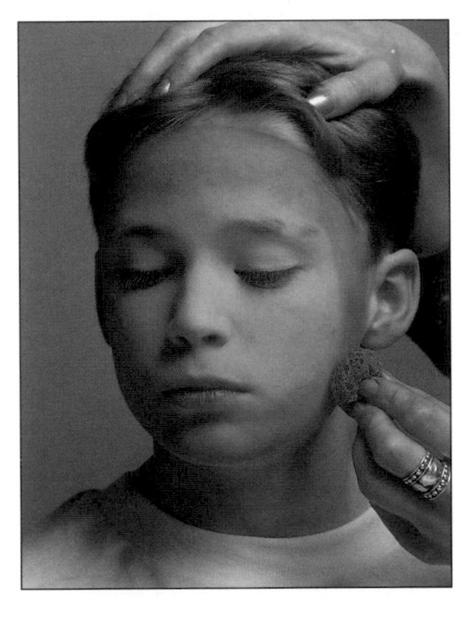

3 Blend an orange border into the yellow by lightly dabbing ("stippling") along the adjoining edge with a barely damp sponge.

TIP: Dark skins can sometimes be difficult to cover. Stipple the base colour over the entire face with a barely damp sponge. Metallic colours can be substituted, and look terrific. They also act as a primer onto which you can apply your base colour.

4 The finished duotone base.

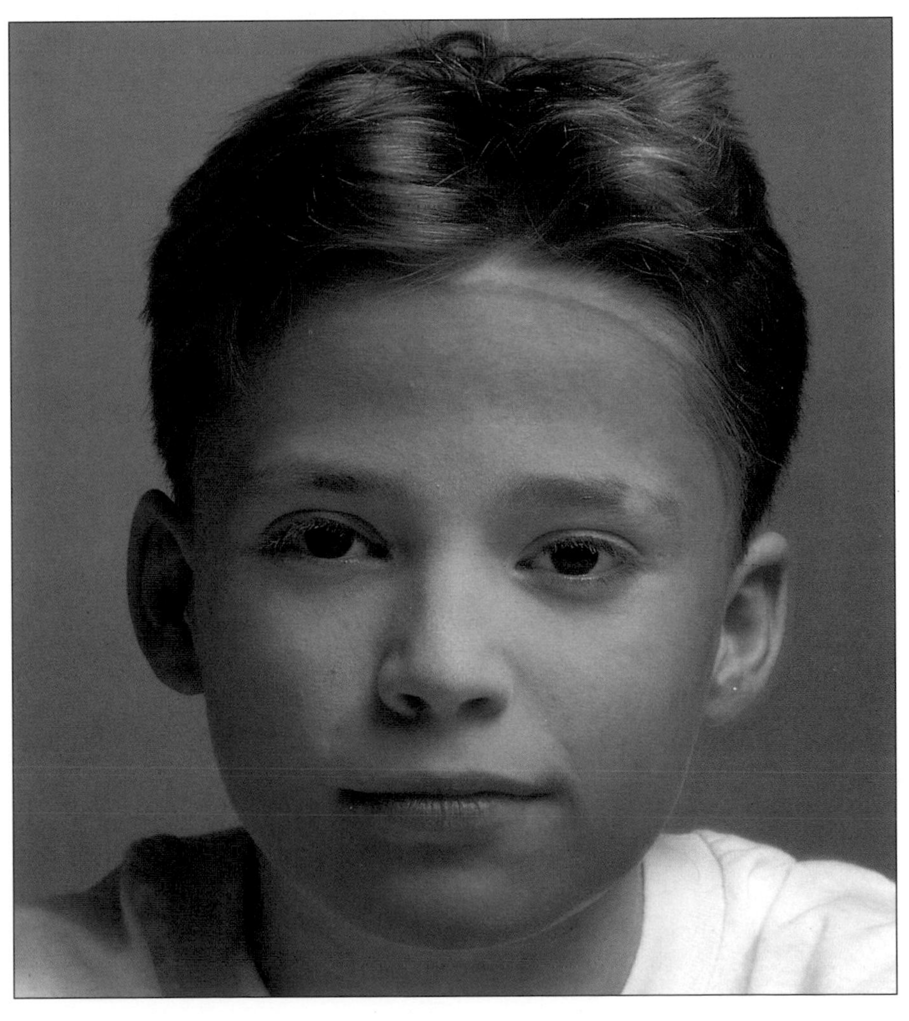

Painting the Eyes

TIP: Always take great care when painting anywhere near the eye. Most of the faces in this book have been designed so that the models can keep their eyes closed throughout the whole procedure. If you need to get closer to the bottom eye-line, ask the model to look up and away from the brush as you do so.

Method 1

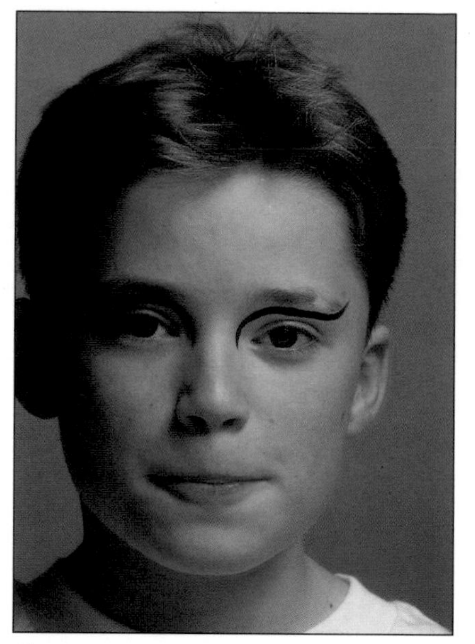

1 This method is ideal for very young children because it starts beside the nose and sweeps across the brow without actually touching the eye.

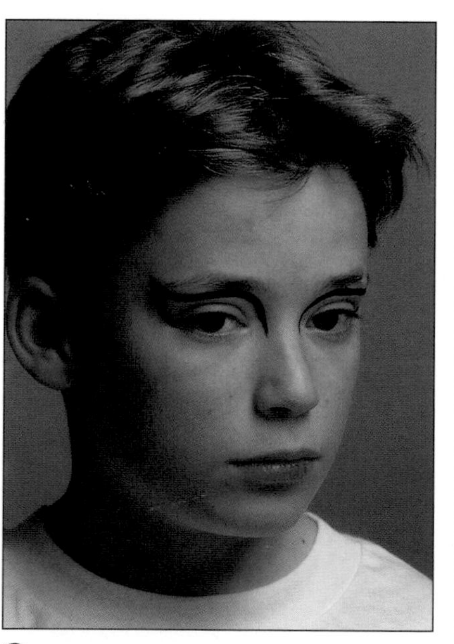

2 You can enhance the effect by simply bringing the end of the line down to meet the outer corner of the eye.

Method 2

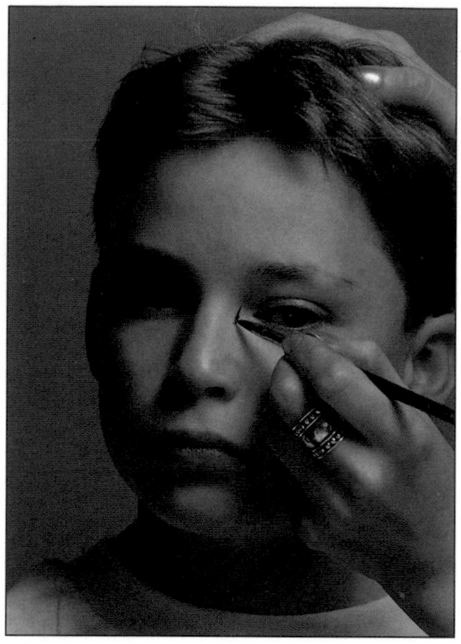

1 For a more elaborate image, use a thin brush and start the top line just below the inner corner of the eye.

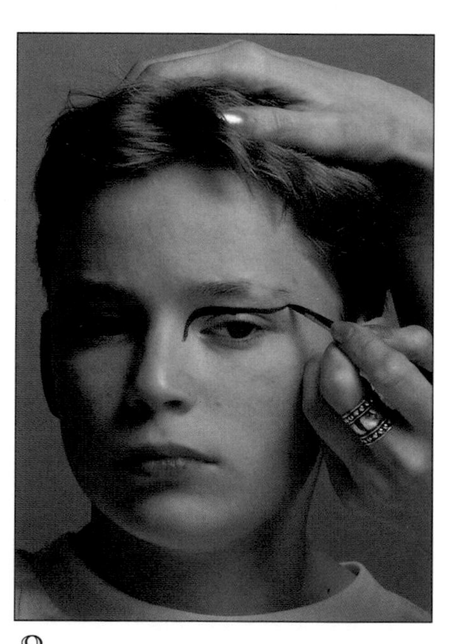

2 Take the line across the eyelid, winging it up slightly at the end.

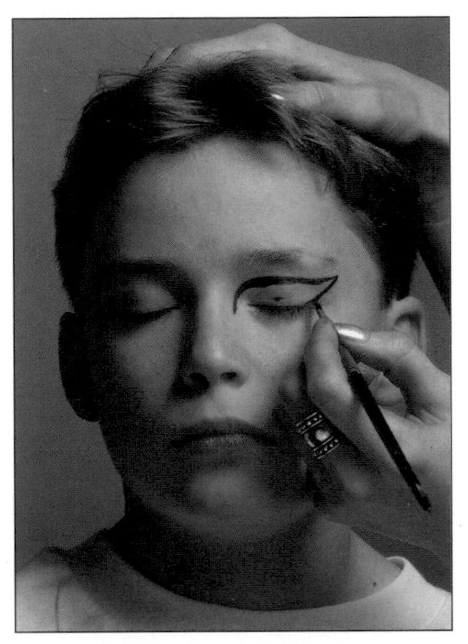

3 Bring the end of the top line down to the outer corner of the eye.

5 Start the bottom line at the inner corner and sweep it beneath the lower lashes to join the outer corner of the top lid.

4 Fill in the outlined area in black.

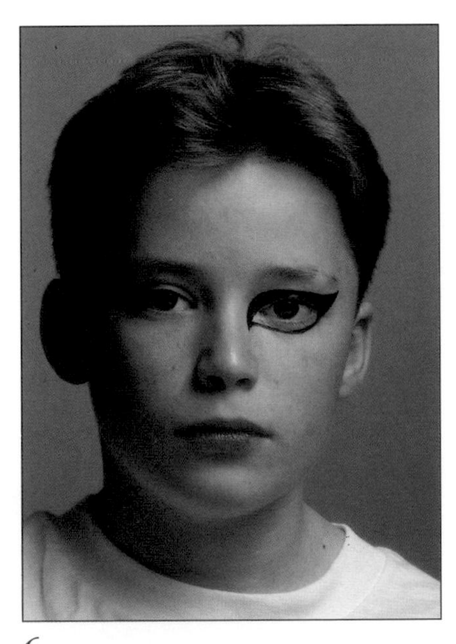

6 The finished effect.

Method 3

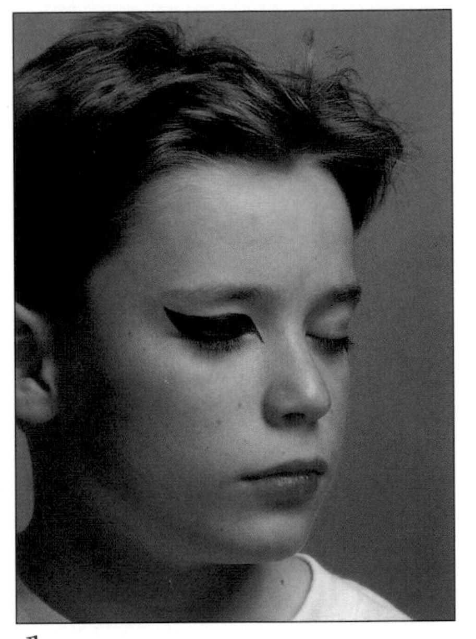

1 Shape the top lid using the method described previously.

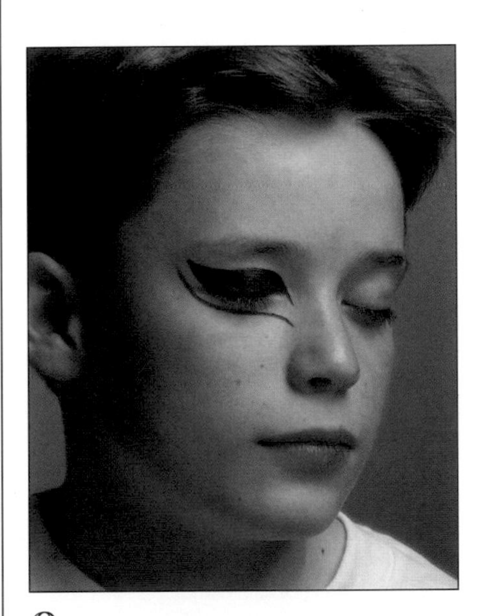

2 Start the lower line below the inner corner and sweep it up, following the direction of the top lid, to finish parallel to but not touching the top line. The space between the two lines can be emphasised with a slick of white paint.

☞ This "open-ended" technique is often used in the theatre because it makes the eyes appear larger.

Five O'Clock Shadow

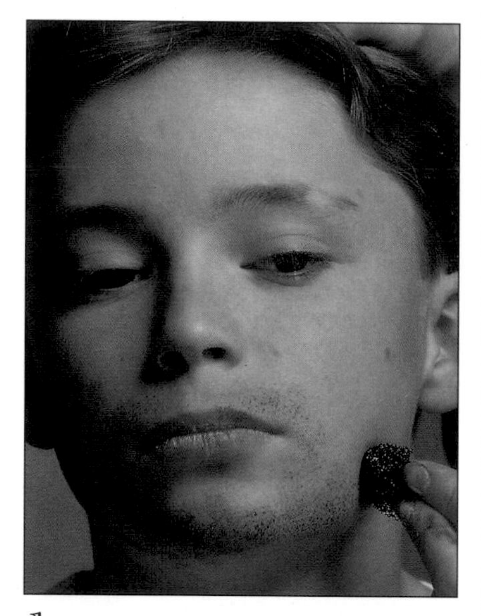

1 To create an unshaven look, use a small coarse sponge to stipple black/brown paint gently over the beard and moustache area of the face.

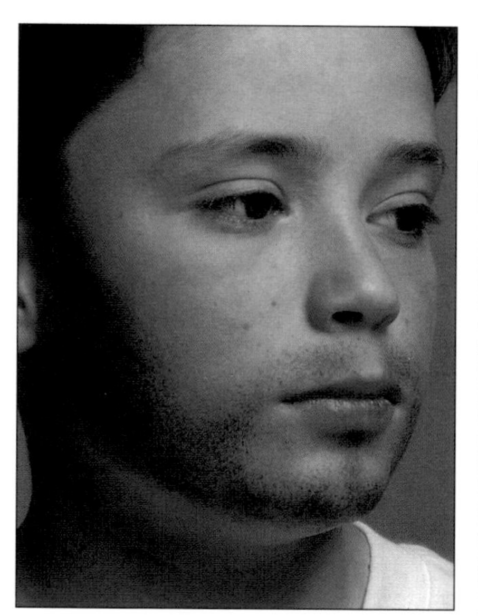

2 The finished effect.

TIP: Build up the depth of colour very gradually. Tap the sponge on the back of your hand before each application of colour to remove any excess paint. If any areas start to look too dark, stipple them lightly with a paler colour.

Eyebrows

A change of eyebrow shape can transform a face into a multitude of different characters. Think about the type of personality you are trying to convey. Make faces in the mirror – of laughter, anger, sadness – and see what happens to your features. Build up a repertoire of shapes based on what you observe.

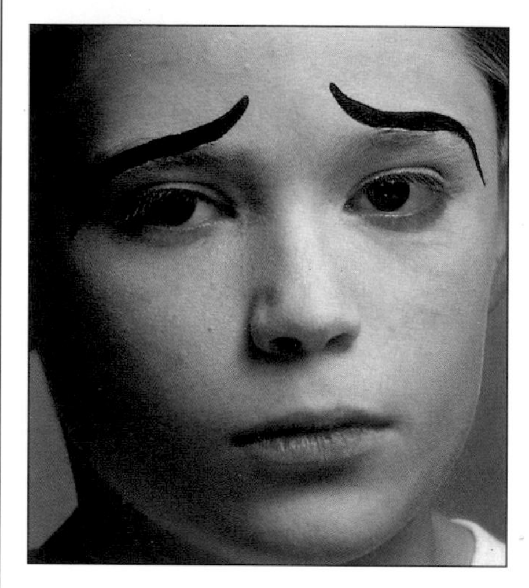

1. Sad.

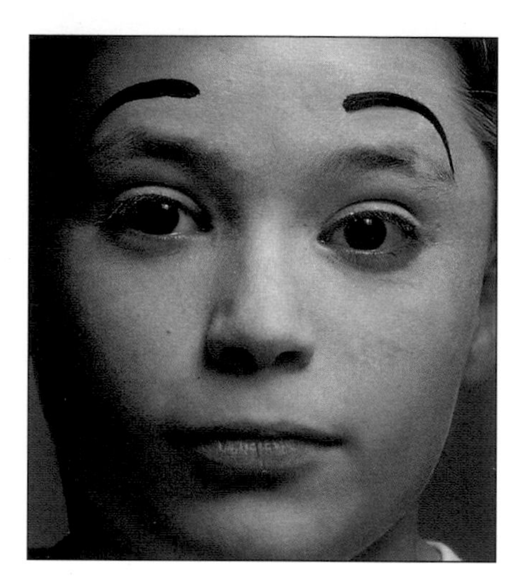

2. Surprised.

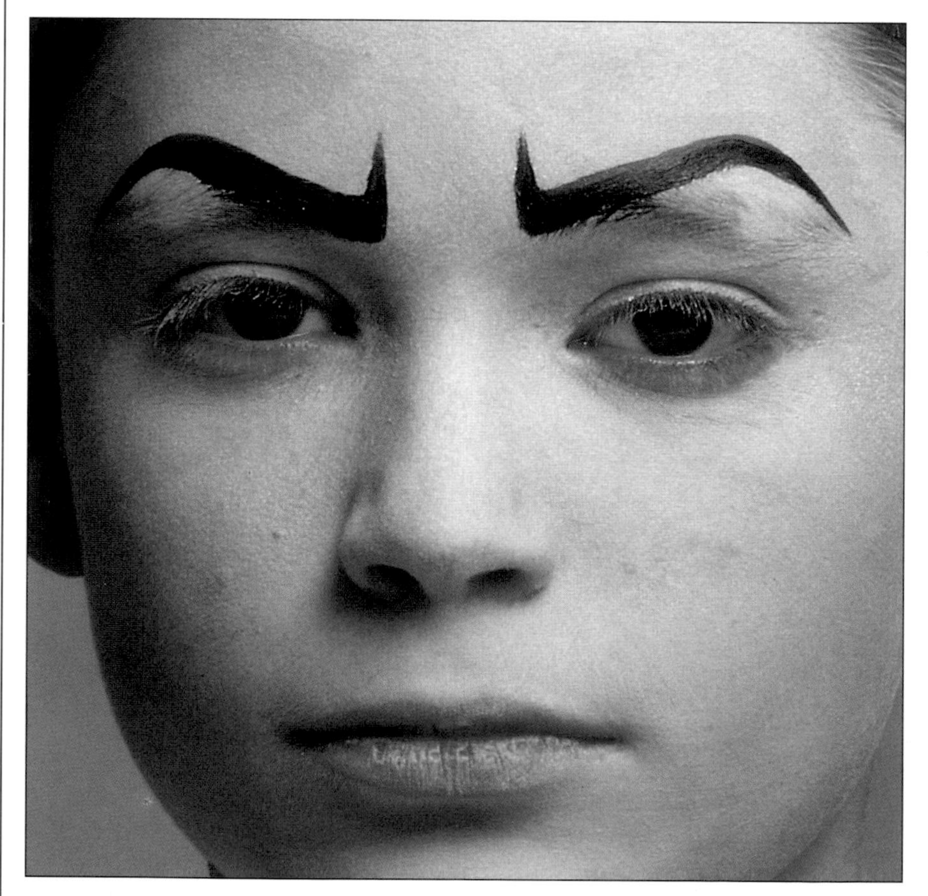

3. Cruel.

Using a Make-up Chart – A Finished Example

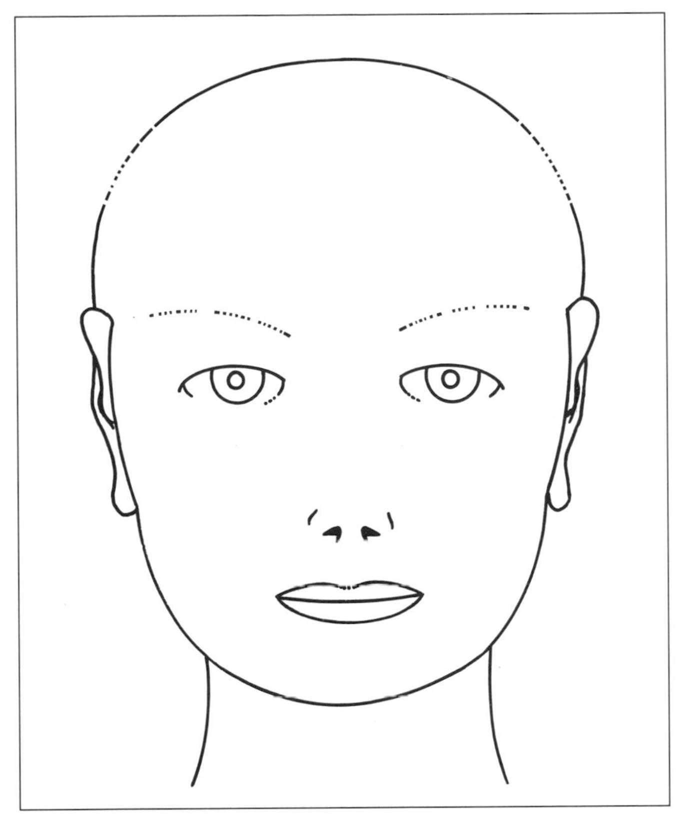

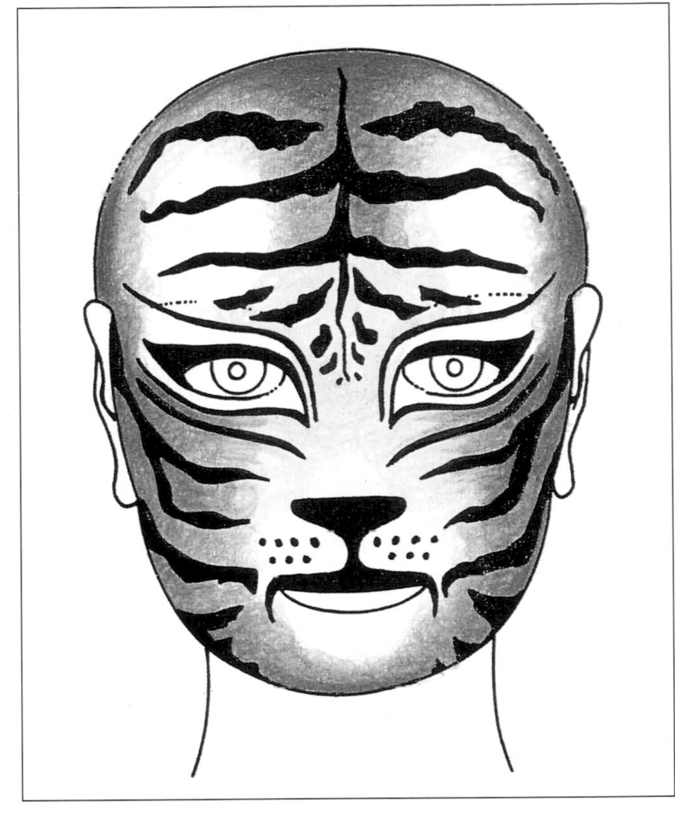

1 You can photocopy this blank chart to help you plan your own creations.

2 Fill in the design with paints, felt tips or coloured pencils.

3 Keep referring to your chart as you apply the make-up.

1 ANIMALS

From time immemorial, people the world over have painted their faces and bodies to imitate animals; either to enhance their physical appearance or perhaps with the hope of acquiring some of the amazing powers of the natural world.

The young men of the Nuba tribes in South-eastern Sudan paint their bodies purely for decoration. The animals represented are chosen for their elegance and beauty rather than their spiritual and physical powers.

In most tribal societies, however, people believe that by painting the body with the stripes of a tiger, for example, or by wearing the feathers of an eagle they will assume the strength and grace of these creatures and increase their own powers beyond their natural limit.

Leopard

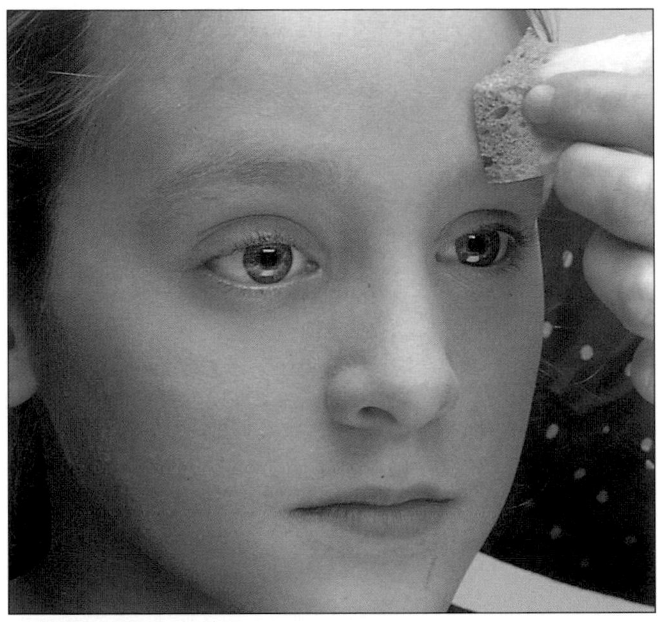

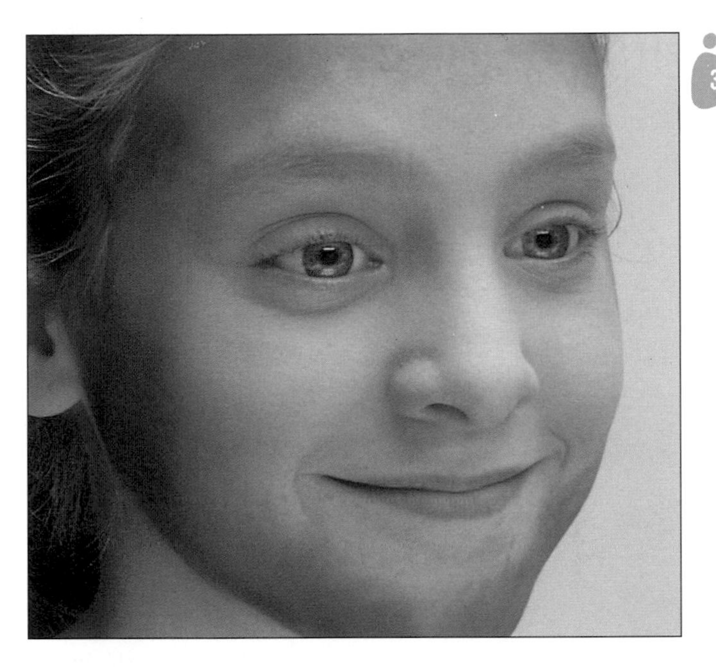

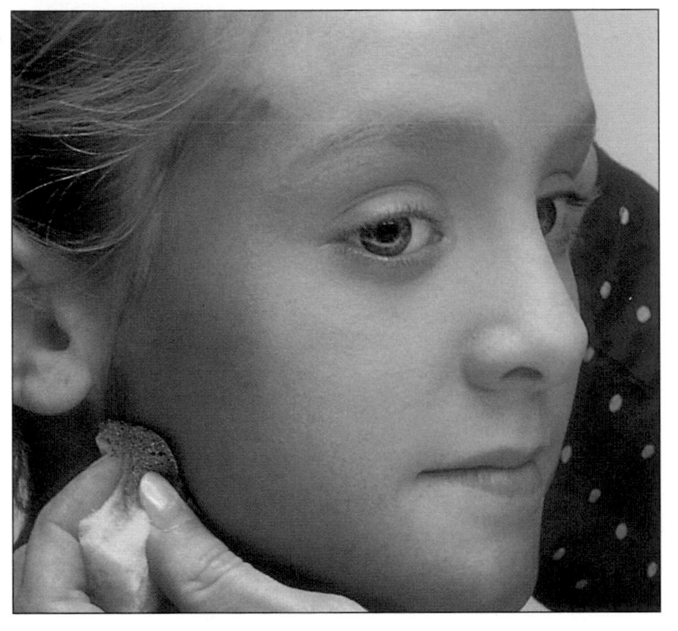

1 Dab yellow base colour over the whole of the face using a sponge.

2 Use another sponge to shade the outer parts of the face with mid-brown.

3 Merge the two colours together by stippling gently with the yellow sponge.

TIP: When stippling colours to blend them, keep the sponge almost dry; squeeze it onto a tissue to remove any excess moisture.

4 Stipple white paint with a sponge over the mouth and chin, and from each eyebrow up to the hairline.

5 With a thin brush, paint black across the whole eyelid. Start at the inner corner of the eye, take the line past the outer corner and wing it up slightly at the end.

- Paint a black line down from the inner corner of the eye and over the cheek.
- Paint a black line below the bottom eyelashes, starting at the inner nose line. Follow the direction of the top lid, sweeping the end of the lower line up to meet it at the outer corner.

6 Paint the tip of the nose black. Draw a thin line from the centre of the nose down to the top lip. Paint the top lip only in black, dropping the ends down at each corner of the mouth. Block out the bottom lip completely with white.

7 Already the model has a real animal look; this is because the main features of the face – the eyes, nose and mouth – have been de-humanised to a large extent. Once this effect has been achieved, the image is set, and any further decoration is incidental. This is why you must follow the preliminary stages so carefully.

8 Having added the whisker spots to the top lip with black, paint on some leopard markings in very dark brown, highlighting them just off-centre with flecks of white.

9 Remember, most animal markings are symmetical.

10 The finished leopard.

Lion

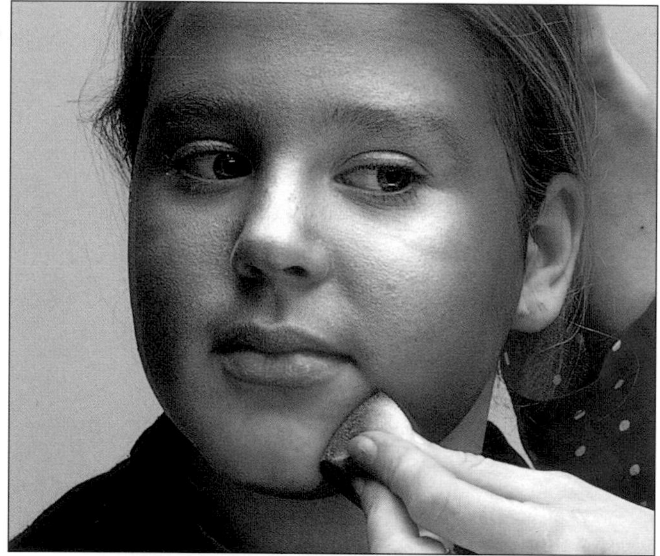

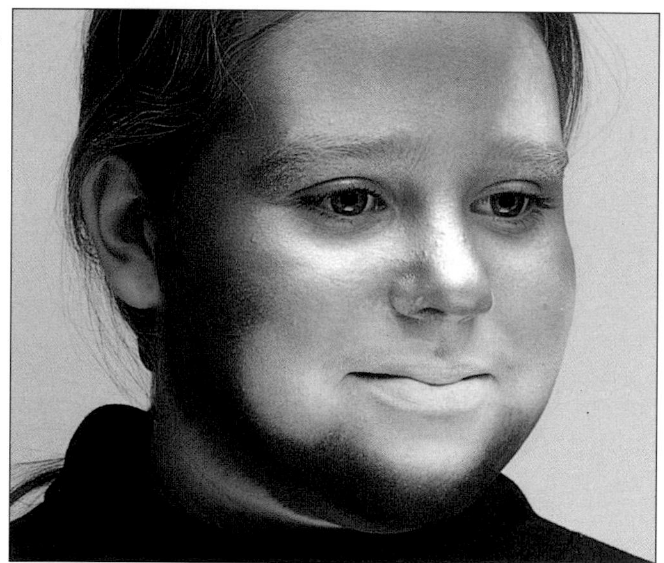

1 The base of this make-up is gold, with dark brown around the edges of the face. Apply the colours with sponges and stipple to blend them together.

2 Using a clean sponge, stipple white paint over each eyebrow, fading it out towards the hairline. Apply the white to the mouth and chin as well, extending it across the cheeks to create a heavy-jowled look.

3 Paint the whole eyelid black, taking the colour underneath the eye and a little way down the side of the nose. Blend the eye colour into the base with fine, sharp brush strokes. This technique is known as "feathering".

The nose and mouth are created in the same way as the leopard (see page 18), but allowing the mouth lines to extend further down the chin to outline and emphasise the lion's jowls.

4 Decorate the outer edges of the face with rough, intermittent lines in dark red. Repeat these lines in very dark brown or black.

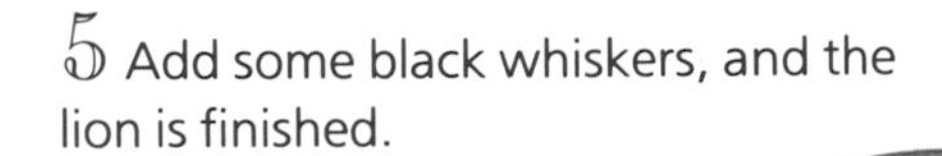

5 Add some black whiskers, and the lion is finished.

Tiger

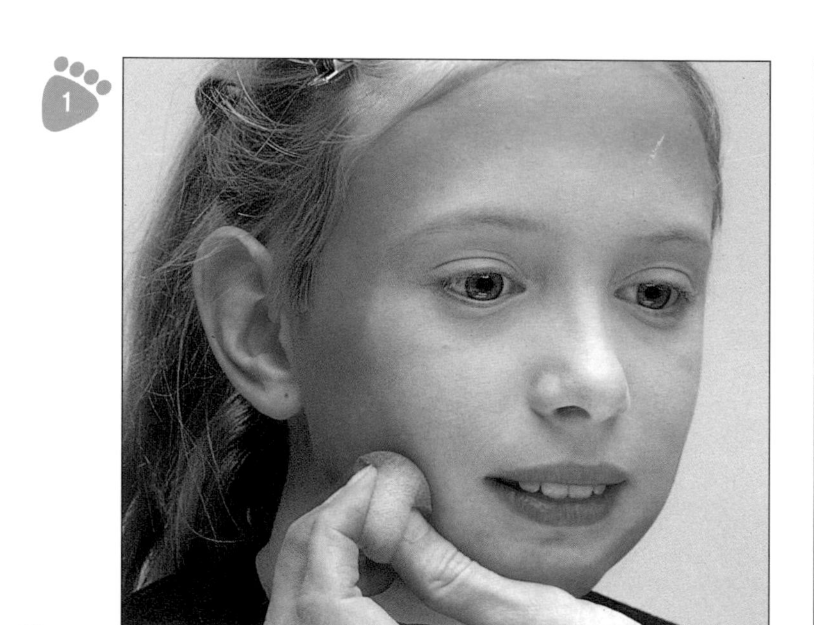

1 Apply a base of yellow with orange on the outer edges. Stipple the colours together with a sponge.

2 Stipple on white patches around the mouth and above the eyebrows. Paint the eyes in black, starting just below the inner corner; take the colour across the lid and wing the line up slightly just past the outer corner of the eye. Paint the lower eyeline below the lashes, following the curve of the top line but leaving the outer end open.
 The mouth and nose are applied in the same way as for the leopard (see page 18) except that the tiger's nose should be extended a little way onto the cheek.

3 For the tiger's stripes, use a narrow brush to paint black lines across the forehead. Finish one side of the face first, then copy the design onto the other side to keep the pattern symmetrical.

4 The finished tiger. Because the markings are so strong, there is no need to add whiskers – these would only clutter the face and spoil the effect.

Dog

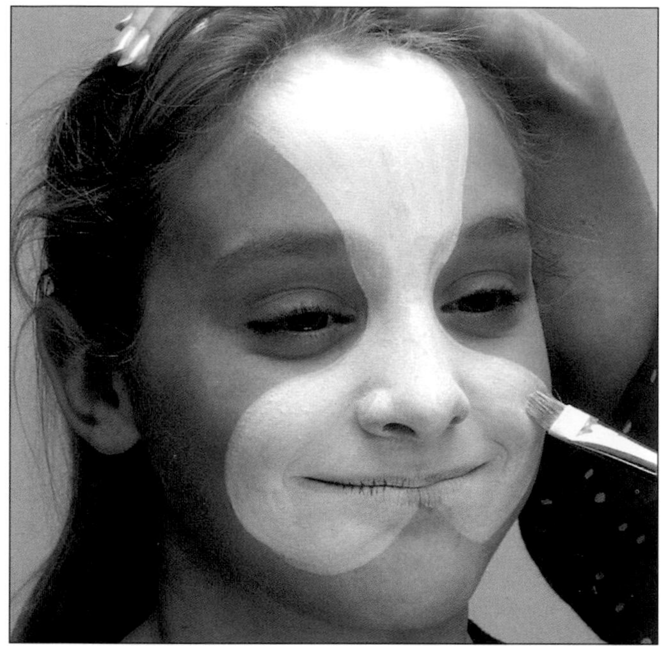

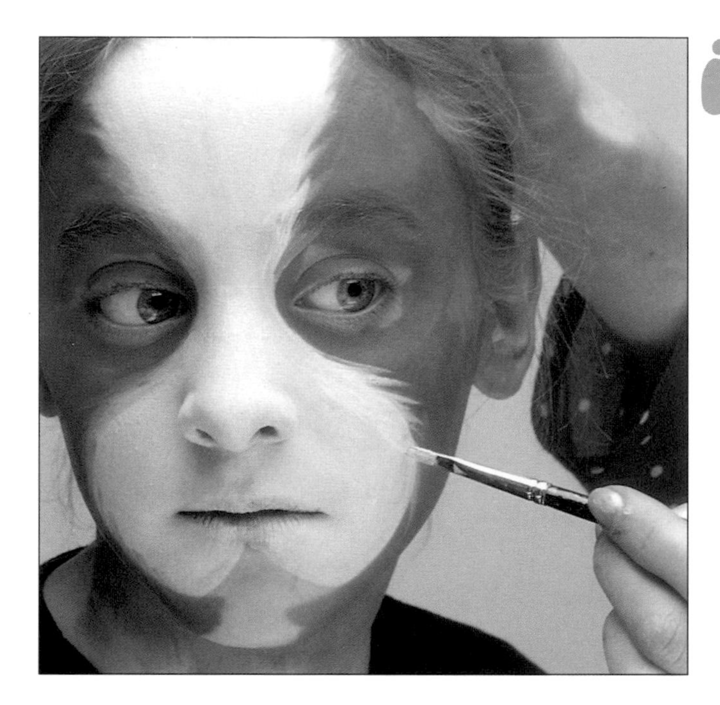

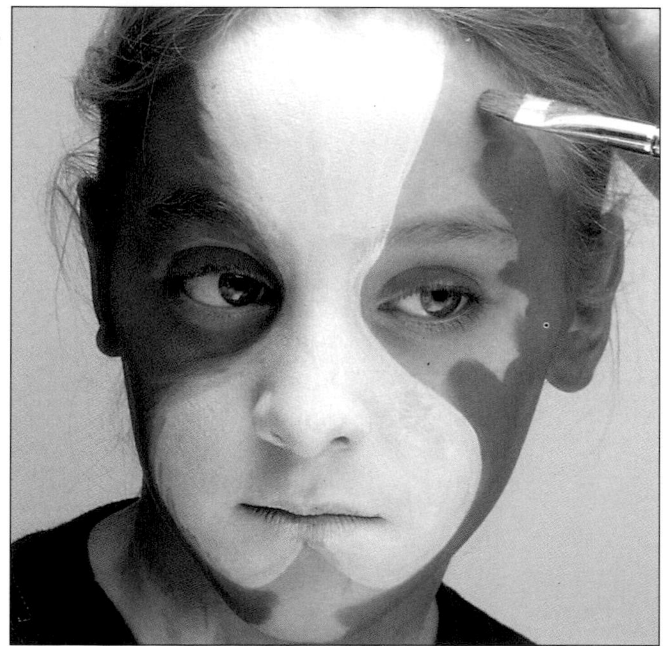

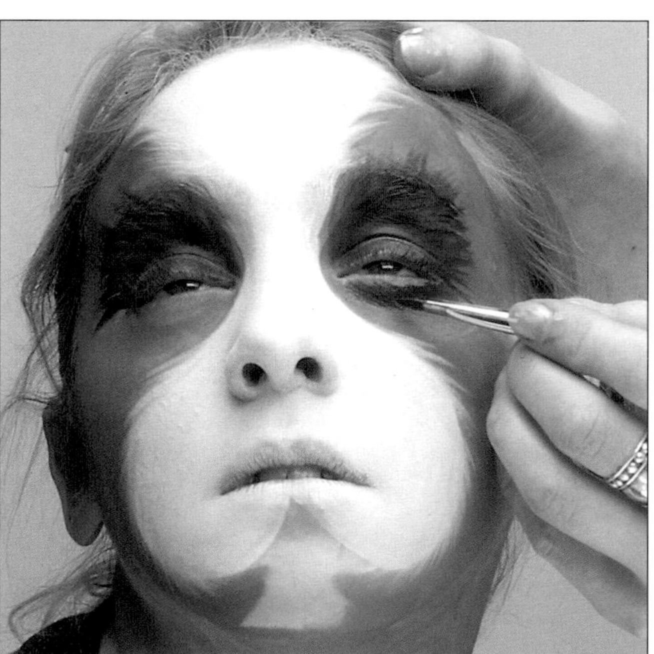

1 Using a flat, wide brush, paint this white shape down the centre of the face.

2 Fill in around the white with a mid-brown.

3 Soften the line where the two colours meet by feathering the white onto the brown with a very fine brush.

4 Paint the eyes in dark brown, using jagged, uneven brush strokes.

5 Use black for the mouth, extending the line beyond the corners of the mouth before dropping it down sharply to the chin. Paint the tip of the nose black and add some black whisker spots.

6 The drooping tongue is dark red. Fleck the eye areas with red and yellow to highlight them.

Rabbit

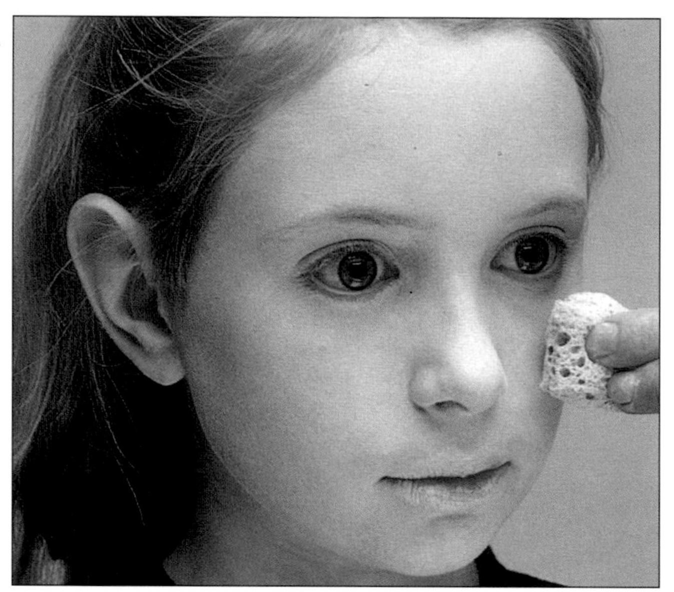

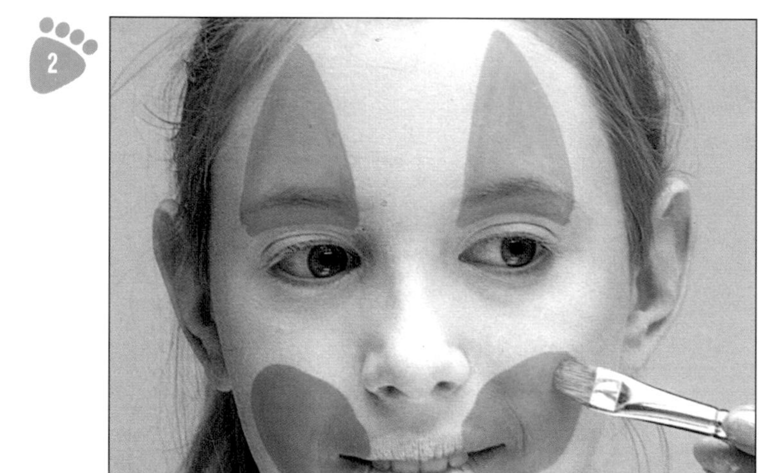

1 Use a sponge to apply white to the whole face.

2 Paint pink circles over the corners of the mouth onto the cheeks and pink eye shapes from the eyebrows to the hairline using a wide, flat brush.

3 Outline the eye shapes with thin purple lines. Extend the bottom lines down the nose a little and sweep the outer ends up towards the temples.

4 Tell the model to close her eyes, and draw a fine slanted purple line underneath the bottom eyelashes. Colour the end of the nose purple, and join it to the mouth with a thin purple line. Outline the natural shape of the model's lips in purple leaving the middle third of the bottom lip free.

5 Draw the outline of the teeth over the bottom lip, using a very fine brush and black paint. Fill in the teeth with white. Add some small black whisker spots, and carefully draw in the fine blue whiskers and brow detail.

6 Paint a neat white line around the inside of the brow shapes to emphasise them.

7 The finished rabbit.

Glam-Cat

1 Cover the face with white paint blended into a red border by stippling with a damp sponge.

2 Paint the upper eyeline in black, starting just below the inner corner of the eye, following the lash line and sweeping the end of the line out and up. The lower line is also black, and follows the curve of the upper one, sweeping up to join it at the outer edge. Fill in the whole eyelid area in black.

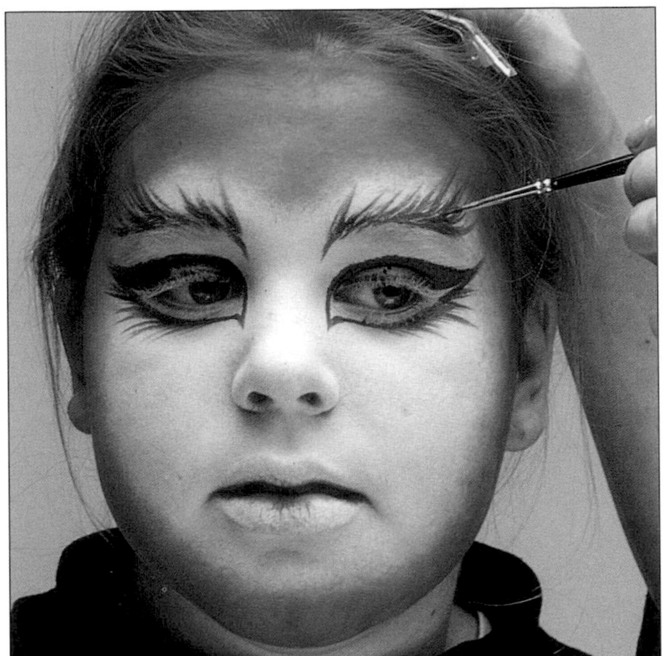

3 Use small, delicate brush strokes to create the eyebrows, making sure their shape follows that of the eyelines. Paint in some similar lines along the outer edge of the lower eyeline.

4 Paint the tip of the nose black, taking the centre line down to the top lip. Paint along the top lip and curl the ends of the line up slightly onto the cheek. Add black whisker spots.

5 Around the edge of the face, apply some rough strokes of grey. Highlight this shaggy effect, and the area below the eyebrow, with patchy dashes of yellow. Draw a small dark red semicircle on the bottom lip.

6 A very glamorous cat.

Black Cat

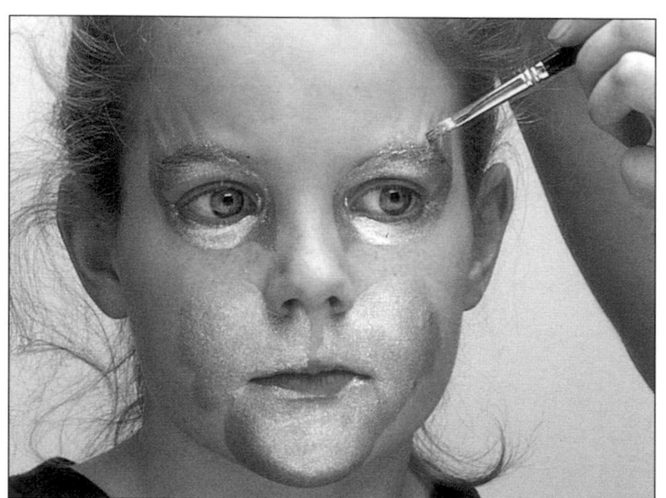

1 Paint silver around the mouth, chin and eyes, making these areas slightly larger than they will eventually be.

2 Square off the end of the nose in pink, and apply the same colour to the lips.

3 Carefully paint round the silver features in black, then fill in the rest of the face.

4 Using a fine brush and sharp, delicate strokes, feather the black paint onto the silver to give a softer, more textured effect.

5 Add black whisker spots, followed by white whiskers and white eyebrow details. Because the paint is easily removed by washing, the colours can be extended into the hair to complete the make-up.

6 The finished black cat.

5

6

Eyes on Eyelids

Ask the model to close her eyes, then paint the upper eyelids yellow, outline the eye socket with a thin line of black and paint a black iris in the centre.

Magic Cat

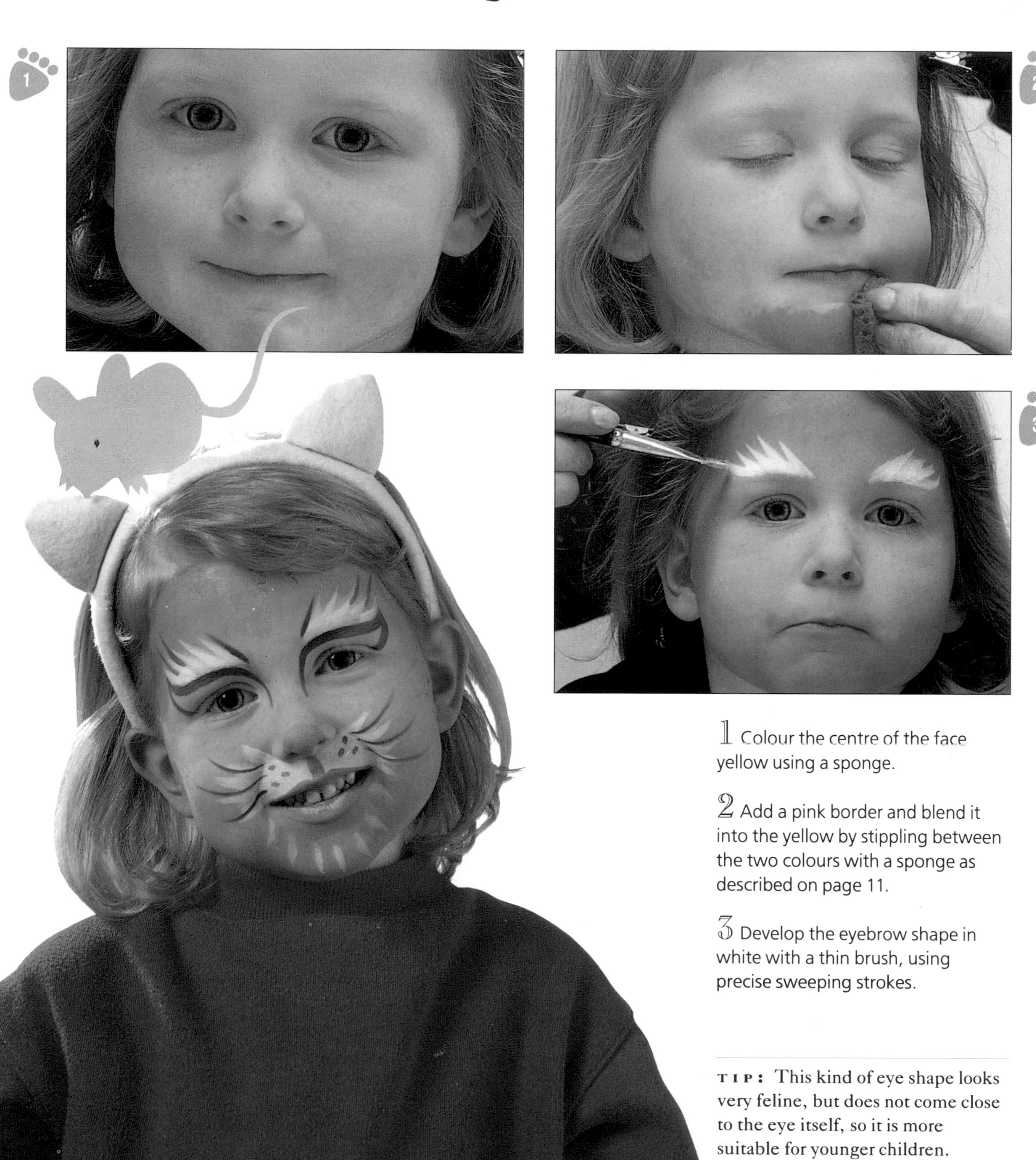

1 Colour the centre of the face yellow using a sponge.

2 Add a pink border and blend it into the yellow by stippling between the two colours with a sponge as described on page 11.

3 Develop the eyebrow shape in white with a thin brush, using precise sweeping strokes.

TIP: This kind of eye shape looks very feline, but does not come close to the eye itself, so it is more suitable for younger children.

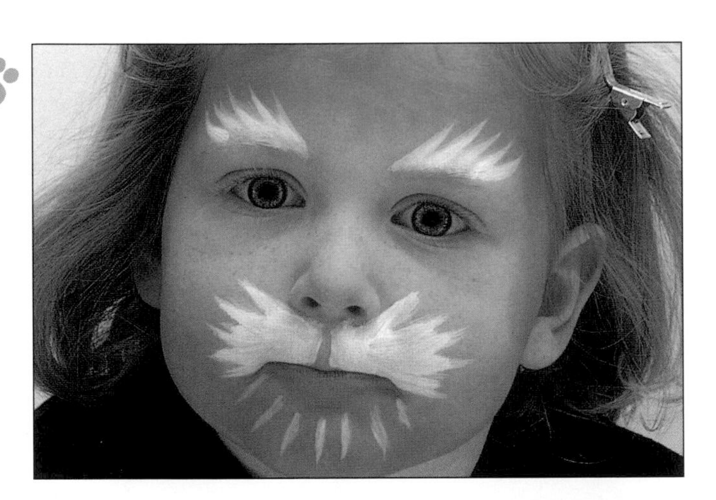

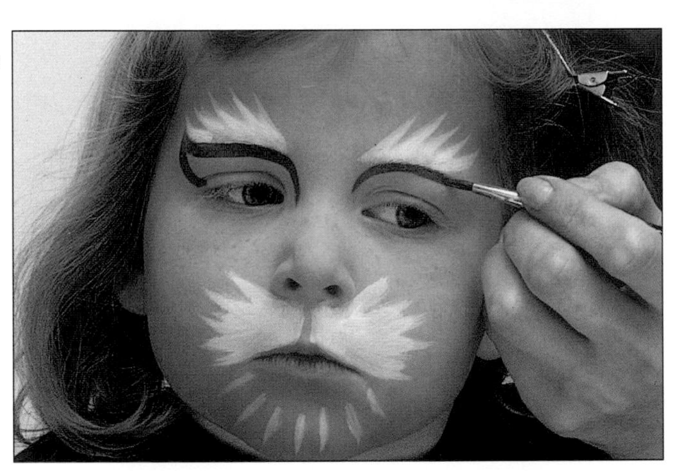

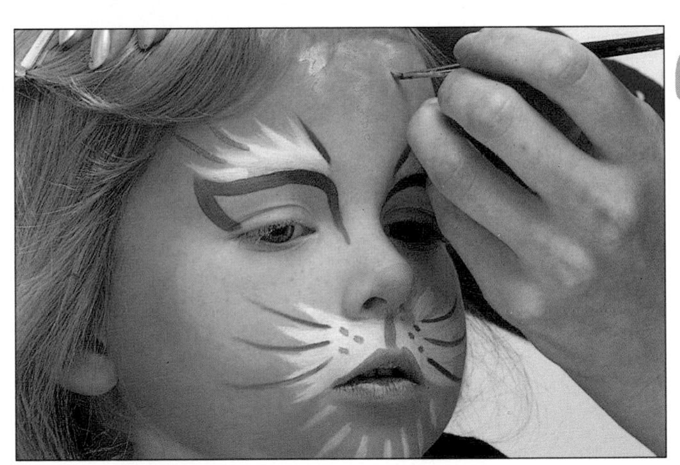

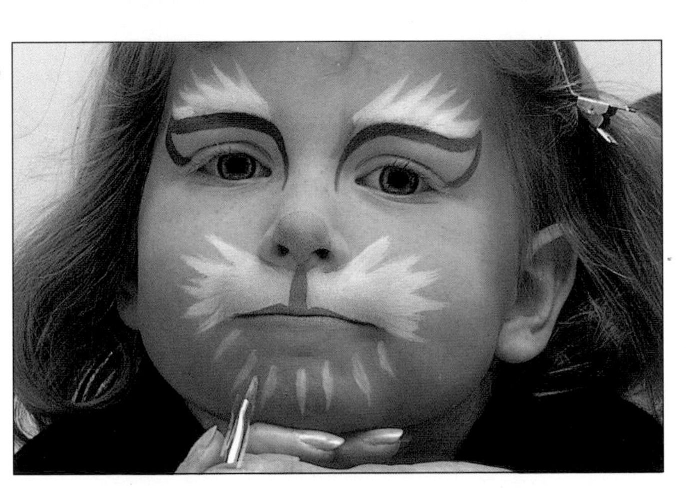

4 Paint white whiskery fluff above the top lip in the same way, adding a few flecks of white to the chin.

5 The eye shapes are outlined in purple, starting beside the nose and sweeping the line along the brow-bone.

6 Paint the tip of the nose lilac and bring the colour down onto the mouth to enhance its natural shape.

7 Use a very fine brush to add blue whisker spots and some brow details.

8 With the same brush, paint a streak of dark red above the inner end of each brow line and add a few delicate red whiskers.

9 Complete the make-up with a few bright green squiggles on the forehead and cheeks.

Frog

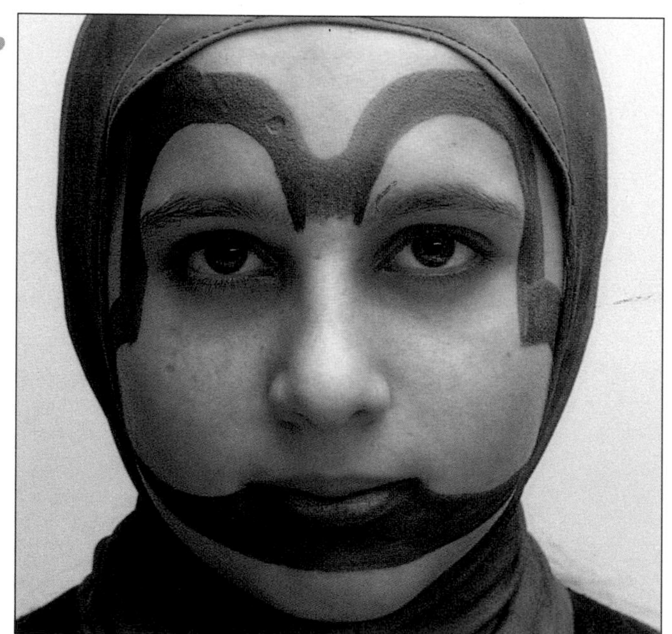

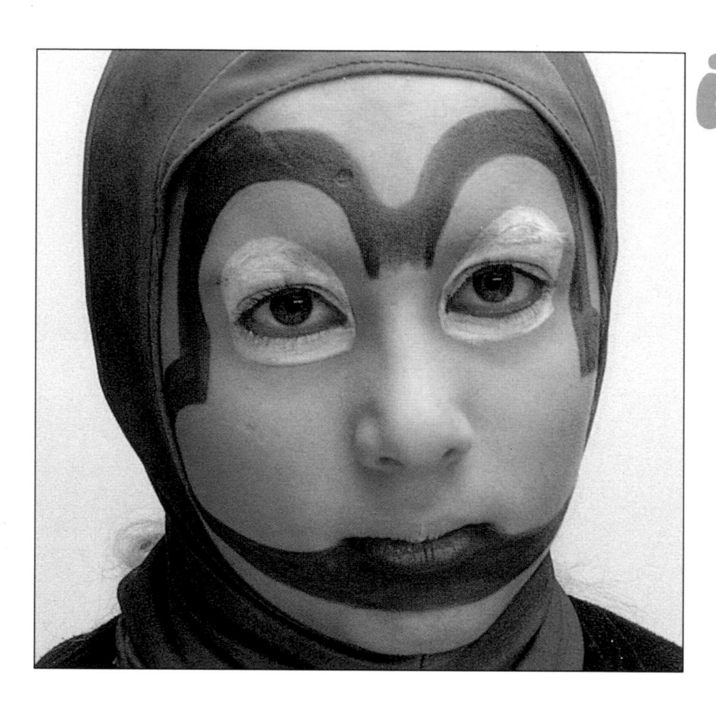

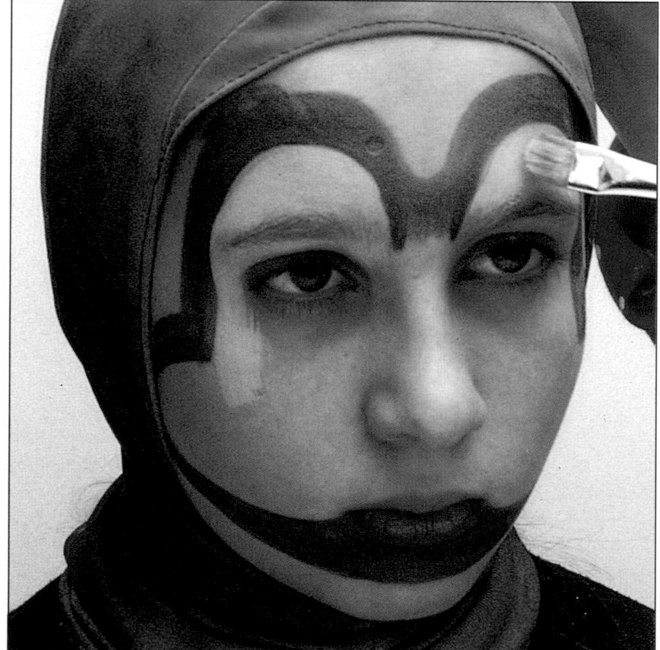

1 The basic outline is applied in green, with the cheek lines extending right out to the ears.

2 Fill the area inside the green lines with yellow, using a flat, wide brush.

3 Leaving a rim of yellow, paint white patches underneath and around the eyes.

4 Paint in the area outside the green lines with a very dark brown.

5 Following the edge of the green, draw a thick black line across the top lip from one side of the face to the other.

6 Use a cotton bud to mottle the nose and cheeks with pale brown.

TIP: Outline the black mouth with white to make it seem more protruberant.

Zebra

TIP: As the markings of a zebra are so repetitive, it is a very good idea to draw this design on a copy of the make-up chart (see page 15) before you begin. This will give you something to refer to if the lines begin to confuse you!

1 Cover the face and neck with white paint, using a sponge.

2 Stipple grey over the nose and mouth area.

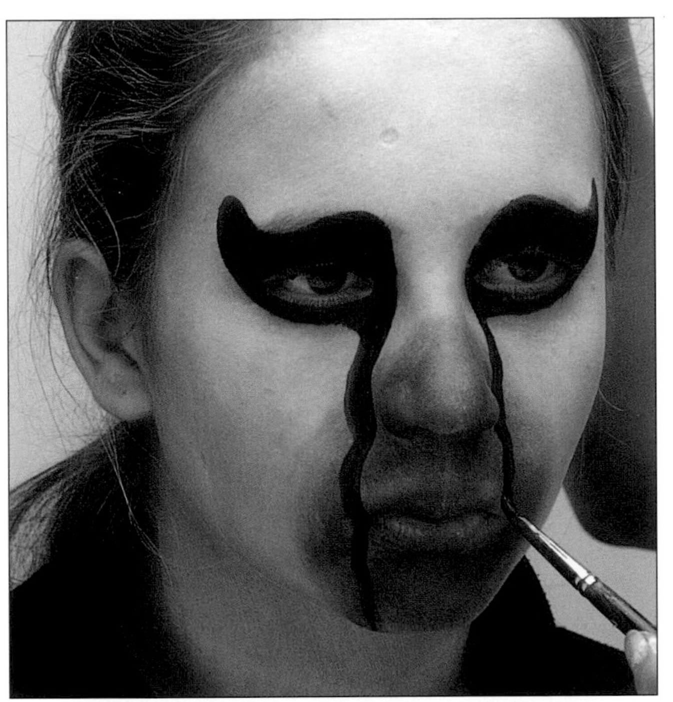

3 Paint the black shapes over the eyes, extending the inner corners right down past the sides of the nose and onto the chin.

4 Draw a rough line down the middle of the forehead and use this as a centre point for the rest of the black markings on the forehead and down the nose.

5 For the zebra, it is easier to work on both sides of the face at the same time, rather than completing one side first. You will find it less confusing, and it will be easier to keep the pattern symmetrical.

6 The finished zebra.

Ladybird

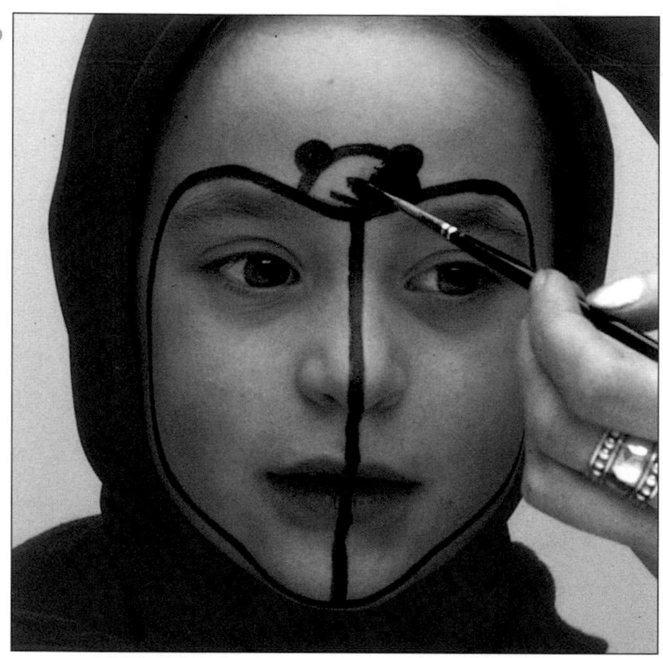

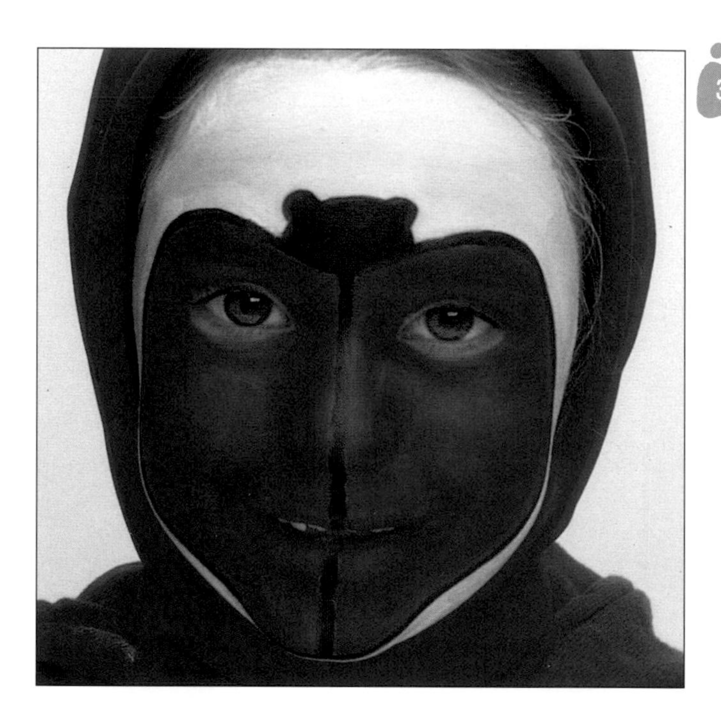

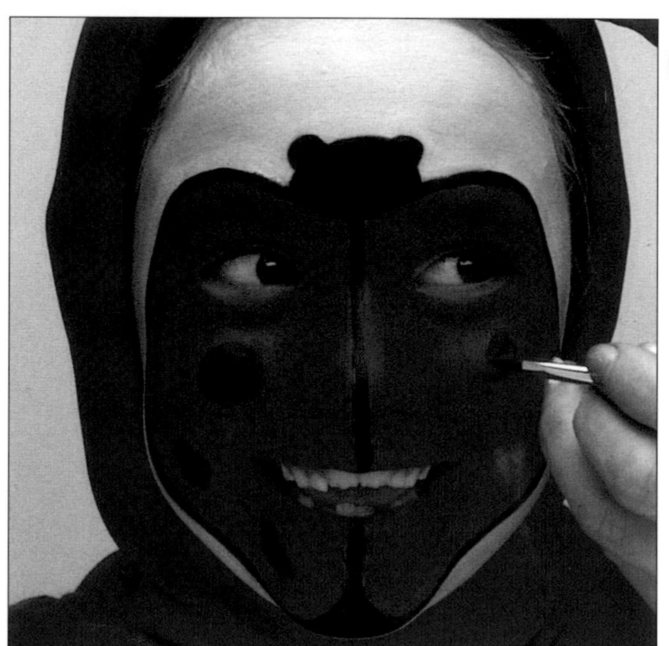

1 Using a thin brush, carefully paint the black outline onto the face.

TIP: It might help to draw the shape onto the face with a grey eye pencil first.

2 Fill in the shape with red, using a flat, wide brush.

3 Paint the borders of the face in white, taking great care not to let the colours overlap.

4 Add the black spots and a small black triangle on the chin.

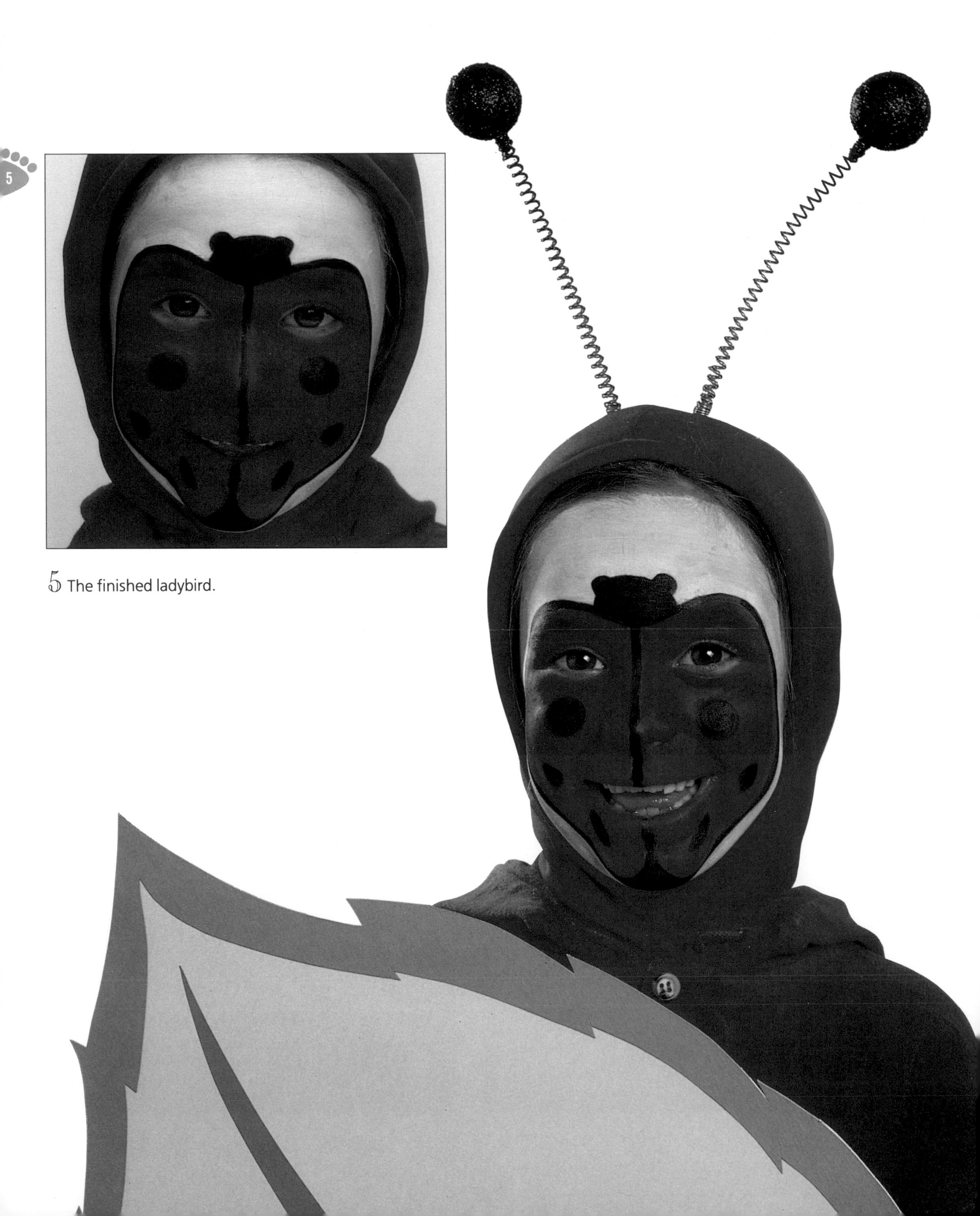

5 The finished ladybird.

2
CLOWNS

The history of the clown is a surprisingly long one – the role dates back over 4000 years, to well before there were such things as circuses. In their earliest days, the clown figures were known as jesters, fools, buffoons or gleemen, and they entertained the crowds at fairs, markets or in other public places. They were also employed by the nobility to entertain private guests, at the Royal Court for example.

Today there are three main types of clown: the Hobo or Tramp, the Auguste, and the White Face. The most well-known Hobo or Tramp clown is probably Charlie Chaplin. The Auguste type of clown is the zaniest of the three and wears the most bizarre and exaggerated make-up. The White Face clown is the graceful, thoughtful one, of which a popular example is the Pierrot.

The Pierrot clown is sometimes known as Pedrolino, and can be traced back to early 17th-century Italy, but the romantic figure we associate with the name today was created in the 19th century by the French mime artist Jean Baptiste Gaspard Deburau. Traditionally Pierrot is sad because the dashing Harlequin has stolen his true love, Columbine – this is the cause of the single tear that always appears under one eye.

Pierrot

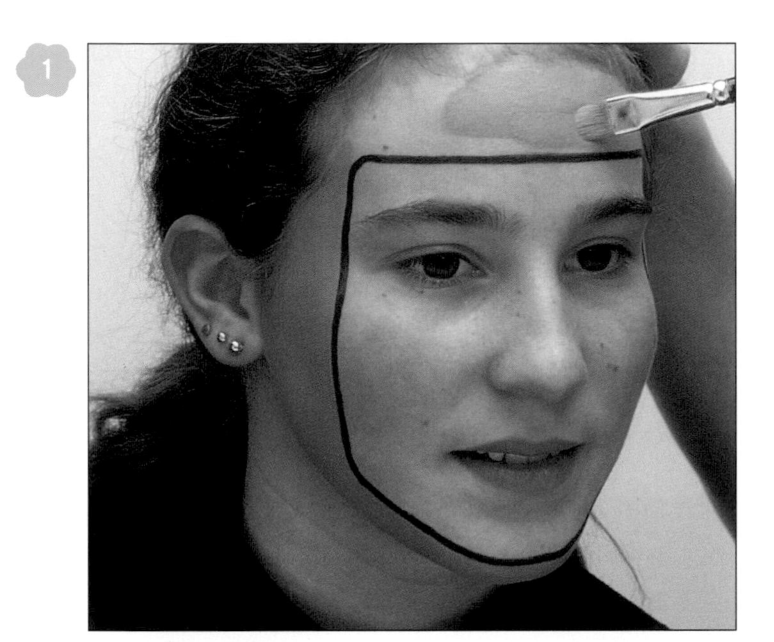

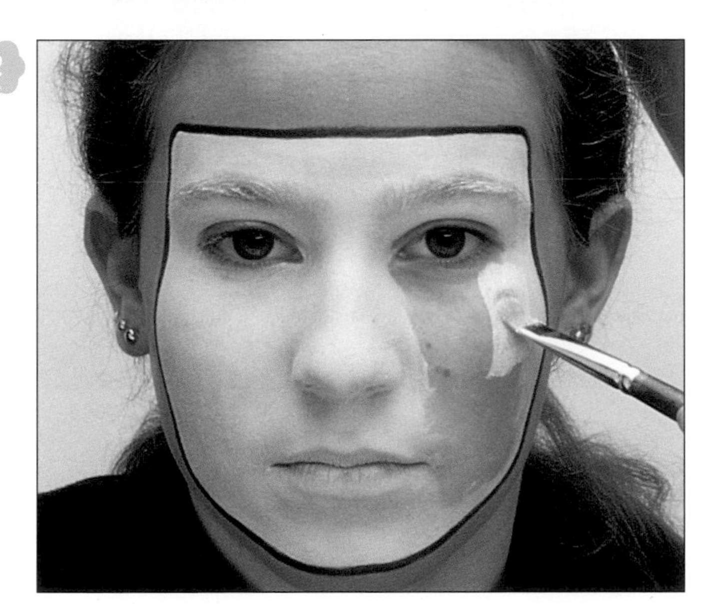

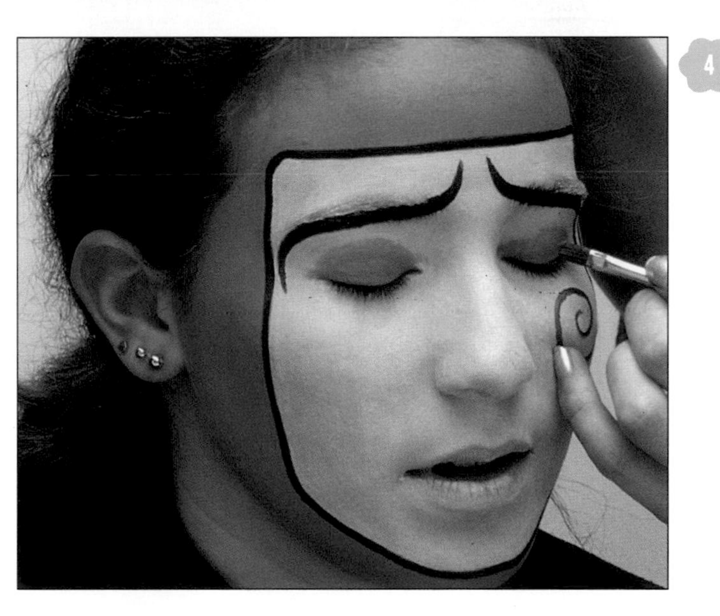

1 You will need a steady hand to paint this outline onto the face; try to keep the line as sharp and even as possible. It might help to draw the shape onto the face with grey eye pencil first before painting the line in black. Paint the area outside the mask in pink using a wide, flat brush.

2 Rinse the flat brush and use it to fill in the mask area in white, taking great care not to go over the black outline. If any white areas seem patchy or streaky, stipple over them gently with a sponge.

3 The eyebrows are an essential part of Pierrot's sad expression. Start the brow line quite high above the natural eyebrow, then drop the line down diagonally to end below the outer corner of the eye. One side has a decorative curl.

4 Paint the eyelids in the same shade of pink as the edges of the face.

5

6

7

8

9

10

5 Use a very fine brush to paint a thick black line across the upper eyelid next to the lashes, ending a little way beyond the outer corner of the eye.

6 With the same brush, paint a thin black line under the bottom row of eyelashes, again extending the line to just beyond the outer corner of the eye. This will make the eye seem larger.

7 Cover the lips with white and paint in the lip shape in black with a very fine brush. You could use a fine black eye pencil if you prefer.

8 Colour the lips pink.

9 Paint the essential Pierrot tears carefully onto one cheek in black.

10 You can add some silver glitter to the teardrops to give them a watery look, or they could be coloured in blue. For extra glamour, add a few dots of silver glitter to the lips and brows.

11 Poor Pierrot.

Baby Clown

1 Paint on a wide red smile, and add a red dot on each cheek and a red tip to the nose.

2 Outline the red mouth shape with yellow. With the model's eyes closed, add a blue triangle under each eye. Make the nose and cheek markings look shiny with some white highlights.

3 Using a thin brush, paint on some arched purple eyebrows and a dash of purple above each eye.

4 A very cheerful clown face.

Funny Clown

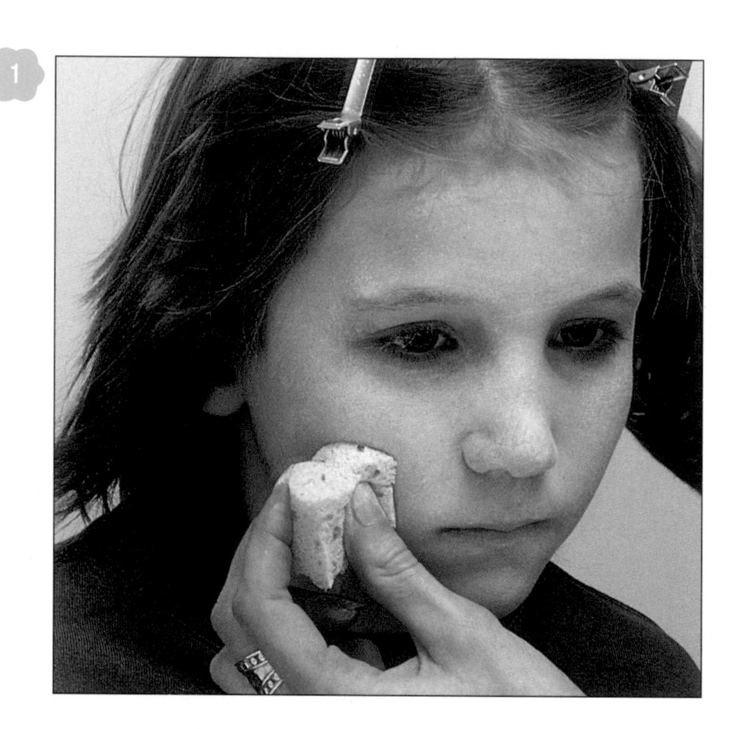

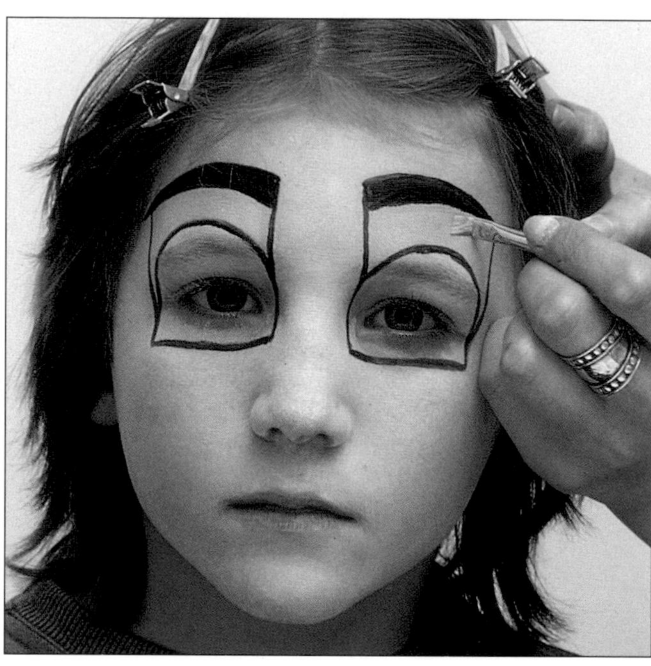

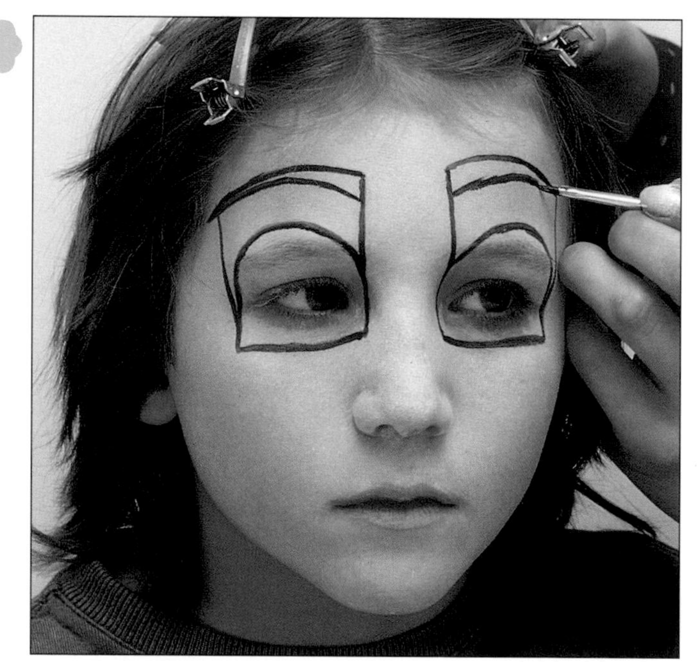

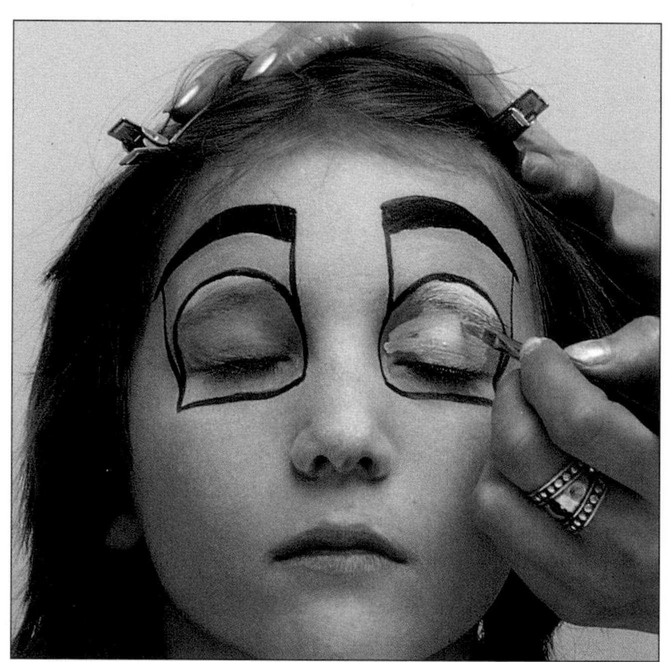

1 Cover the whole face in white paint using a sponge. Stipple lightly over any patches that seem streaky to make a really smooth finish.

2 Draw in the main eye shapes with a very fine brush, and add the eyebrows.

3 Fill in the eyebrows in black. The space underneath each one is filled in with blue.

4 Cover the main eye area carefully in white.

5

8

6

7

5 Paint the end of the nose red, and use a thin brush to outline the shape of the clown's mouth.

6 Fill in the mouth shape with yellow and outline the red border with light blue.

7 Add some coloured spots of assorted sizes to each cheek and draw a black rectangle in the centre of each eyelid.

8 The nose and cheek spots will benefit from some white highlights.

Card Clown

1

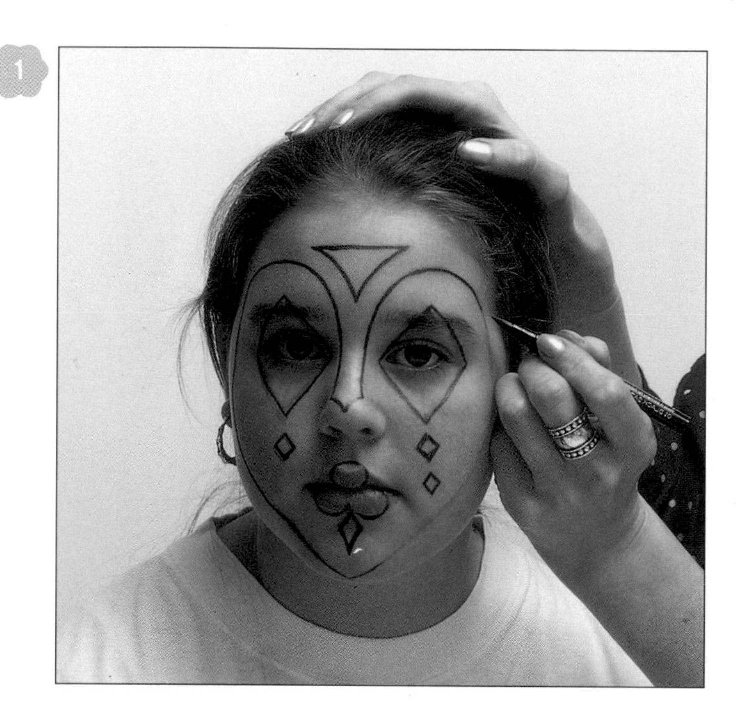

3

2

4

1 Sketch the design lightly onto the face with a grey eye pencil. Once you are satisfied that both sides of the face are even, trace over the design with either a very fine brush or a black liquid eyeliner pen.

2 Use a fine brush to make a white outline around all the inner shapes of the design.

3 Fill in the remaining areas with white.

4 Paint the diamond shapes black, including the eye shapes but leaving the eyelids blank.

5 Colour the shape on the lips in red.

6 Carefully paint the borders of the face and the stripe down the nose in red.

7 Outline the eyes in white. Whenever you are working close to the lower lid, ask the model to look up and away from your hand.

3
HALLOWE'EN

Hallowe'en falls on 31 October – the day before the Christian Feast of Hallowmas or All Saints' Day. However, long before Christianity, it was a Pagan Festival called *Samhain*. 31 October marked the end of the Harvest and the Summer and the start of Winter and the Celtic New Year.

It was also on this night that witches and warlocks held their great *Sabbat*. People believed that on this night the gateway between the Supernatural world and this world was opened and that the spirits of the dead walked the earth. Gifts of food were left on doorsteps to appease restless ancestors and ritual bonfires were lit in the fields to keep evil spirits at bay. Turnip lanterns with menacing faces carved into them were hung outside houses to frighten away ghosts, and the people dressed up as demons or goblins with the belief that by imitating the other-worldly creatures, they would protect themselves from the powers of evil.

Devil

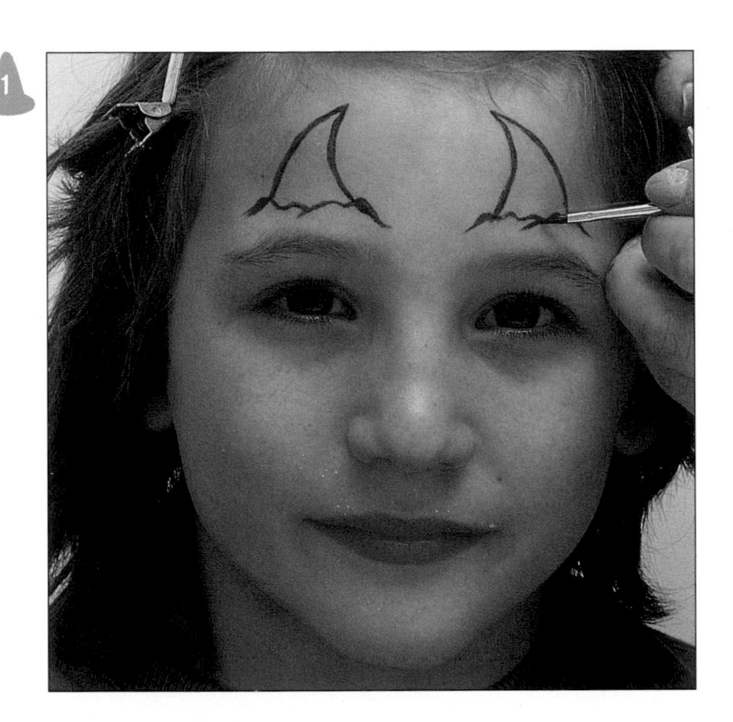

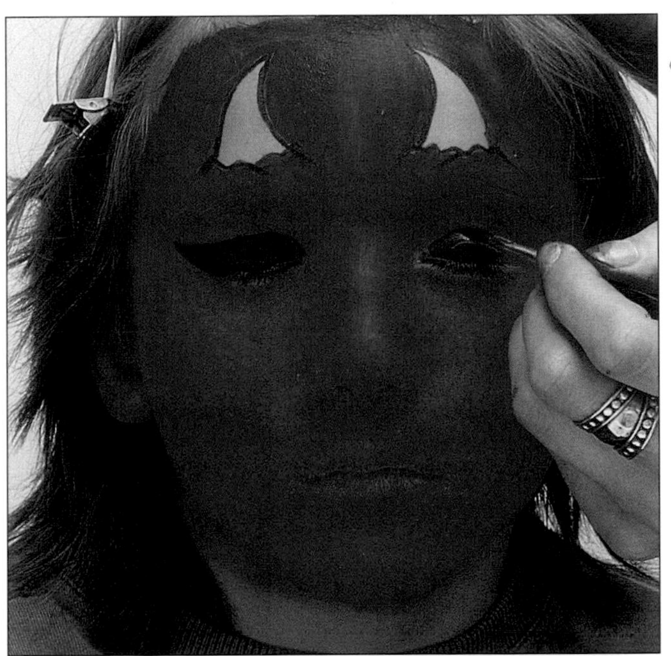

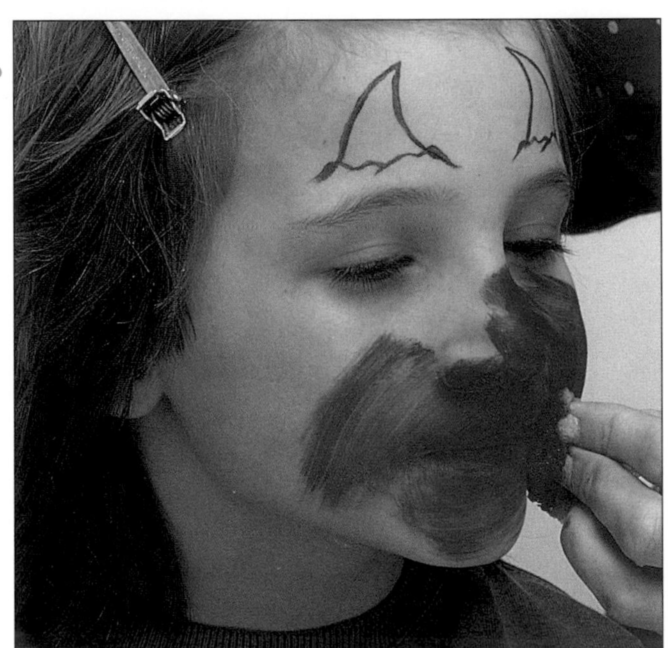

1 Sketch the horn shapes on the forehead with a very fine brush.

2 To keep a neat edge, use a brush to start painting the red area around the horns, then finish the rest of the face with a sponge.

3 Starting at the inner corner of the eye, paint the top lid black, winging the outer ends up slightly.

4 This may well be enough eye detail for younger children.

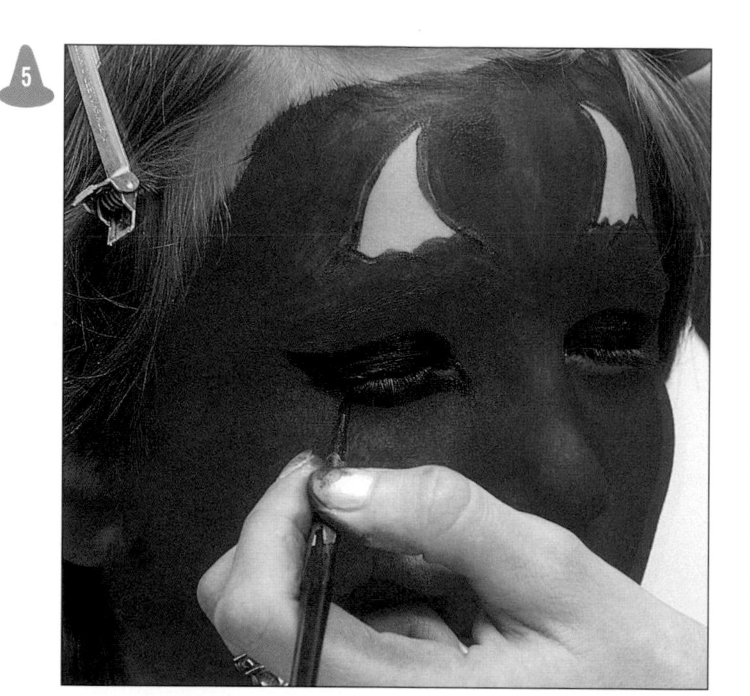

5 Add a thick black line under the bottom eyelashes, making a point at the inner corner and sweeping the line up to meet the top one at the outer corner.

6 Use black paint to make the nostrils look flared by extending them a little way up the nose.

7 The moustache and beard are built up with small sharp strokes of a fine brush, starting above the centre of the top lip.

8 Draw the eyebrows with the inner ends turned up into a frown. Add a line from the nose to the side of the mouth, following the natural crease in the model's cheek. Feel for the model's cheekbones, then enhance them by painting a black curve just below the bone. At a point beneath the centre of the eye, taper the line down onto the jawline.

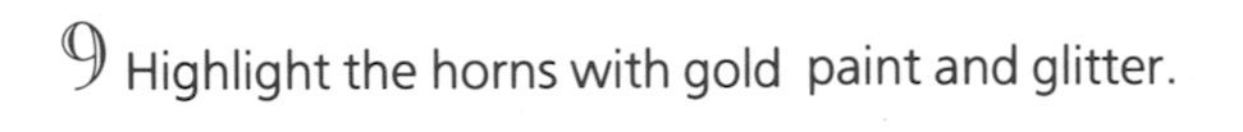

9 Highlight the horns with gold paint and glitter.

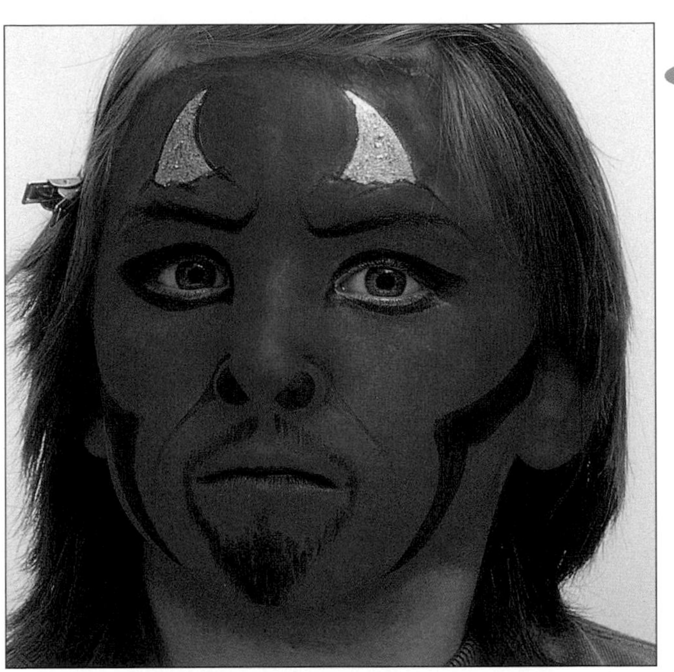

10 A fearsome devil.

Pumpkin

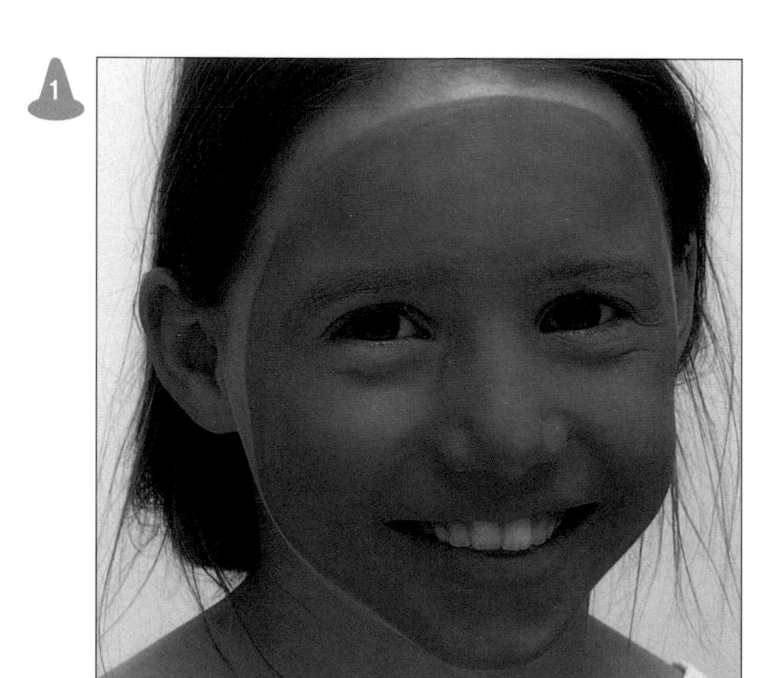

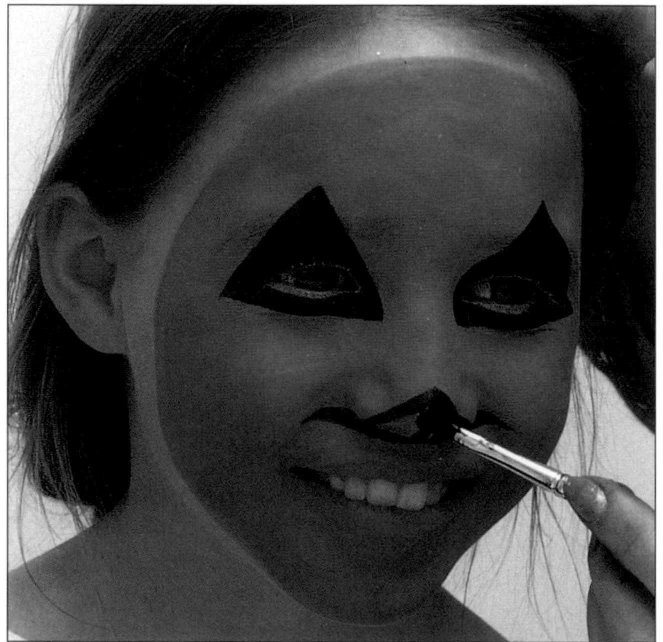

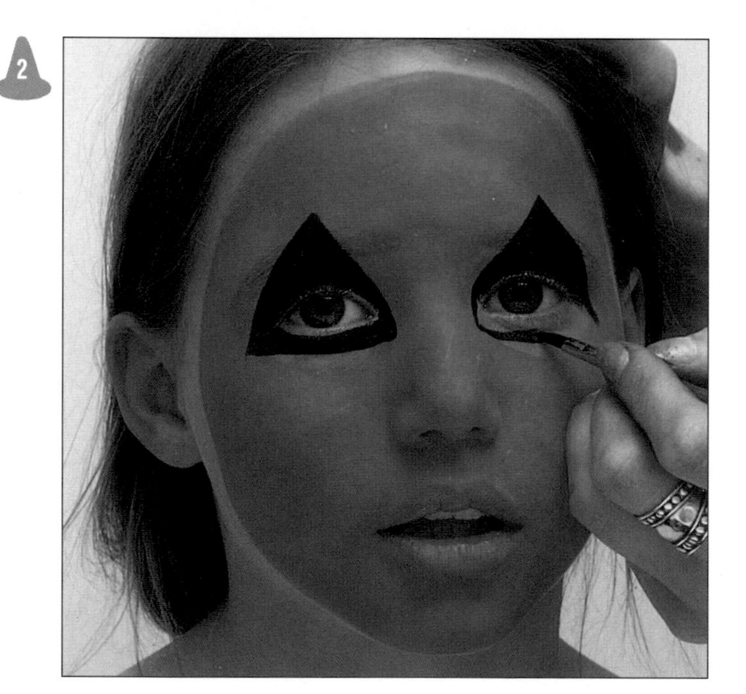

1 Paint a large orange circle over the whole face, filling in the colour with a sponge.

2 Add a black triangle over each eye, using a fine brush. Extend the points of the triangle below the line of the lower lid and carefully fill in the centre leaving a margin around the eye.

3 Paint another triangle on the tip of the nose and extend the sides out onto the cheeks.

4 Outline a huge smile in black and make the top edge a zig-zag line.

5 Fill in the whole mouth shape with black.

6 Design a small green stalk in the middle of the forehead and run some segment lines down from it, following the curve of the orange outline.

Wicked Witch

1 Paint the whole face white, stippling over any streaky areas with a sponge. Draw on the eyebrows with a very fine brush, taking the line up and away from the natural shape to form an arch. Turn the inner ends up to create a scowl.

2 Paint the eyelids black, starting at the inner corner of the eye and flicking the outer ends up towards the temples. Add a thin black line under the lower lashes, following the shape of the top line.

TIP: For safety, ask the model to close her eyes while you paint anywhere near them.

3 The lips are painted in luminous green. Add a line of the same green along the top edge of each eye.

4 On one side of the face, neatly draw three black lines that intersect.

5 Slowly and carefully develop the web pattern, keeping the lines as sharp as possible. Add the spider dangling on a thread – remember spiders have eight legs!

6 On the other cheek, draw a few stars and crescent shapes in black.

7 Decorate the eyebrows, lips and stars with gold or silver glitter.

Hag Witch

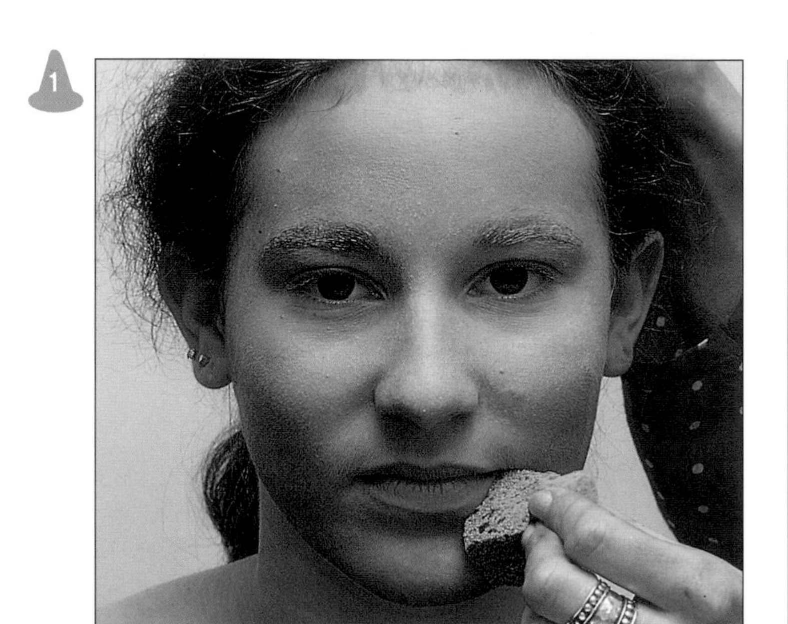

1 Use a sponge to cover the whole face in green. (Yellow or pale grey also work well for this make-up.)

2 Starting above the inner corner of the eye, paint a sharp diagonal line in black, sweeping up towards the temples. Feather the top edge of the line using small sharp strokes to suggest a coarse hairy eyebrow.

3 Paint the eyelids and inner corners of the eyes in dark brown, extending the colour down the sides of the nose to a point just above each nostril.

4 Start to create the folds and creases in the face; take the dark brown paint down along the folds of the cheeks to a point level with the mouth. Paint bags under the eyes by following the lower line of the eye socket at both the inner and outer corners. Feather all these lines with a damp brush.

TIP: When trying to age a young face, only apply lines in a downwards direction – lines that are drawn upwards will only lift the face and counteract the effect you are hoping for.

5 Add some creases across the forehead and two vertical frown lines. Blend these lines slightly with a cotton bud.

6 Paint some small wrinkles around the outer corners of the eyes and shade the hollows of the cheeks to make them look sunken.

7 Small black semicircles on both top and bottom lids will give a beady-eyed look.

8 Block the mouth in green and draw a crooked black line across the lips, dropping the ends down at each corner of the mouth.

9 Add some fine wrinkle lines all round the mouth and a touch of shading to the cleft of the chin.

10 The hag witch is finished, and the model will hardly recognise herself!

Evil Queen

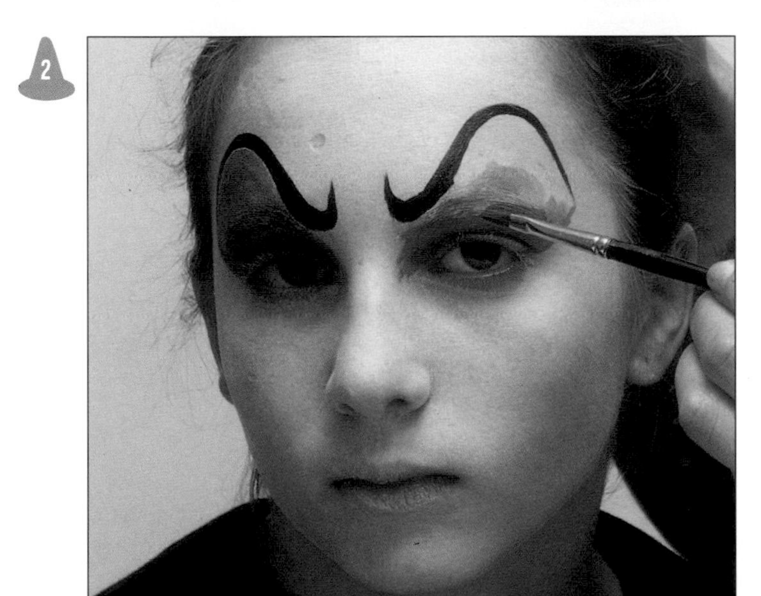

1 Use a sponge to colour the face and neck white, stippling gently over any streaky areas. Ignore the natural brow line – instead, create very exaggerated eyebrows that arch dramatically and turn up at the inner end forming a scowl.

2 Paint the whole eyelid and brow area in purple, joining the colour to the eyebrow line sharply at the outer corner of the eye.

3 Extend the purple right down each side of the nose, blending the outside edge away from the nose and into the base colour.

4 The frown has been accentuated by adding sharp-edged blocks of purple to the forehead with a slightly damp brush. Now paint the eyelids black, blending the line upwards onto the brow-bone and into the purple. The eye sockets now seem much deeper and the expression is suitably evil.

5 Draw a black line under the lower eyelashes starting just below the inner corner of the eye and sweeping up to end at the outer end of the eyebrow line.

6 Shade the hollows under the cheek bones with purple using a soft brush.

TIP: Aqua-Colours are sometimes tricky to blend, so you may prefer to use an ordinary powder eye shadow for this. However, powder shadows aren't usually recommended because they lack staying power and density of colour.

7 Give a sharp black outline to the lips with either a very fine brush or a sharp eye pencil. Fill the mouth shape in with purple.

8 The Evil Queen is finished.

Skull

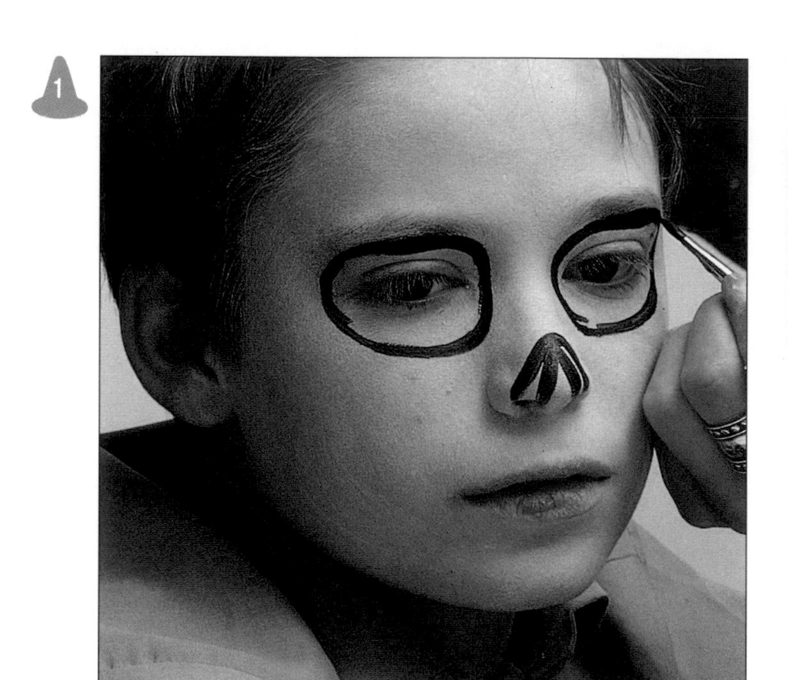

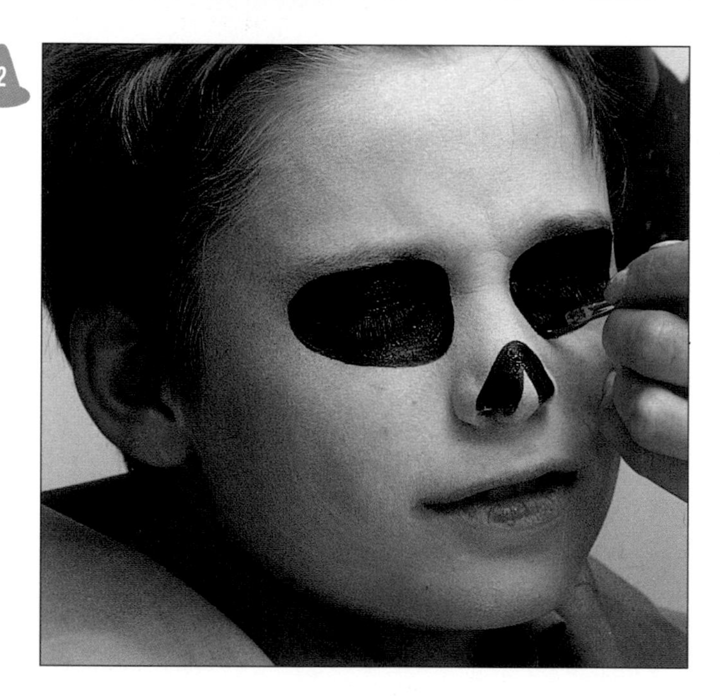

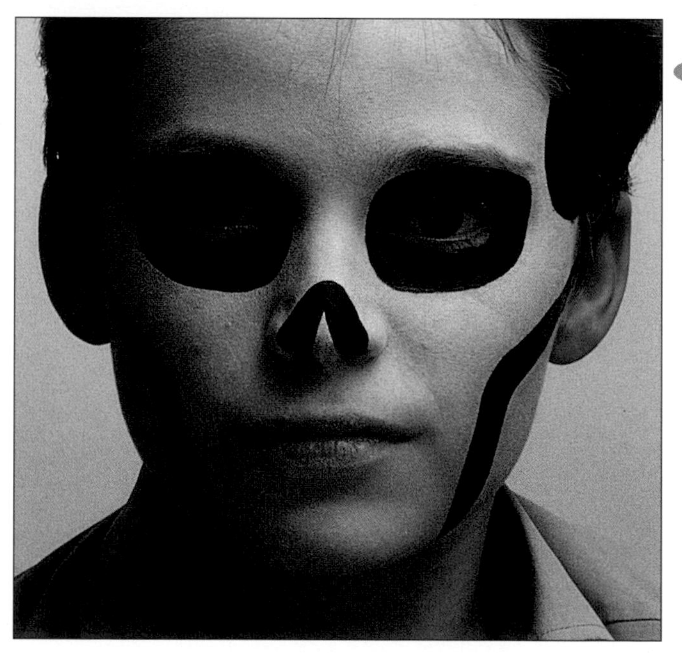

1 Cover the whole face in white using a sponge. Draw in the outlines for the nose and eye sockets in black.

2 Fill in these areas in black, leaving a small segment of white showing at the centre of the nose.

3 Feel for the model's temple hollows and emphasise them by painting a black semicircle over each one.

4 Feel for the cheekbones and paint along the underside, stopping approximately level with the centre of the eye. Then drop the line downwards to the jawline. Fill in the area behind this line with black.

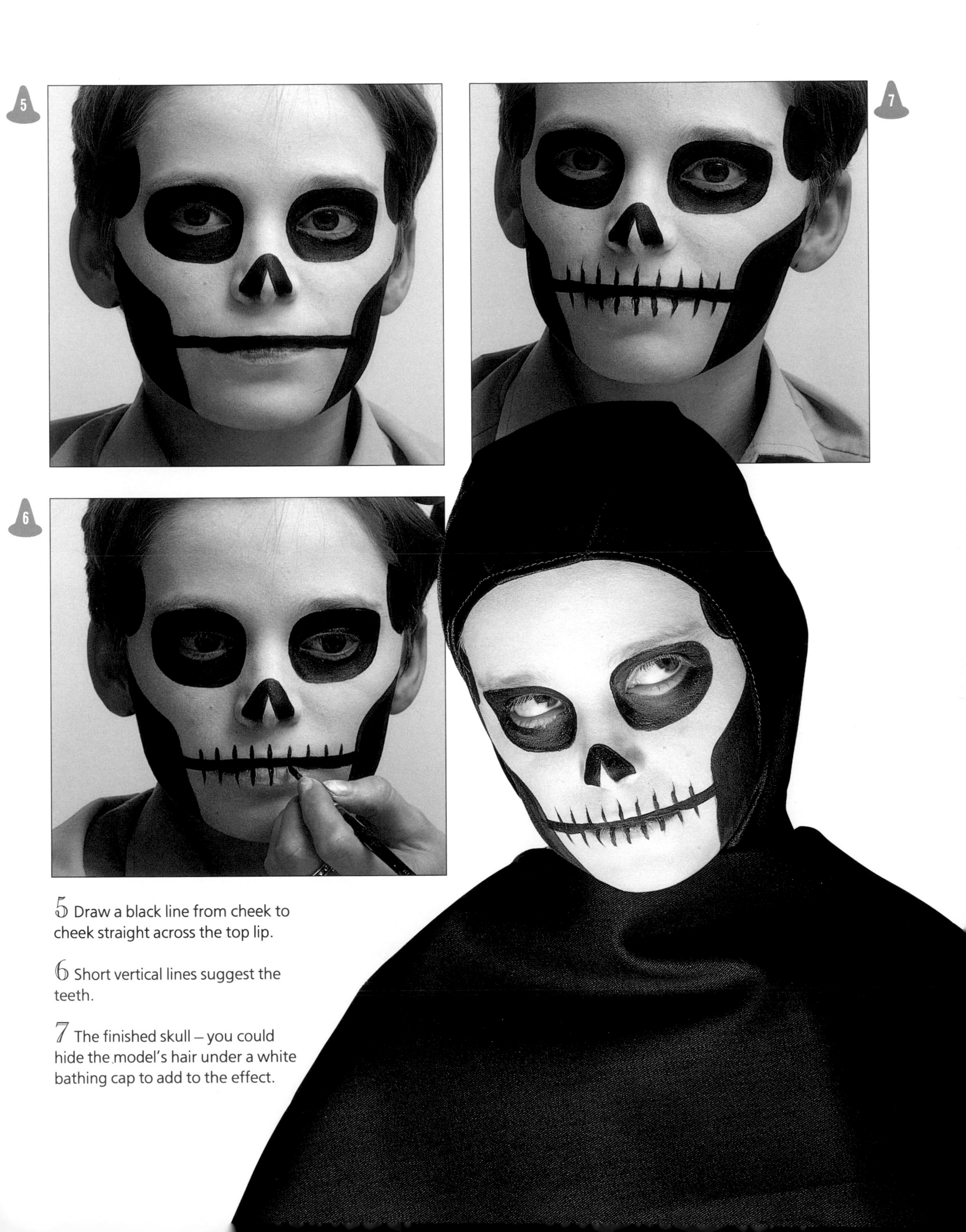

5 Draw a black line from cheek to cheek straight across the top lip.

6 Short vertical lines suggest the teeth.

7 The finished skull – you could hide the model's hair under a white bathing cap to add to the effect.

Dracula

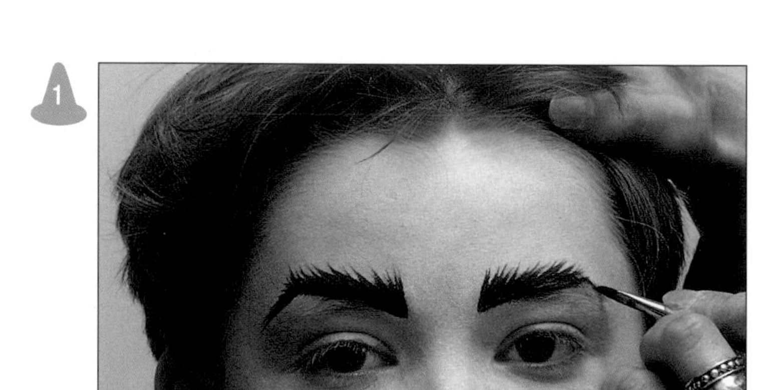

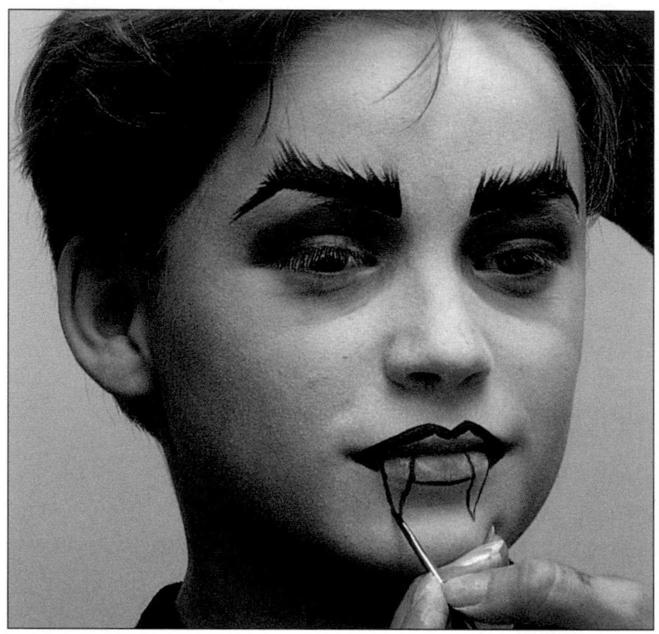

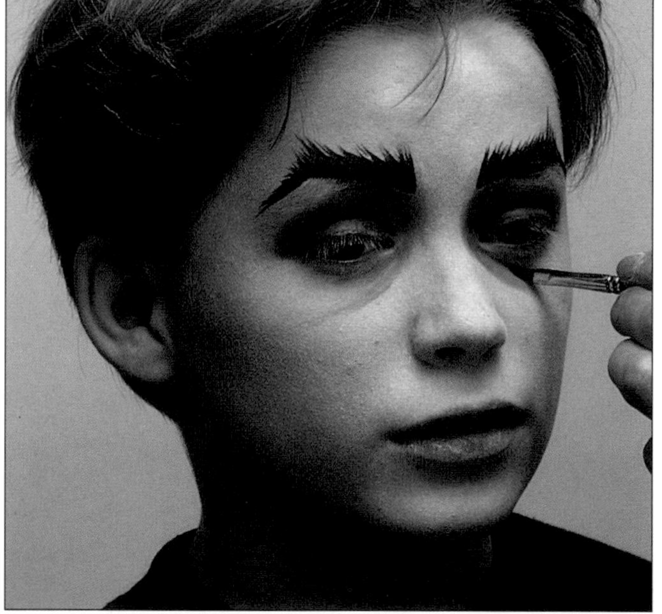

1 Cover the face with white, gently stippling over any patchy areas with a sponge. Add some angular black eyebrows, brushing upwards with light feathery brushstrokes.

2 Paint some grey over the top eyelid, round the inner corner of the eye and along the lower socket line. Blend the edges with a clean damp brush.

3 Draw the outline of long pointed fangs over the bottom lip, using a fine brush or a sharp black eye pencil.

4 Fill in the fangs in white and the surrounding lips in black.

5 Use a brush or a cotton bud to smudge some red paint along the lower eyelash line. The model should look up and away from you while you do this. Shade the cheek hollows with light grey using a sponge or a brush. Powder eye shadow could be used instead of paint, but powder colours are usually less dense than paint and do not last so long.

6 Add trickles of blood from the fangs and corners of the mouth.

Midnight Bat

1 The base for this make-up consists of bands of colour stretching right across the face. Blend purple into blue and blue into green using the stippling technique described on page 11.

2 Draw the outline of the bat, starting at the top of the nose. Estimate where the points of each wing should fall and mark the place with a dot of paint – this will help you to make the shape symmetrical. Outline the eyes with a thin line in a feline shape that sweeps up at the outer corners and extends onto the nose slightly at the inner corners.

3 Fill in the bat shape in black, leaving the area round the eyes.

4 Use a fine brush to sketch the outlines of the moon and stars onto the forehead and cheeks.

5 Paint the area round the eyes in silver.

6 Fill in the moon in silver, and the stars in silver and gold. Add some horizontal streaks of silver around the moon to suggest a moonlit sky.

7 Decorate the stars and sky with glitter. The midnight bat is ready to fly.

4
SPECIAL EFFECTS

The use of special make-up to simulate blood, guts and gore has been used for many years in both the theatre and on film and the effects now achieved are sophisticated and horribly realistic, even under close scrutiny.

Now you have a chance to learn the tricks of the trade yourself. You will need a few bits of specialist equipment, such as wax and fake blood, available at theatrical suppliers, but the main ingredients are your imagination and ability to observe the gory world around you.

Try the projects in this chapter and then experiment with your own ideas – what about a wart made from puffed rice cereal – to shock your family and friends.

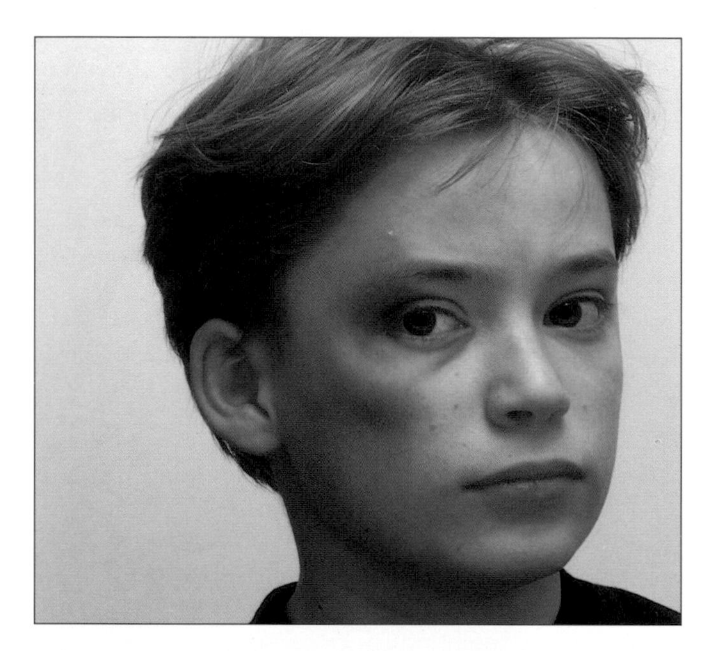

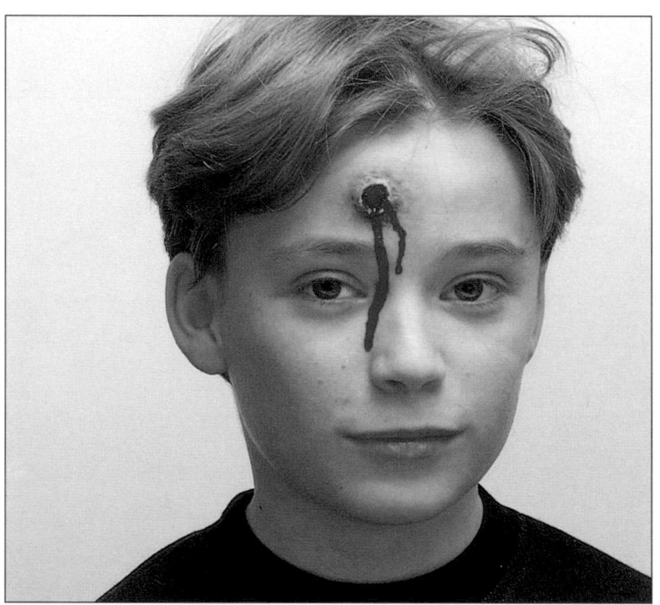

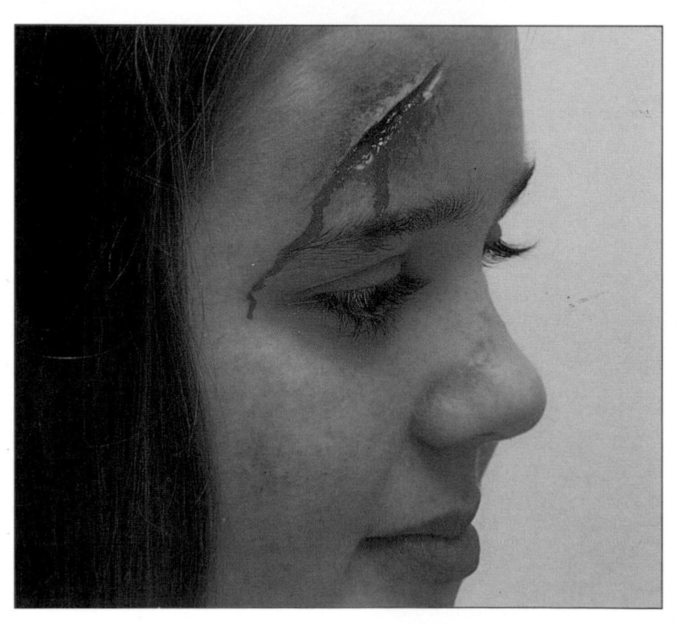

Black Eye

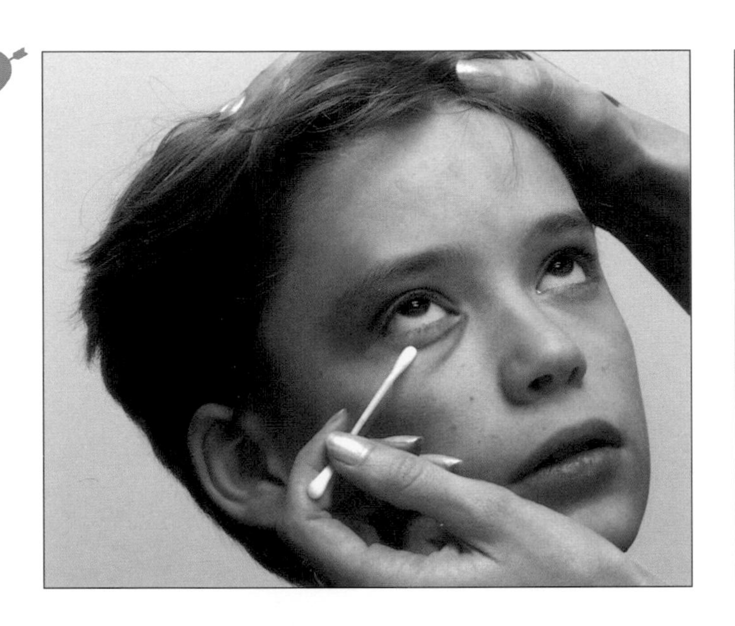

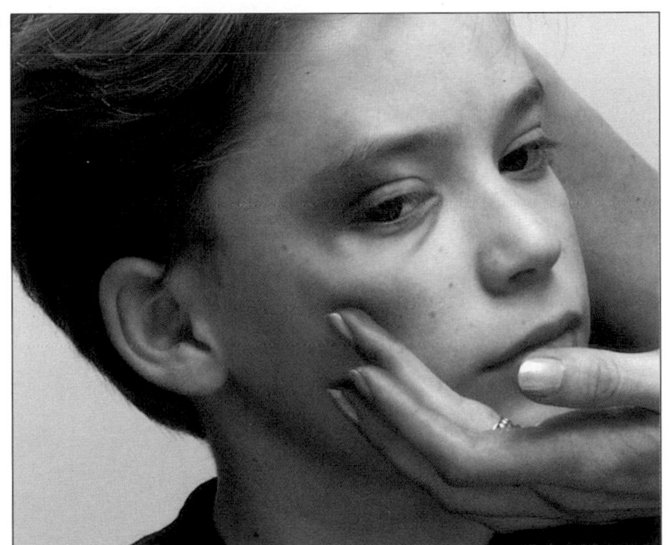

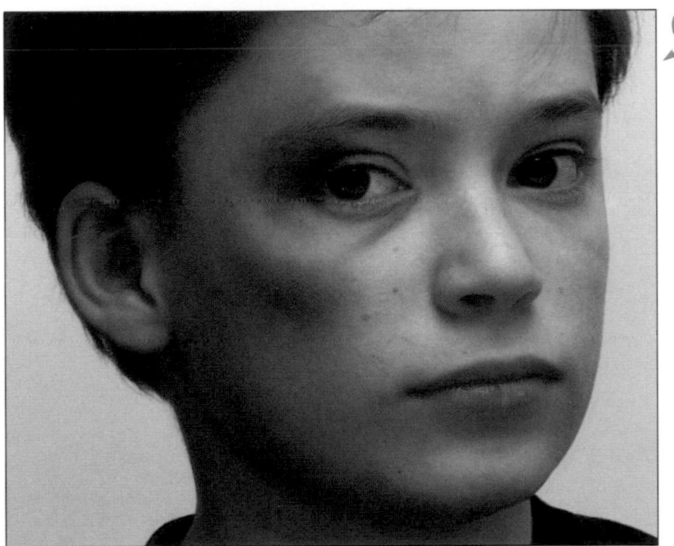

1 Mix dark red paint with a dash of grey and dab the colour over the outer eyelid and brow bone with your finger or a sponge. Using a brush, paint into the lower eye socket line at both the inner and outer corners of the eye. Blend the edges carefully with a cotton bud.

2 Feel for the cheekbone and dab some colour along the underside, fading out towards the temple.

3 Go back over the same areas with a touch of dark blue, allowing the colour to be a little heavier around the outer corner of the eye.

4 The finished black eye looks painfully realistic.

TIP: To make an eye look bloodshot, paint red along the inner rim.

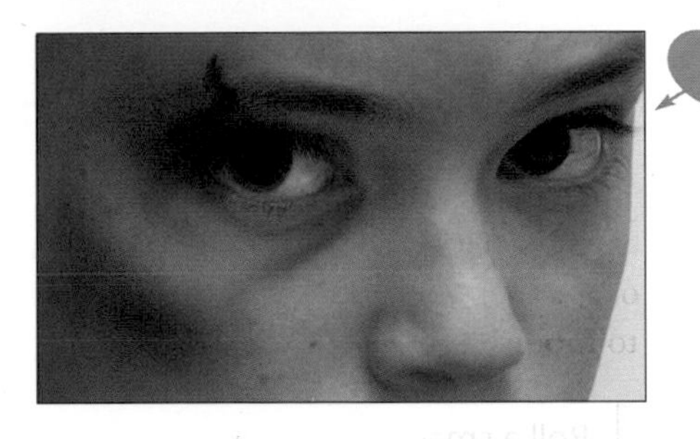

5 For even more realism, add a small jagged red scar painted just above the eyebrow.

Bullet Hole

1

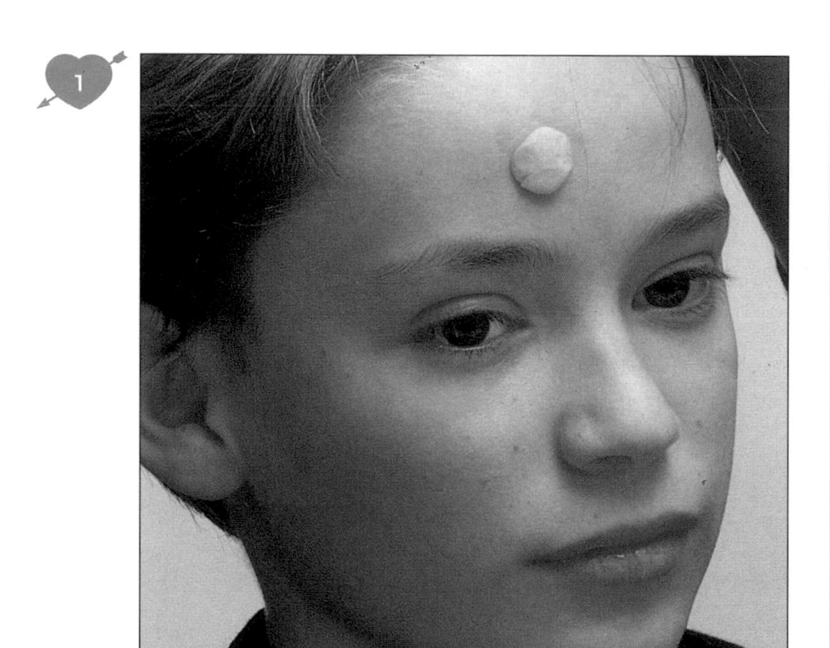

3

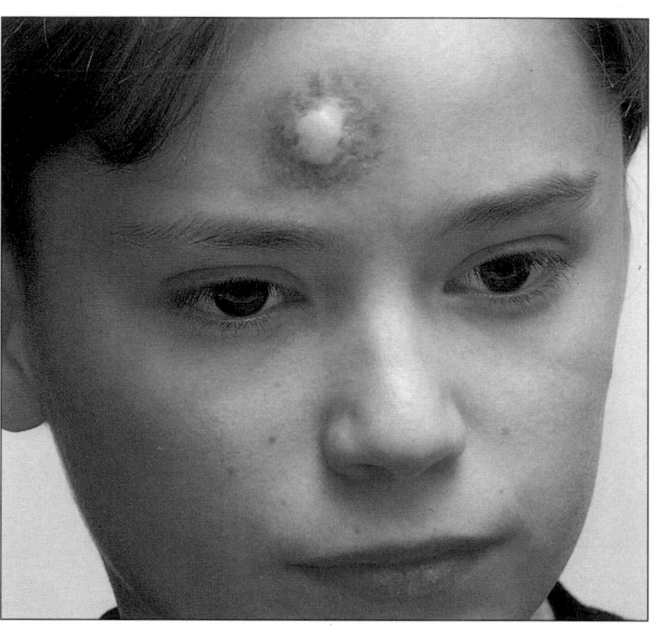

2

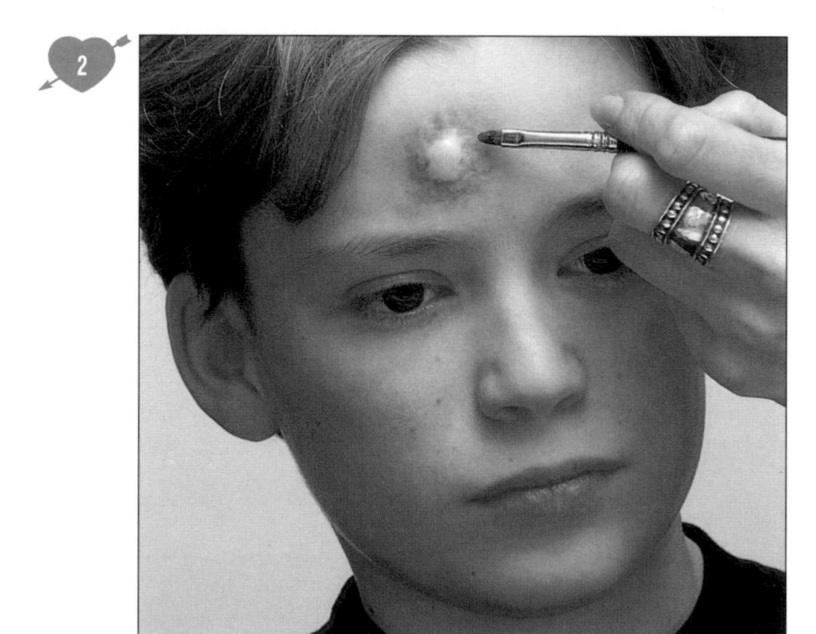

4

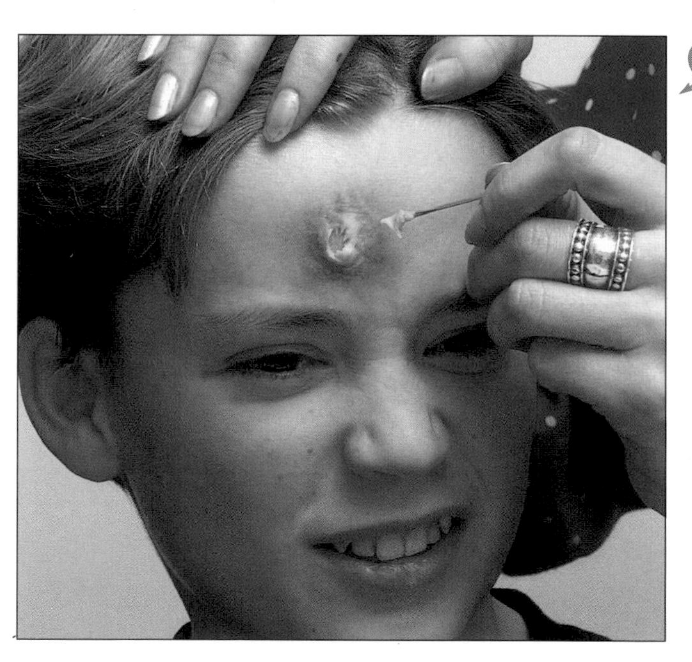

TIP: Don't handle wax for too long or it will become too soft and sticky to mould into shape.

1 Roll a small amount of wax into a ball and press it gently but firmly into place. Use a spatula or brush-end to blend the edges onto the skin.

TIP: A little cold cream used very sparingly will help to smooth and shape the edges.

2 Using a brush, colour the wax and the surrounding area in a dark red. Add a few dots of dark blue, blending the outer edges of the coloured areas into the skin, but leaving the part closest to the wax slightly mottled.

3 At this stage the wax still looks like a lump on the skin.

4 Use a toothpick or orange stick to pick the centre of the wax away.

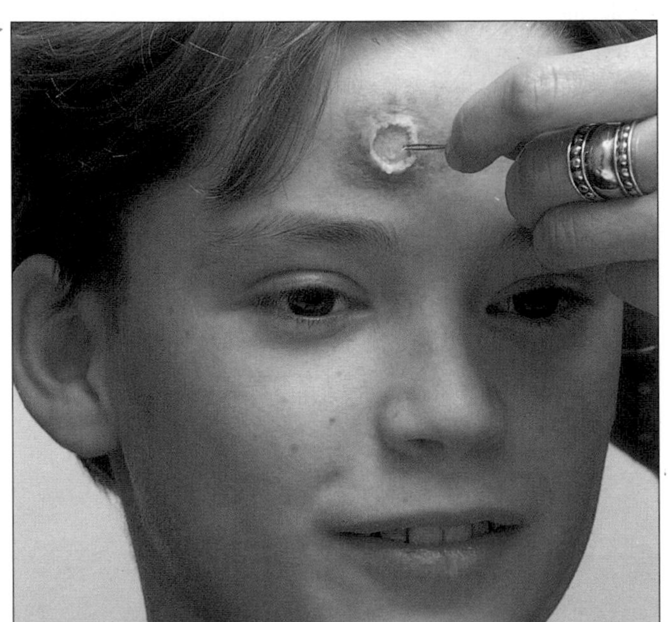

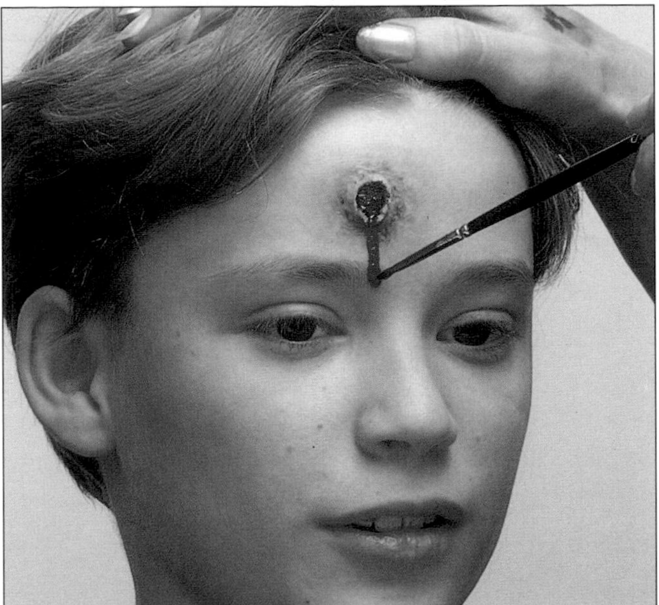

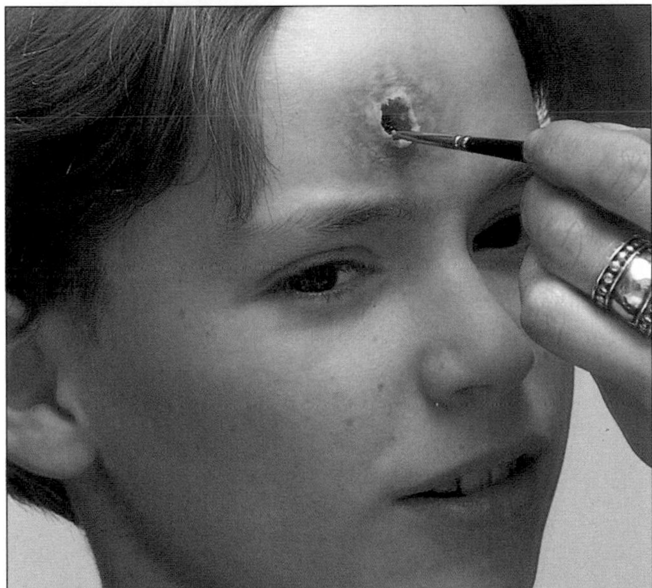

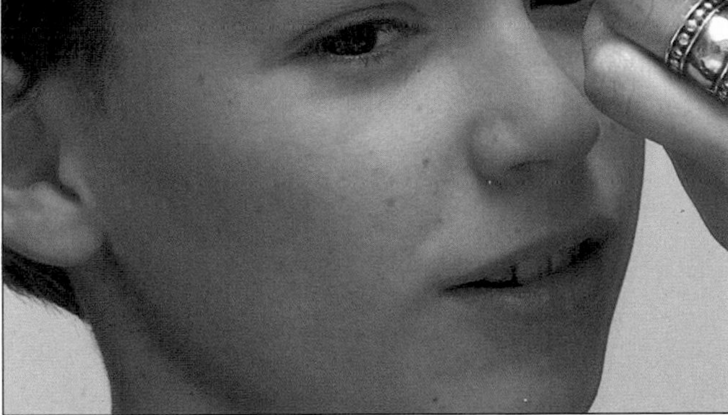

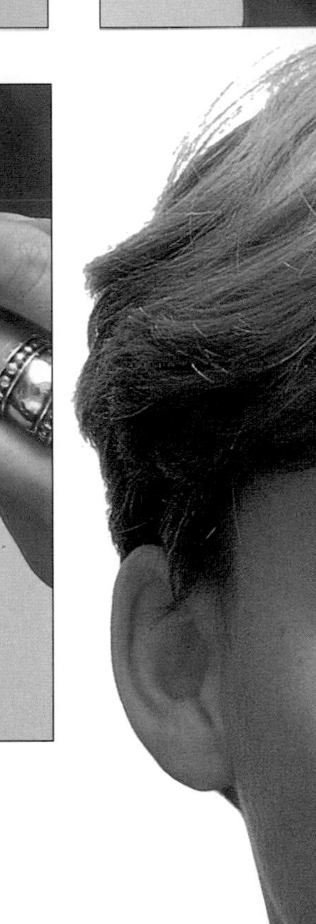

5 Create a hole, leaving the edges rough.

6 Paint the inside of the hole dark red and add some flecks of black randomly around the edge.

7 Apply plenty of fake blood. Take care not to get the fake blood on your clothes or the model's.

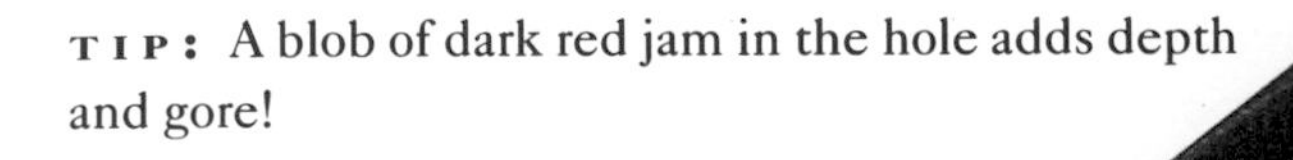

TIP: A blob of dark red jam in the hole adds depth and gore!

Open Cut

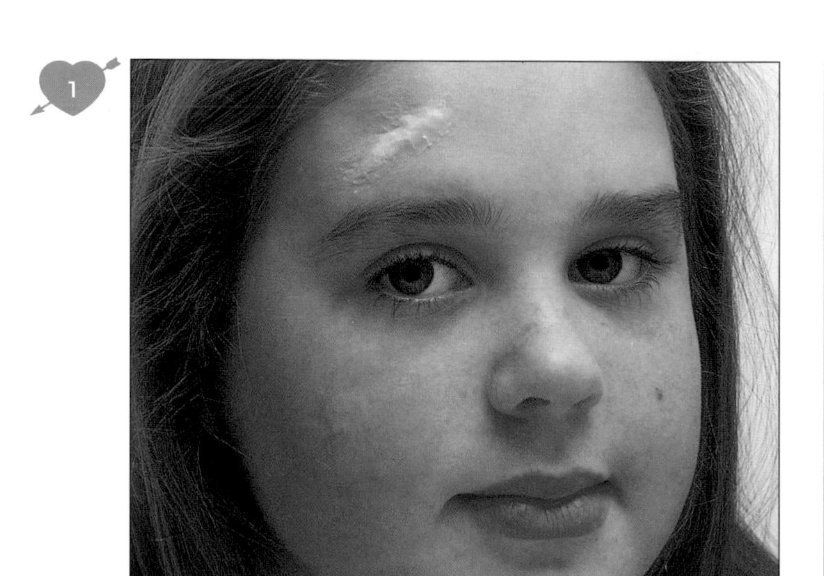

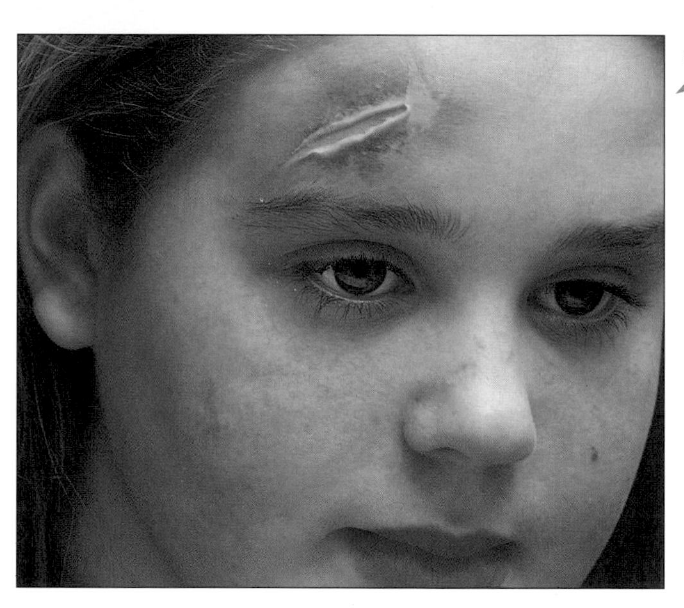

TIP: Avoid handling the wax too much, as it will become too soft and sticky to work with.

1 Mould a small amount of wax into the basic shape of the cut you are going to create. Press it gently onto the skin.

2 With a spatula or the back of your fingernail, shape and thin out the edges of the wax so that they blend onto the skin.

TIP: A tiny touch of cold cream will help to smooth out the edges.

3 With your finger or a small brush, lightly colour the wax and the surrounding area in dark red. A hint of dark blue can be added to suggest bruising. The colours will look more effective if they are left mottled rather than blended together too much.

4 Pick away the wax to form the cut, using either the end of a spatula or brush, or a toothpick or orange stick.

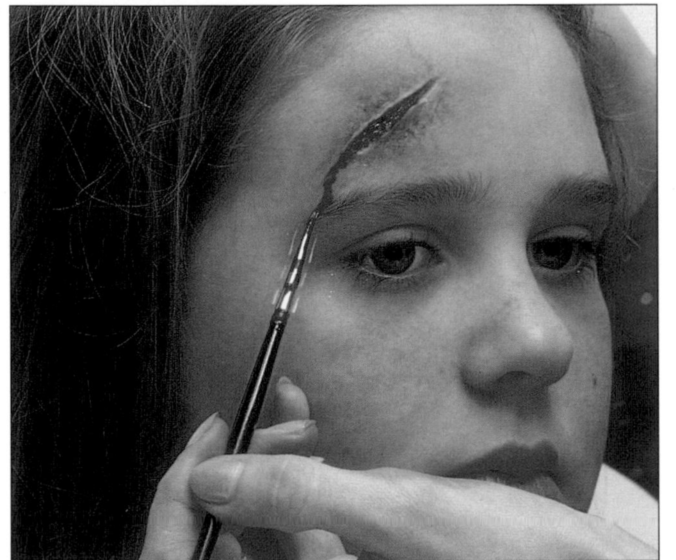

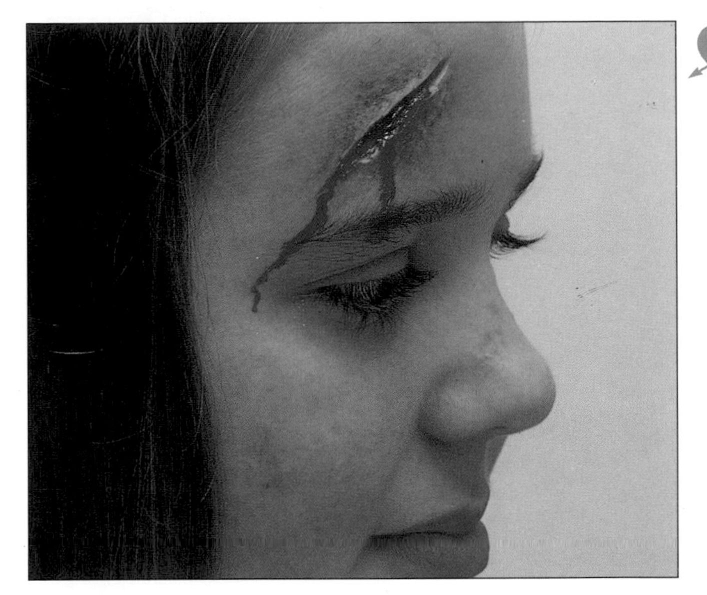

5 Line the centre of the cut with dark red using a fine brush. A few drops of fake blood help to make the cut look real.

TIP: If the fake blood appears too pink or orange mix in a little grey paint.

6 The finished wound.

Scab

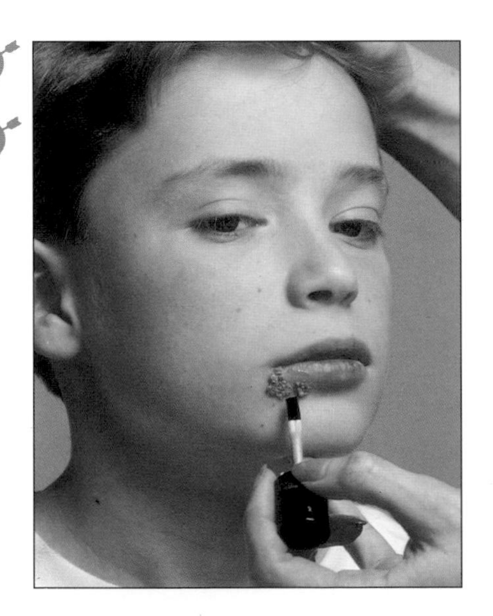

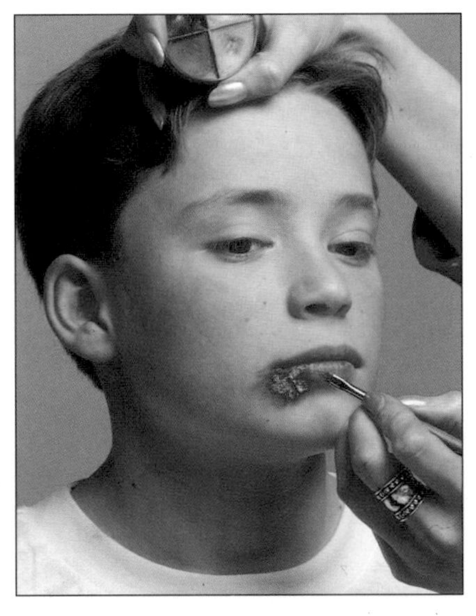

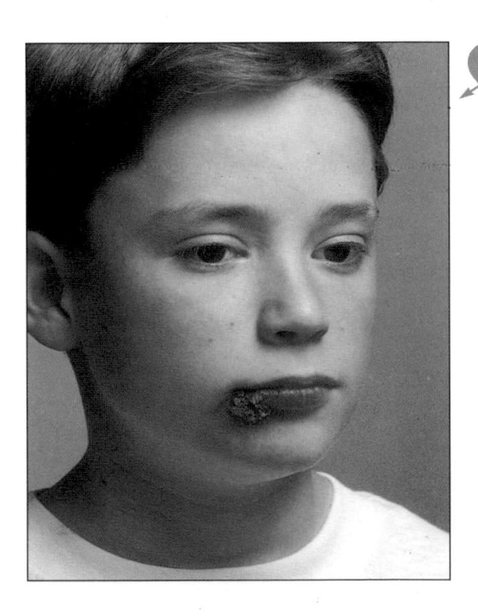

1 Crush a bran flake or cornflake into small pieces and stick them onto the skin using a tiny dab of surgical or water-soluble adhesive.

2 Discolour the area around the flakes by applying dark red with a brush, adding a few spots of grey/green here and there. Blend the edges of the colours into the skin with a cotton bud.

3 The finished scab.

TIP: The same method can be used with puffed rice to make very realistic warts and blisters.

Tattoos

1

2

3

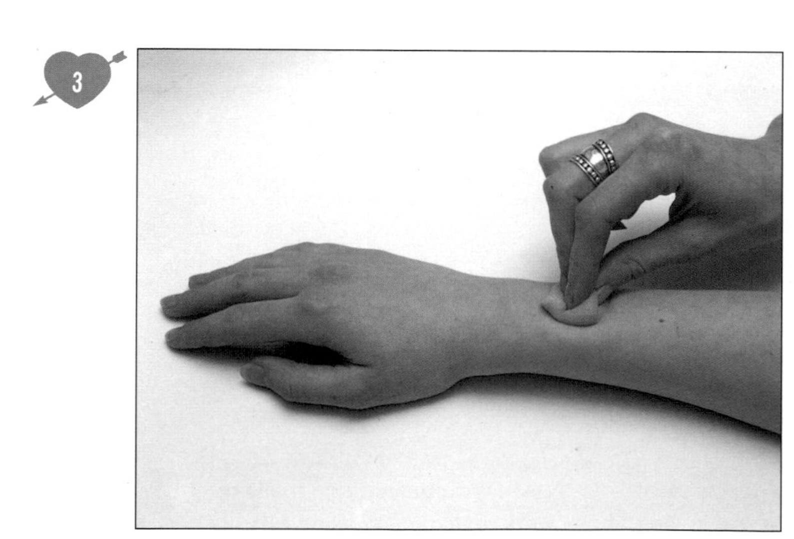

4

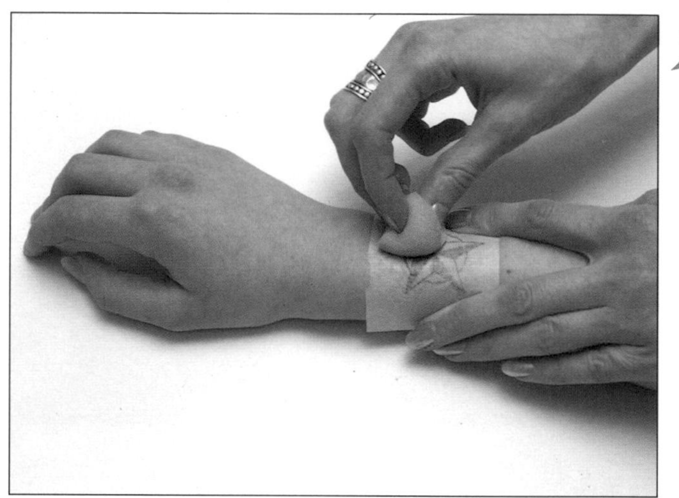

5

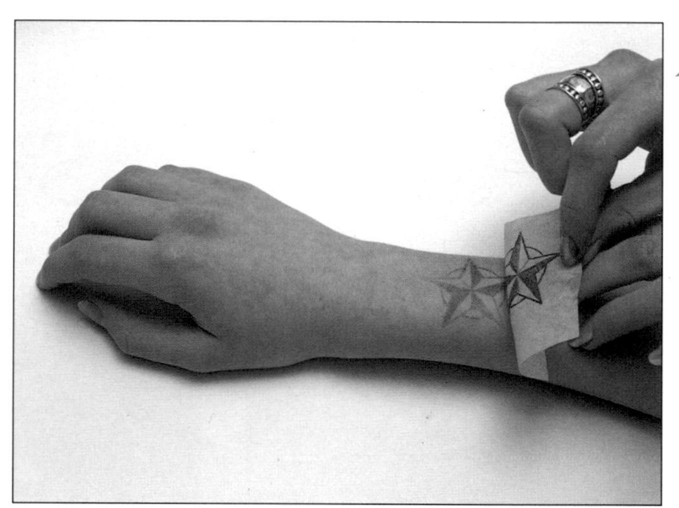

6

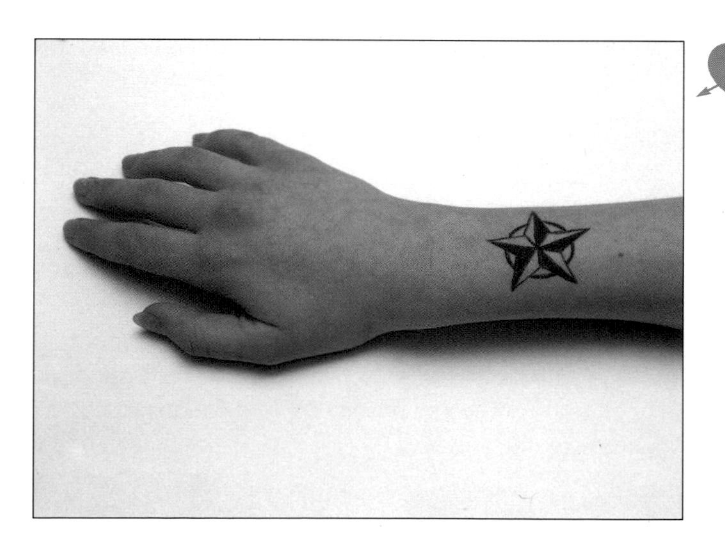

1 Trace your chosen design onto tracing paper or greaseproof paper.

2 Go over the outline with a very soft lead pencil, pressing very hard. If the design contains lettering, do this back to front so that the letters will eventually be the right way round.

3 Decide where the tattoo is to go, and dampen the area slightly.

4 Put the tracing pencil-shaded side down onto the skin and moisten the back with a sponge, holding the tracing very firmly in place.

5 Slowly pull back the paper. The design will have transferred to the skin.

6 The lines can be sharpened and areas filled with colour using paint or make-up pencils.

TIP: To avoid the risk of lettering appearing back to front you could add the letters directly onto the skin.

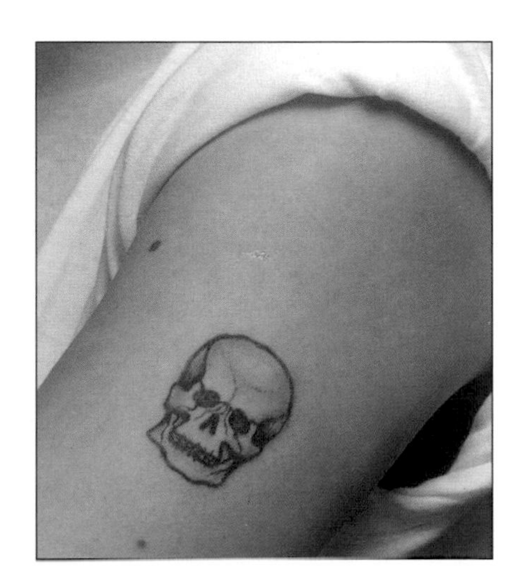

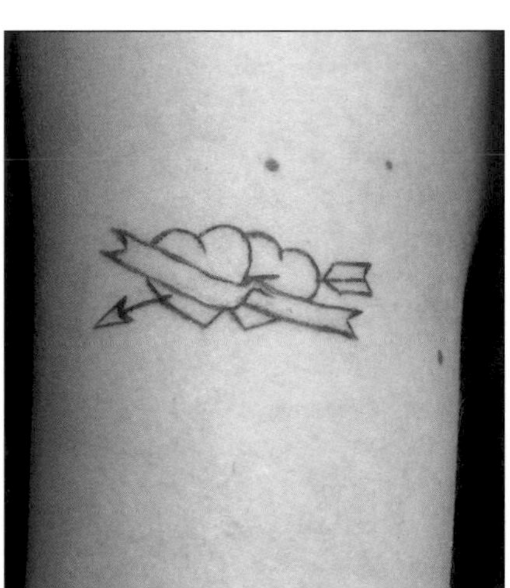

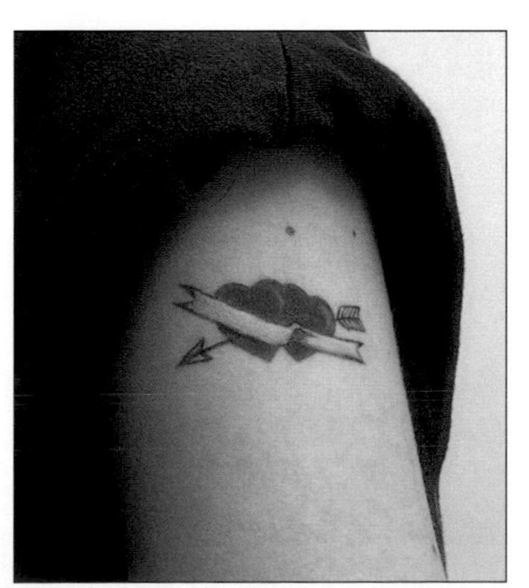

An example of a traditional tattoo, coloured with paint.

Some designs for you to trace or copy (see also Cheek Designs page 94).

5
CARNIVAL

The word carnival is believed to be derived from the Latin words *carne* (meat) and *vale* (farewell). The word was first used for the celebrations that take place before the beginning of Lent – a period of fasting and penance in the Christian Church. There had been festivities at this time of year long before Christianity. Originally February was celebrated by the Ancient Greeks as the end of Harvest and to honour *Dionysus*, the God of wine, fruitfullness and vegetation. Similar celebrations were taken up by the Ancient Romans under the name *lupercalia*, referring to *Lupercas*, the God of flocks.

The connection between Carnival and masks derives from sacred rites performed at the start of the new farming season. The masks represented the souls of the dead who emerged to inspire fertility in the soil. These masks later became essential to the Carnival celebrations since they allowed all the party-goers, whether peasants or nobles, to go unrecognized as they took part in the wild street parties.

By shrouding our bodies in costume and paint we instil in ourselves a sense of invincibility and cast aside our inhibitions.

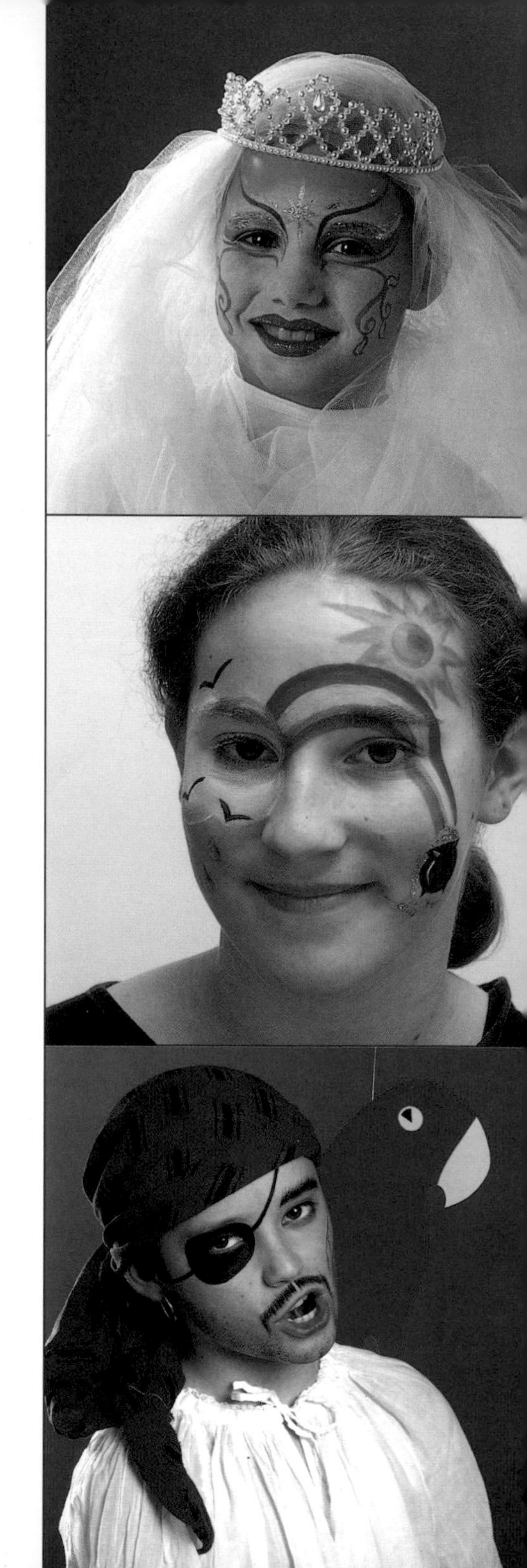

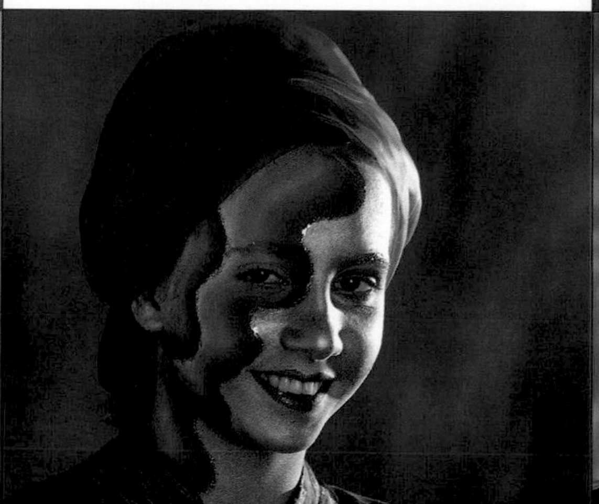

Batman

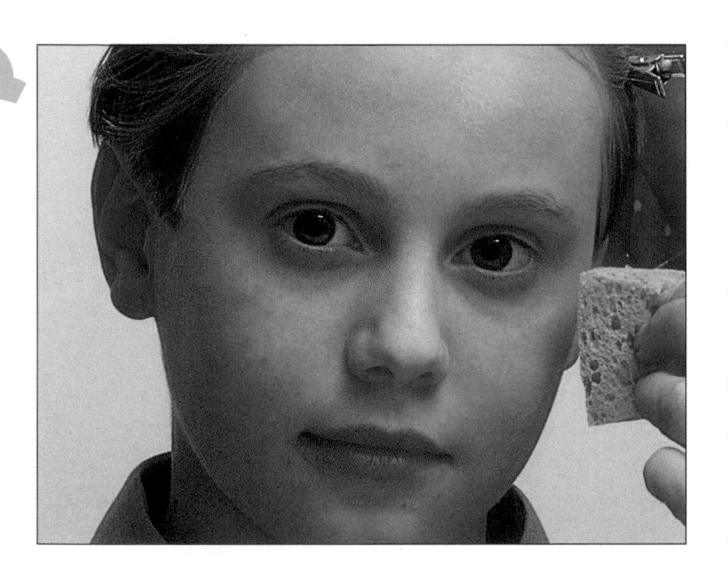

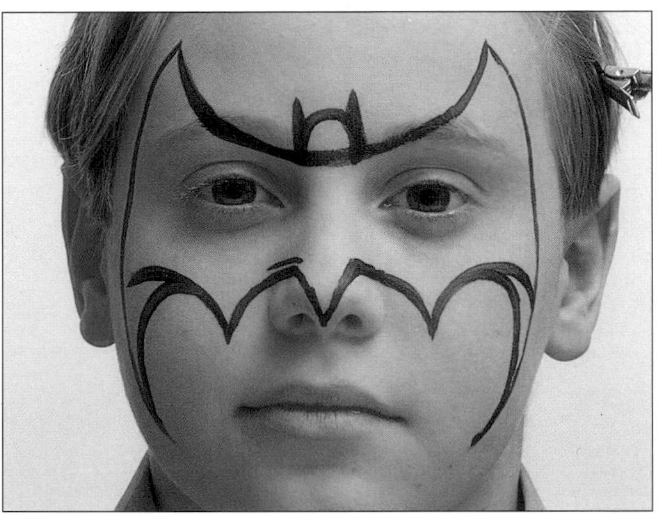

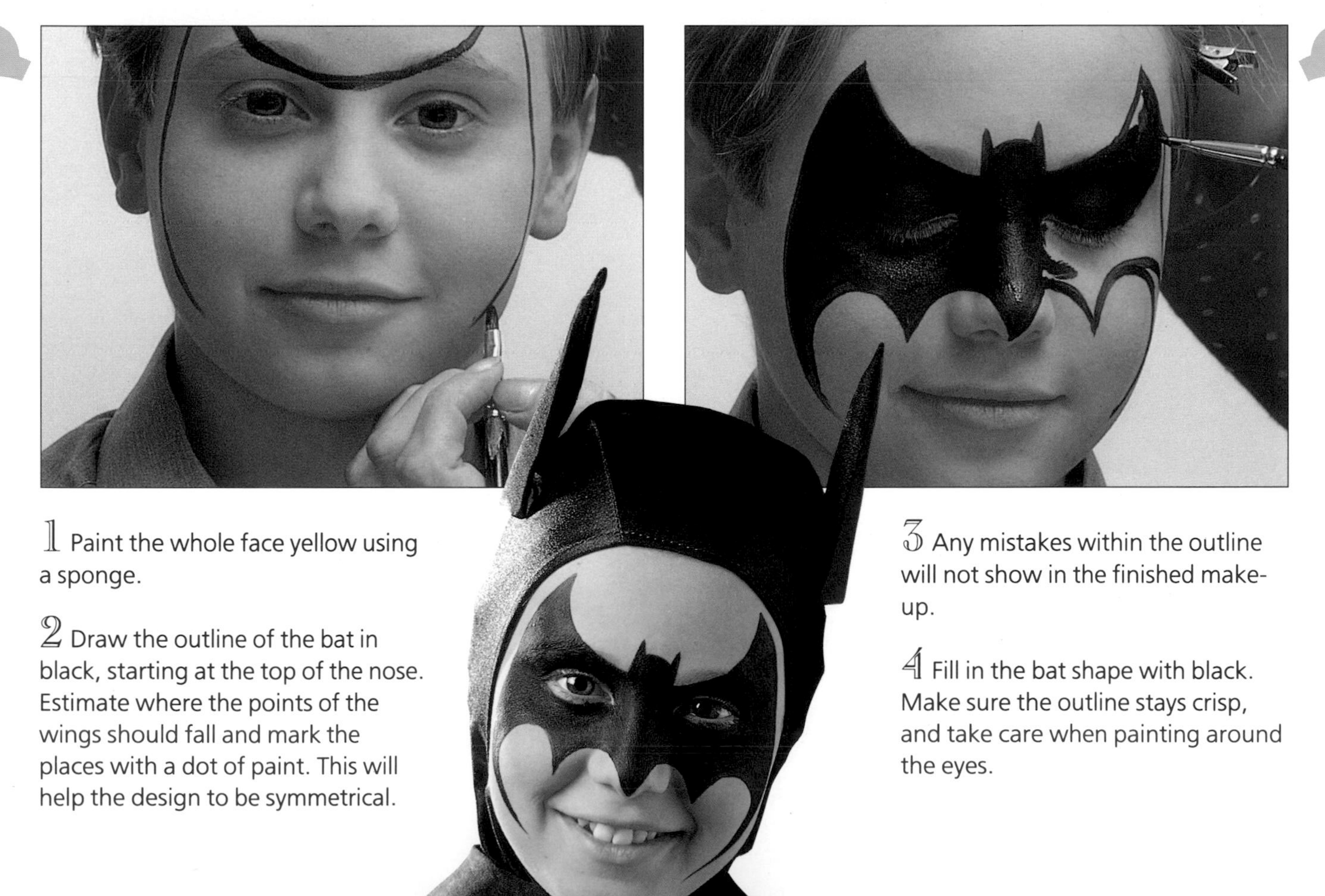

1 Paint the whole face yellow using a sponge.

2 Draw the outline of the bat in black, starting at the top of the nose. Estimate where the points of the wings should fall and mark the places with a dot of paint. This will help the design to be symmetrical.

3 Any mistakes within the outline will not show in the finished make-up.

4 Fill in the bat shape with black. Make sure the outline stays crisp, and take care when painting around the eyes.

Fairy Princess

1

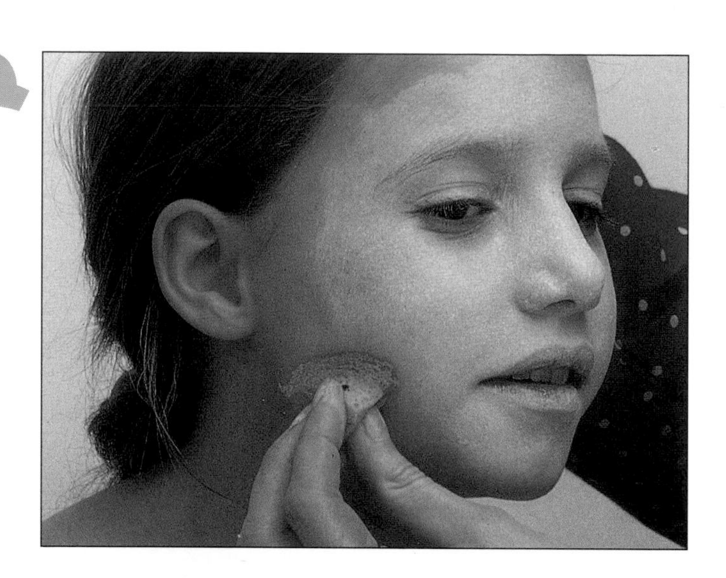

2

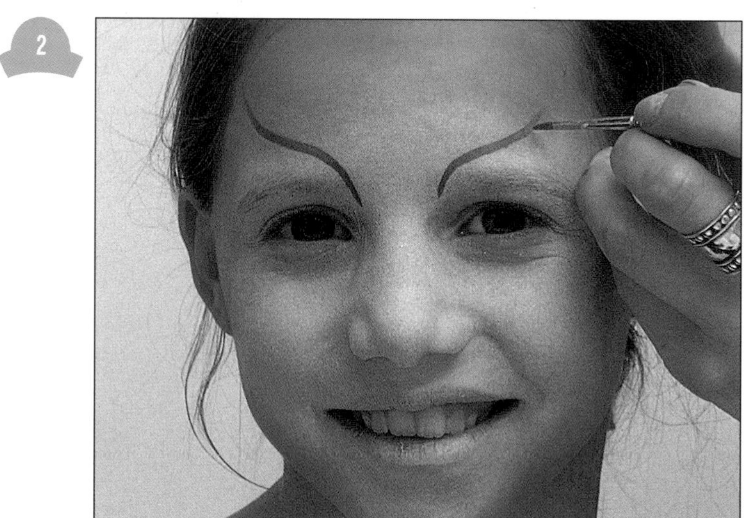

3

4

5

6

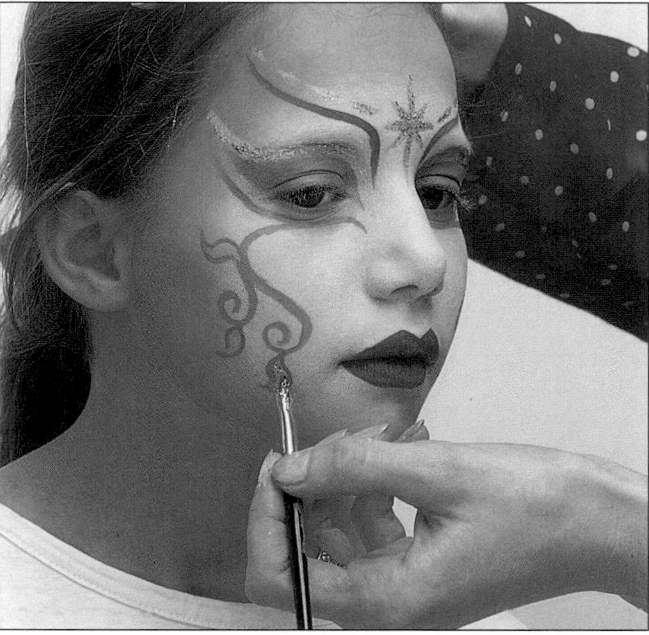

6 Enhance the natural shape of the lips with dark red. Decorate the cheeks with gold and add a star and other details to the forehead.

7 For an extra touch of magic, add some glitter to the star, leaves, lips and browlines.

1 Make a base of white, blending into a pink border. Use the stippling technique described on page 11.

2 Add thin purple eyebrows, sweeping the line up past the temples.

3 Paint the eyelids blue, starting just below the inner corner of the eye and winging the line up at the outer corner to echo the curve of the eyebrow line. Highlight the blue by painting gold along the top edge.

4 With the model's eyes closed, add a fine lilac line under the eye, starting below the inner corner and sweeping up following the same curve as the top line.

5 Using a very fine brush, design some delicate curls and leaves that descend from the lower eye lines.

Cowboy

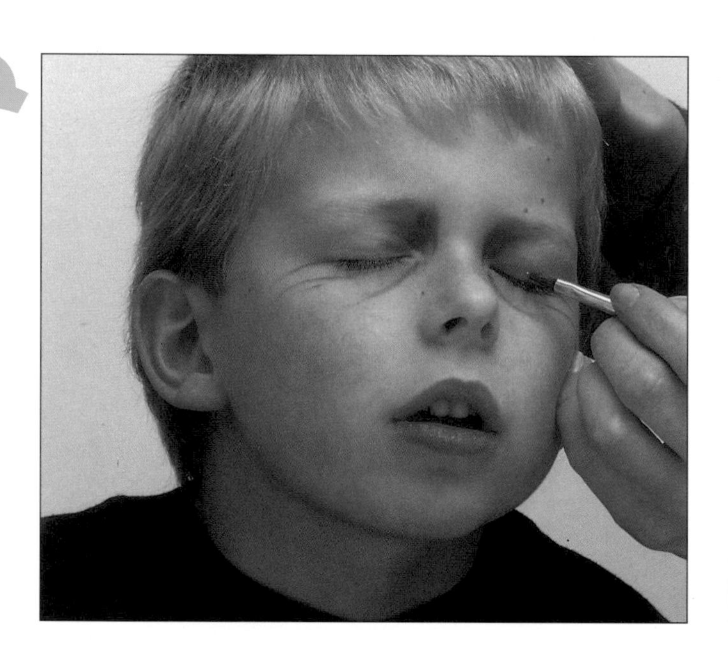

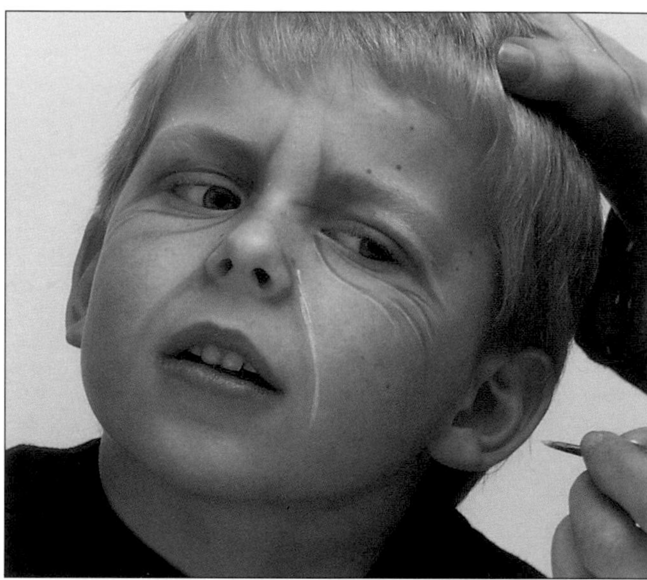

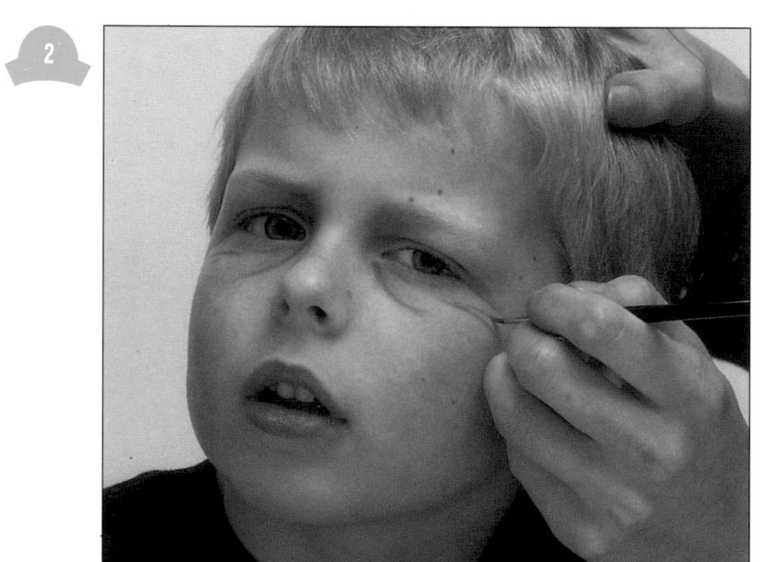

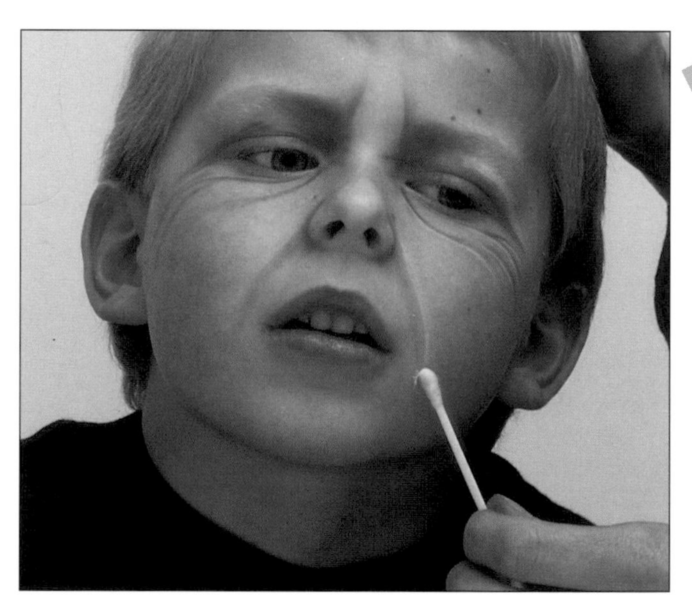

1 Using a thin brush and mid-brown paint, shade the eyelid and the inner corner of the eye, blending the colour down the sides of the nose slightly. Add a subtle line of colour to the lower part of the eye socket.

2 Add some wrinkle lines in their natural positions: downwards from the outer corner of the eye, from the nose down to the corners of the mouth, in the crease of the chin and across the forehead, as well as two vertical frown lines above the eyebrows.

3 Highlight the lines and wrinkles by painting a little white alongside them. To make the eyelids look droopy, paint a white diagonal line along the fold of the upper lid, starting at the eyebrow and ending below the outer corner of the eye.

4 Blend any hard edges using a slightly dampened cotton bud.

5 Create an unshaven look by stippling the beard and moustache area with a coarse sponge and some brown paint (see instructions on page 14). Build up the effect gradually, using only a small amount of colour. Dab the sponge on the back of your hand to remove any excess paint. Darken the eyebrows if necessary. This subtle make-up will enhance any cowboy fancy dress costume.

Rainbow

1

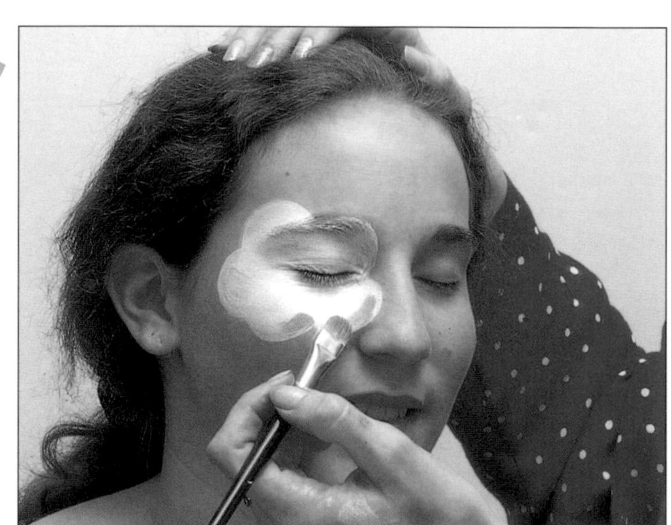

3

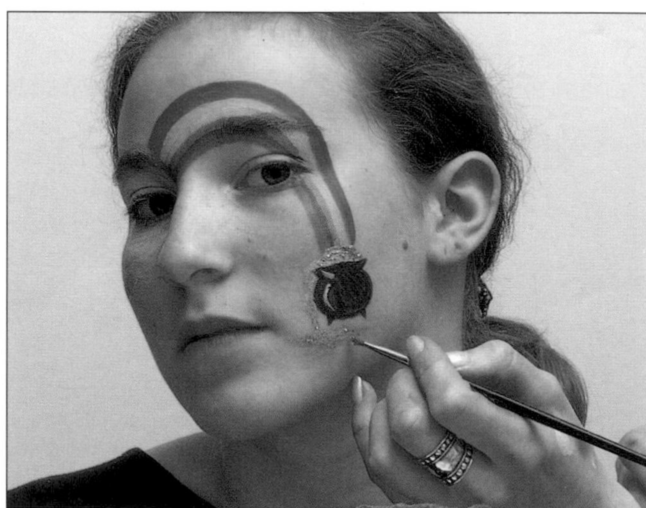

2

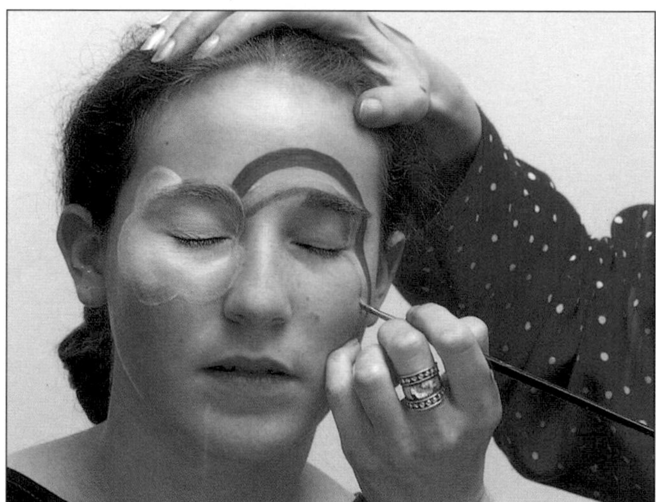

4

1 Paint the shape of a cloud in white over one eye and emphasize it with dashes of blue paint, blended into the white.

2 Paint the rainbow tapering down onto the cheek.

3 Draw a small black cauldron and paint a mound of gold brimming over the edge. Highlight the gold with flecks of glitter.

4 Finishing touches: pairs of curved strokes in black suggest birds flying over the cloud; add three small blue raindrops below the cloud; use a blend of red, yellow and orange to paint the sun behind the rainbow.

North American Indian

1

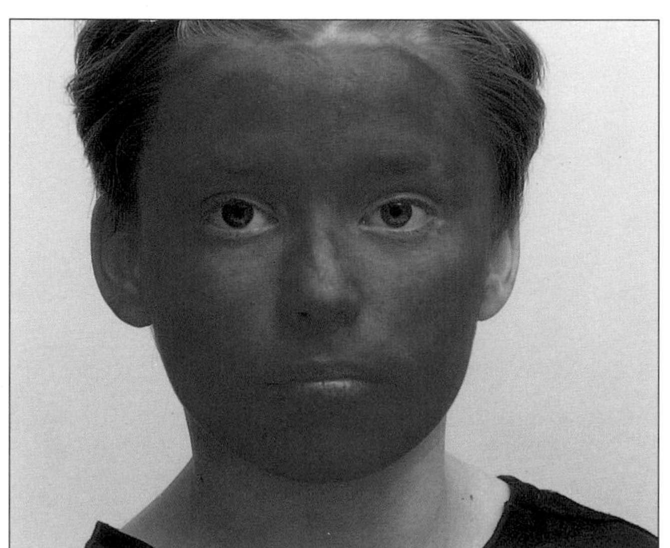

3

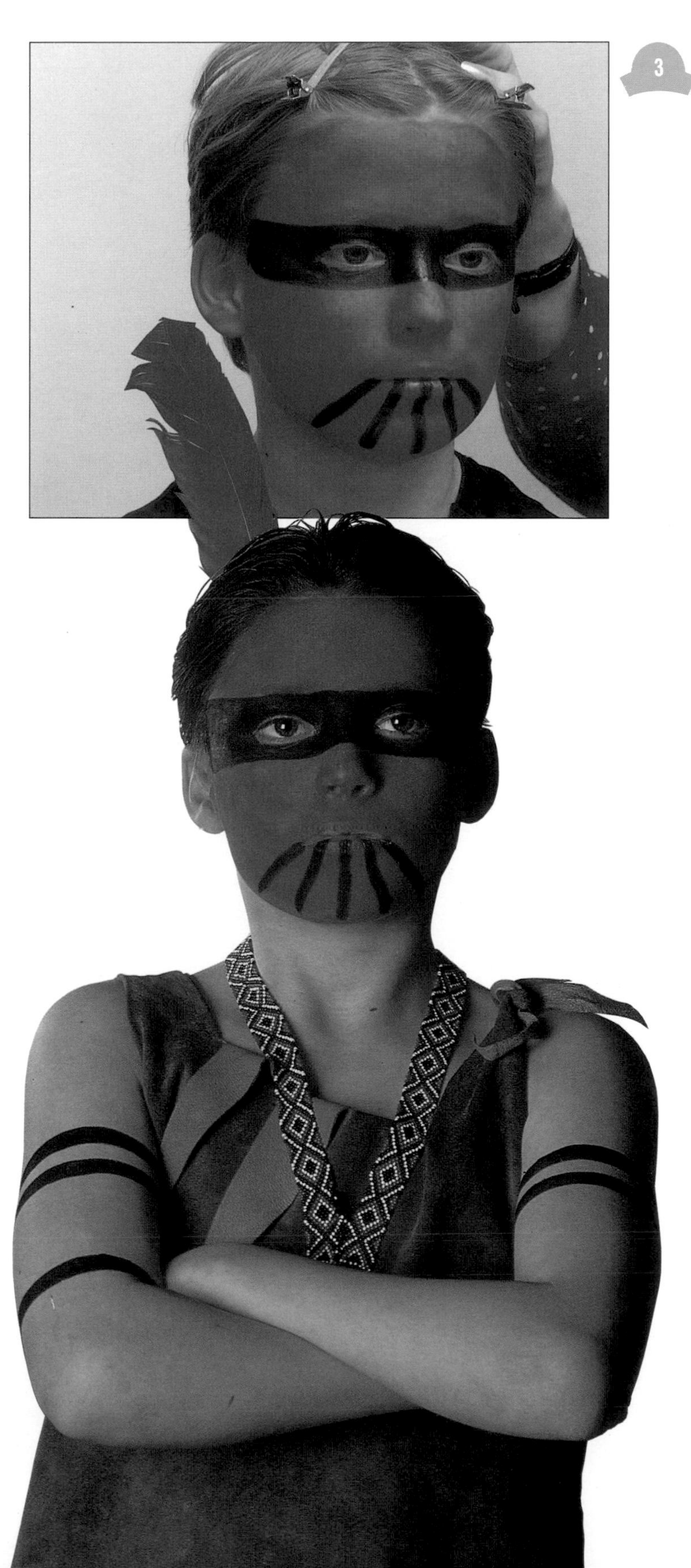

2

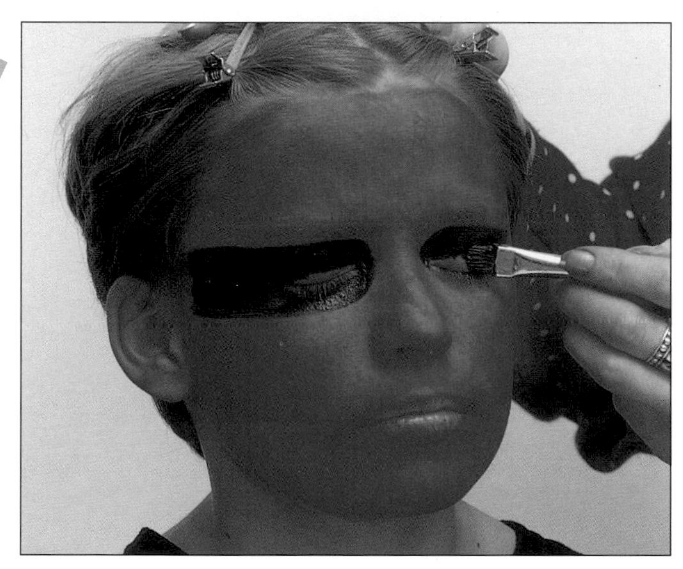

1 Paint the whole face red using a sponge.

2 Add a thick black stripe running straight across the face over the eyelids.

3 Finish the face with black lines from the bottom lip to the chin. The result looks very warlike.

TIP: The most effective Indian ritual masks use bold colours that traditionally represented the four directions: white for North; yellow for South; red for East; and black for West.

Pirate

1

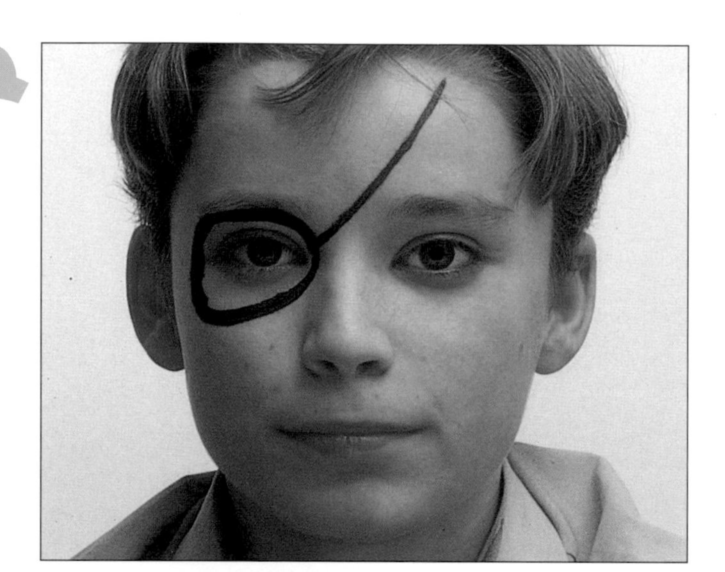

2

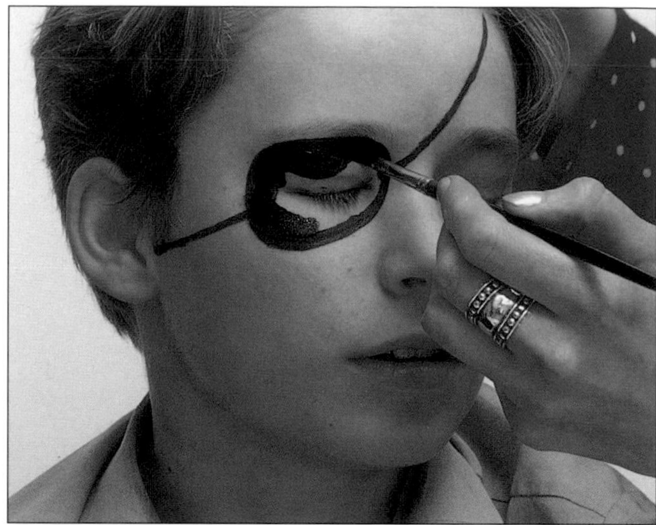

3

1 Draw the outline of the eye patch with a fine brush.

2 Fill in the outline with black and draw in the ties.

3 Create an unshaven look by stippling black paint gently onto the lower face with a sponge (see page 14 for full instructions).

TIP: Build up the colour gradually and don't overdo it.

4

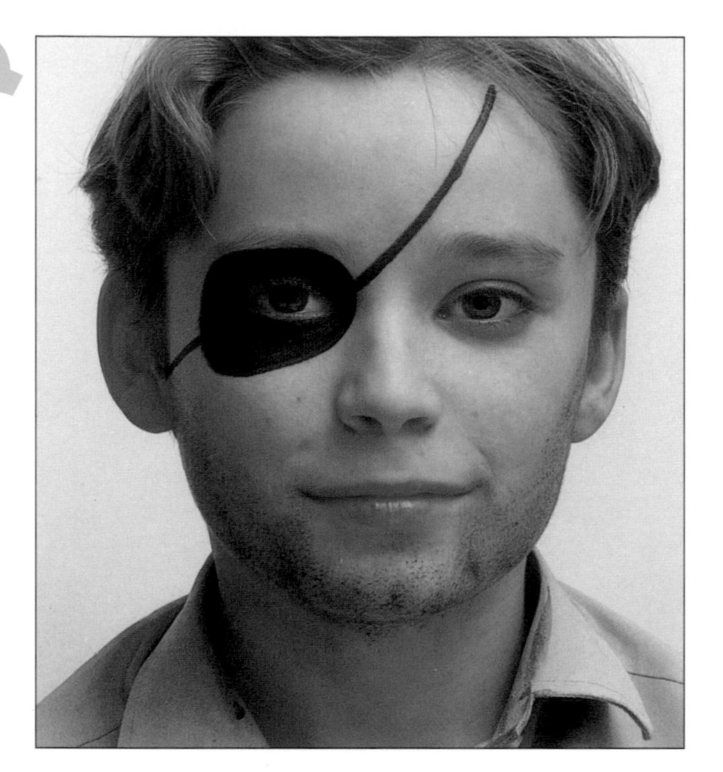

6

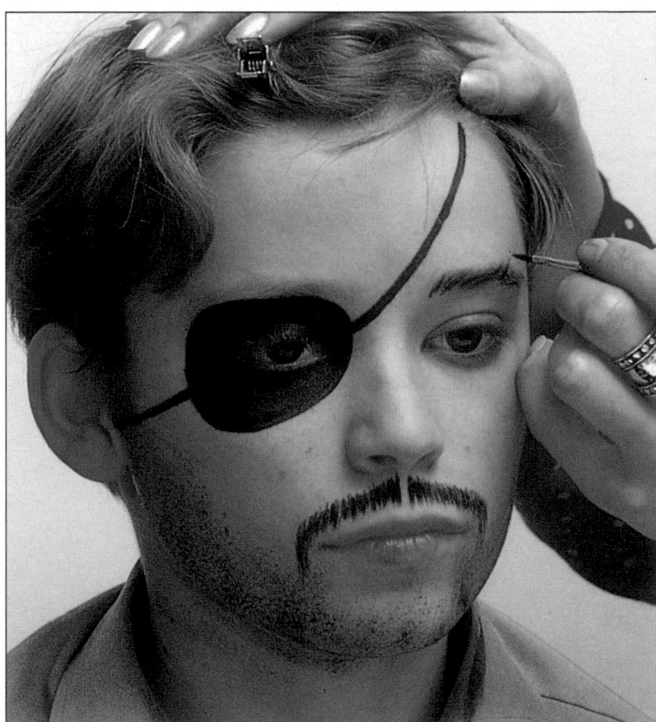

5

7

4 A realistic five o'clock shadow is beginning to emerge.

5 Paint on the moustache with a very fine brush using small sharp strokes.

6 Emphasise the model's eyebrows using the same sharp brush technique.

7 Create a scar by painting a thin dark red line and outlining it in white to achieve a 3-D effect. Paint on a few drops of fake blood.

Spiderman

1 Cover the face and neck with red paint using a sponge. Fill in the eye socket area above and below the eye in black.

2 Make a dot on the end of the nose and use this as a centre point to draw four thin black lines across the face:
1 right down the centre of the face;
2 straight across the face from ear to ear; **3** left to right diagonally from forehead to chin; and **4** right to left diagonally.

3 Begin to develop the web, starting near the centre and repeating the pattern at regular intervals.

4 The web continues right up to the edge of the face.

TIP: A spiderman costume would probably include a red hood but as the Aqua-Colours used here are easily washable you could gel the hair flat and continue the red paint over it.

Arabian Nights

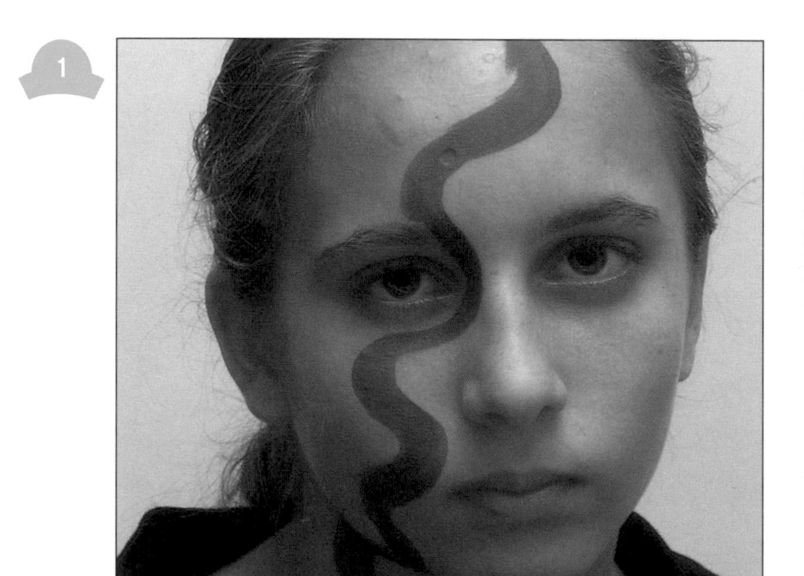

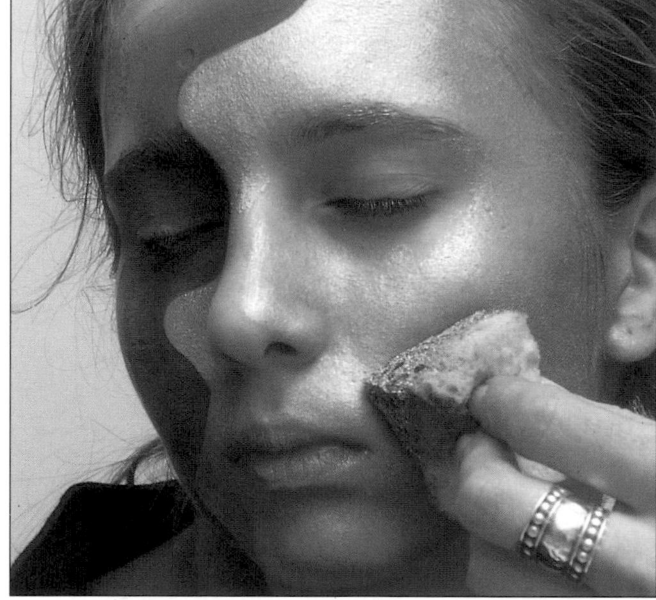

1 Paint a wavy line in purple from the centre of the forehead down onto the neck.

2 Outline the purple in gold. Use a brush along the edge to ensure a neat line, then fill in the rest of the face with gold.

3 Beside the purple, add a strip of pale blue following the same shape, then one of lilac before repeating the whole pattern starting again with purple.

4 Leave the outermost edges sharp, and blend all the other colours into each other using a wide flat brush.

5 The effect so far.

6 Shade the opposite eyelid in purple, fading it into blue on the brow bone. Colour the lips purple.

7 Dab gold glitter along the hard edges of the purple shapes, across the opposite eyebrow and over the lips.

Venetian Mask

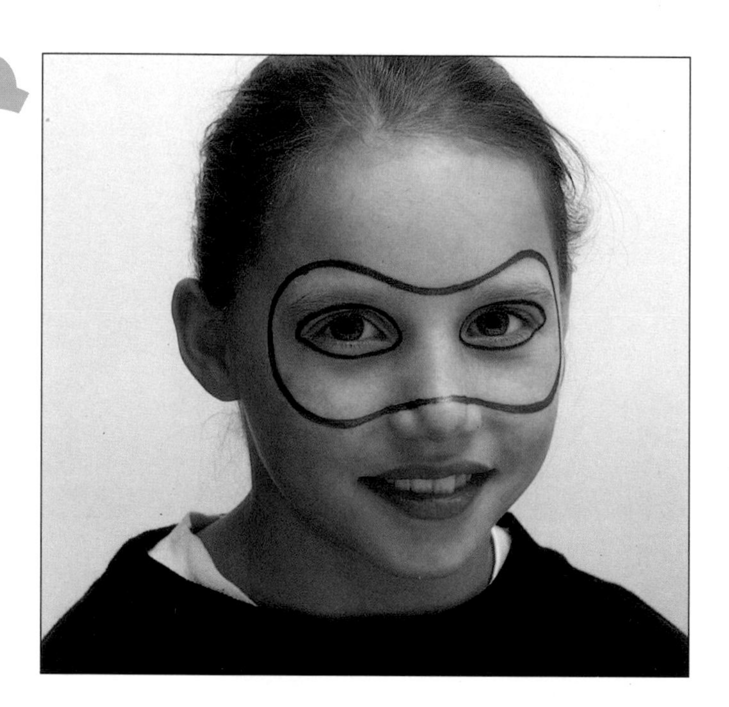

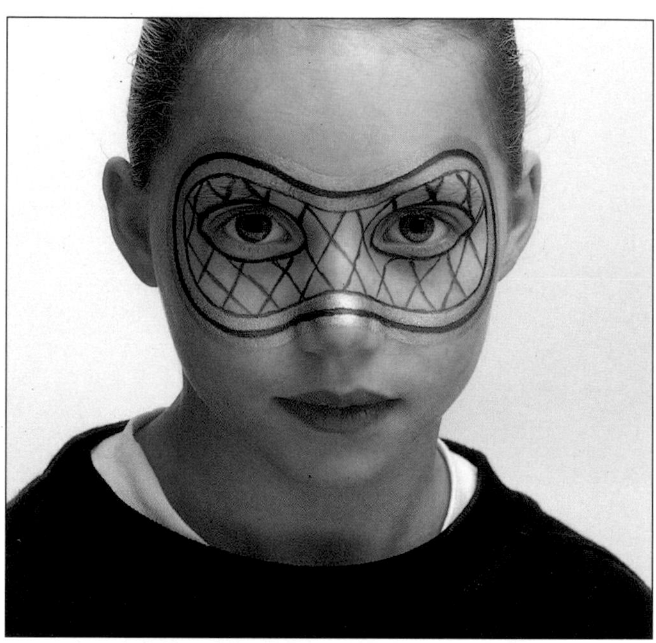

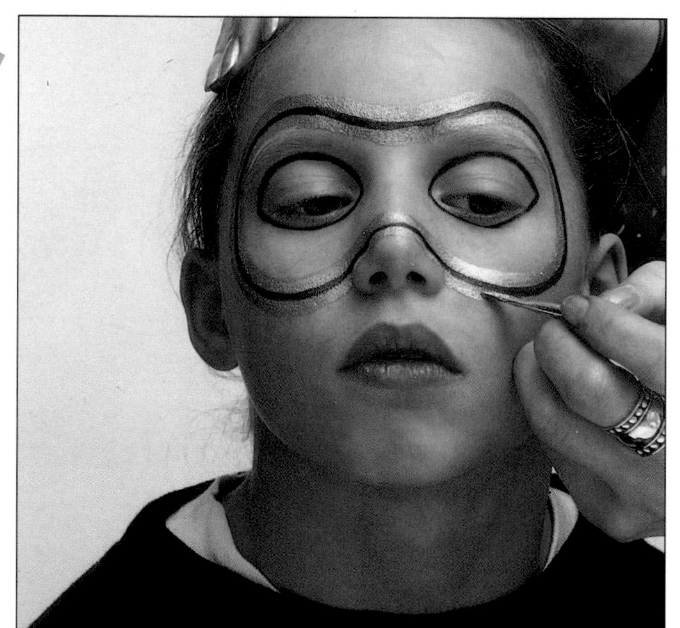

1 Sketch the outline of a mask onto the face with a grey eye pencil – make sure the shape is symmetrical. Outline the eyes in an almond shape. Trace over the grey outlines in black with a fine brush, or use a black eye liner.

2 Neatly paint a gold line around the inside and outside of the mask outline.

3 Carefully draw evenly spaced diagonal black lines across the mask in one direction only. Leave the shape marked out around the eyes blank. Repeat on the opposite diagonal.

4 Paint fine black triangles all round the edge of the mask to represent a frill.

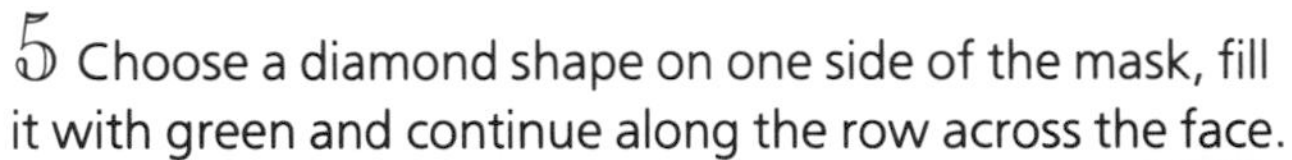

5 Choose a diamond shape on one side of the mask, fill it with green and continue along the row across the face.

6 Miss a row, then colour another row green. Fill in the intervening rows with red. Paint the lips red and draw a whirly line extending from the mask down the sides of the face to represent ties.

Cheek Designs

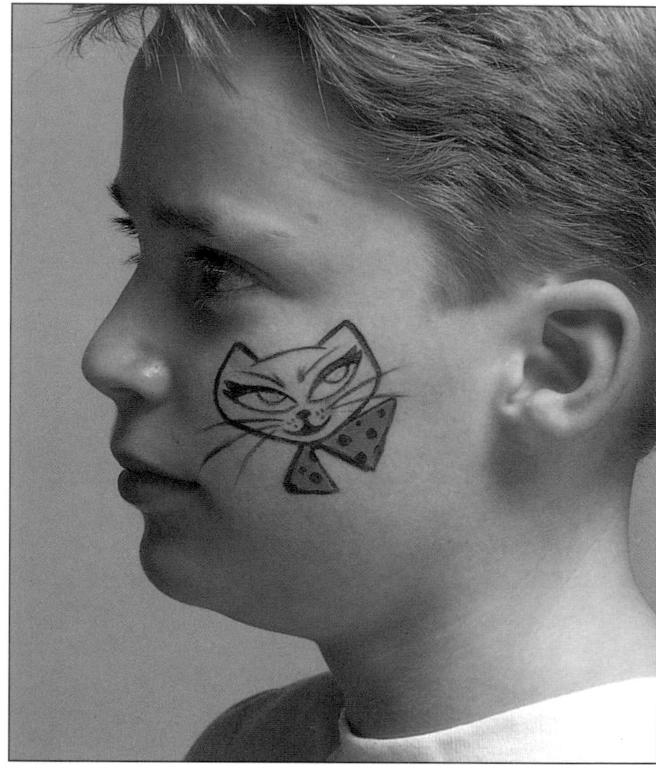

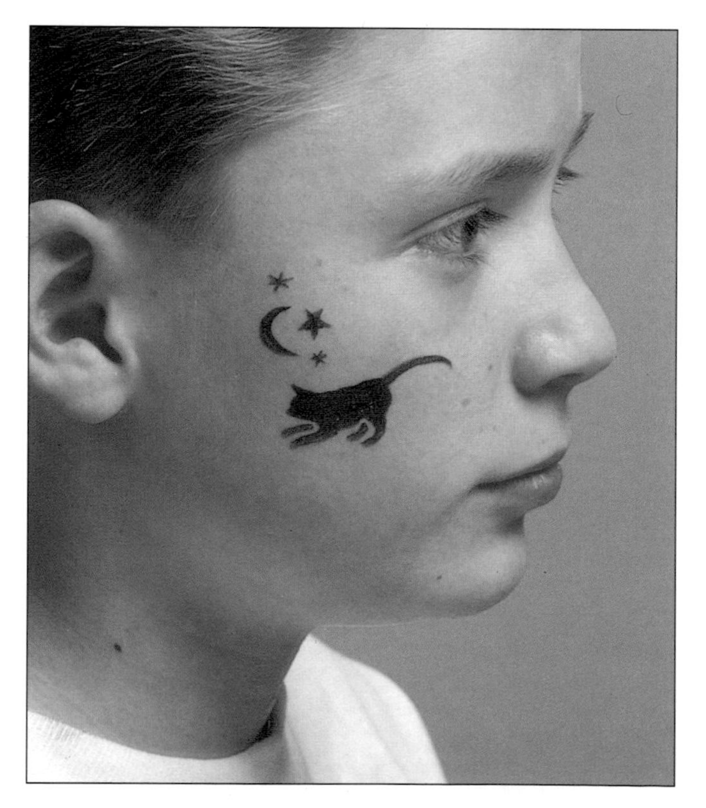

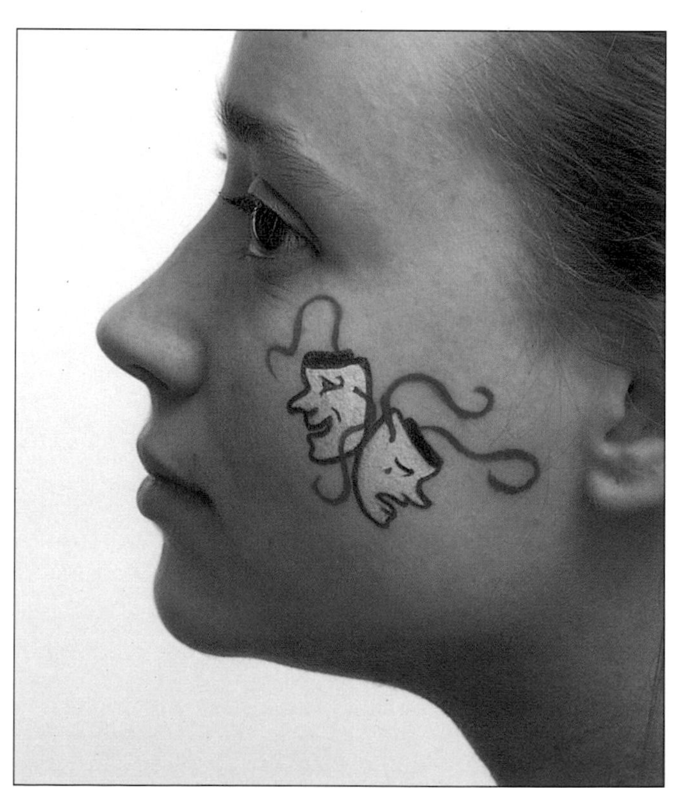

These little designs are quick and fun to do. Of course they don't have to go on your cheek – you could decorate your arms, legs, even your feet. Anything goes! The only basic rule to remember is that once you have drawn out the main outline, always apply the lightest colours first.

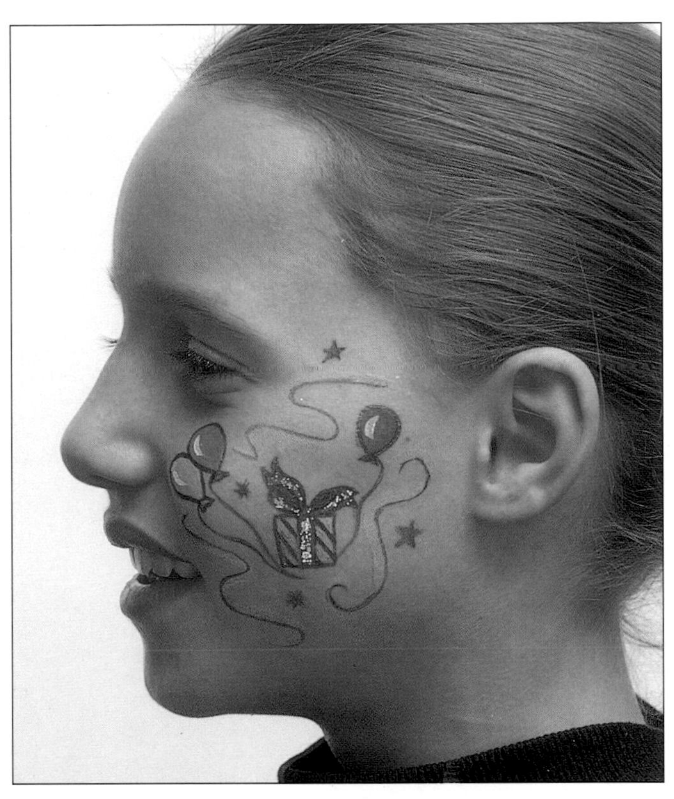

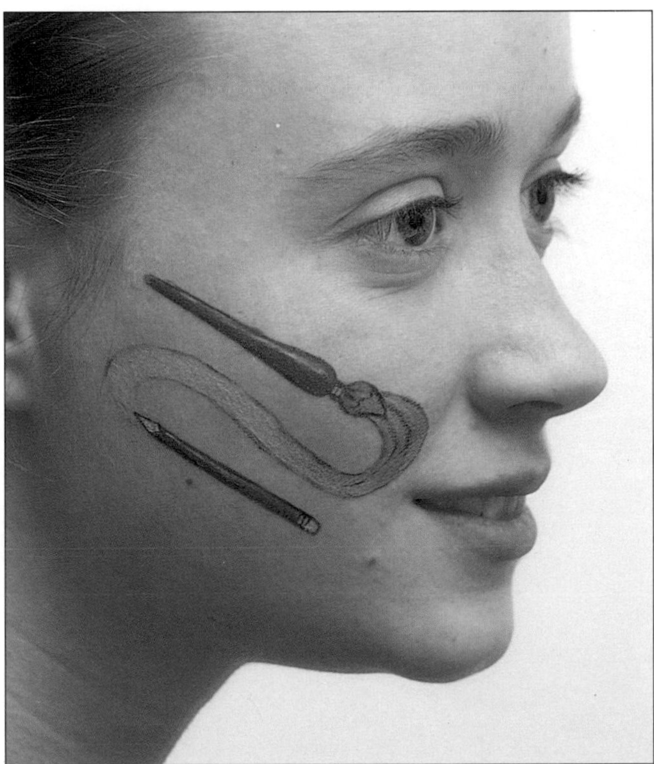

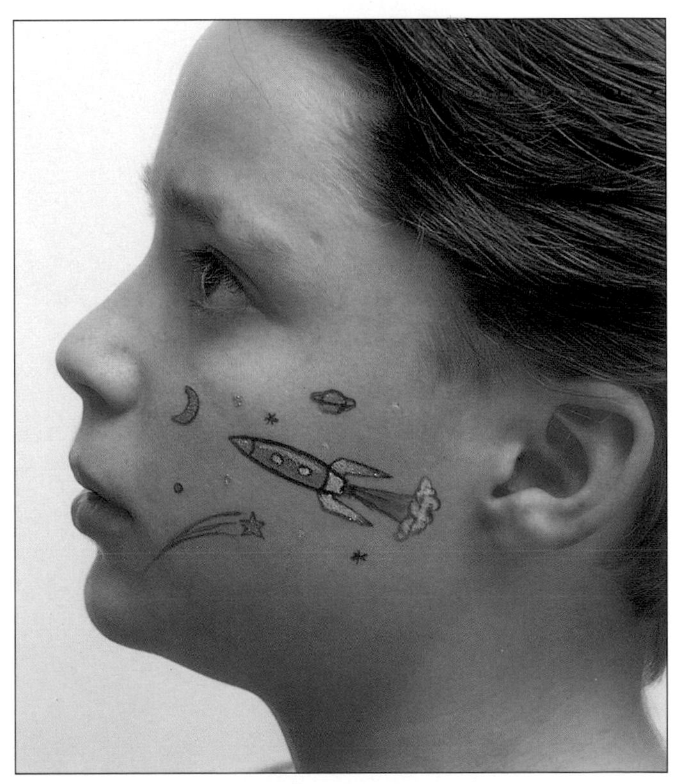

HOW TO DRAW AND PAINT

THE OUTDOORS

MOIRA BUTTERFIELD

Contents

How to Draw and Paint The Outdoors

Paints, pencils, and pots...

HERE WE SHOW YOU some of the most useful kinds of paints, crayons, pencils, and brushes. It is nice to build up a big collection if you're going to paint seriously, but you only need a few paints and some good brushes to make a start!

Powder and poster paints

Powder paint comes in pots or in blocks. When you want to use it, you mix a little of the powder with water. Poster paint can come in jars or plastic bottles. You can use it straight from the container if you want it really thick, or thin it down with water.

Watercolors

Watercolor paint is sold in blocks, which are easy to find and not expensive. Or it comes in tubes as "gouache," which is more professional and therefore a bit more expensive. You don't need a huge range, because you make different colors by mixing.

Watercolor blocks in a palette

Powder paint

Poster paint

Watercolor tubes

Brushes

You need a range of brushes for different techniques and effects - at least a fine pointed one, a middle thickness one, and a really thick one. Nylon is best for thinner paint, as it's soft; choose stiffer ones made of hog's hair for thick paint. You can also recycle household brushes for interesting effects. Try old toothbrushes and nailbrushes for spattering, and decorating brushes for big murals.

Pencils, crayons, and pastels

Colored pencils are cheap to buy and come in a big range. For drawing, buy soft lead pencils, marked with B. A soft lead is much easier to rub out and won't leave a ridge in the paper if you don't press too hard. Also try wax crayons, chalks, pastels, and charcoal.

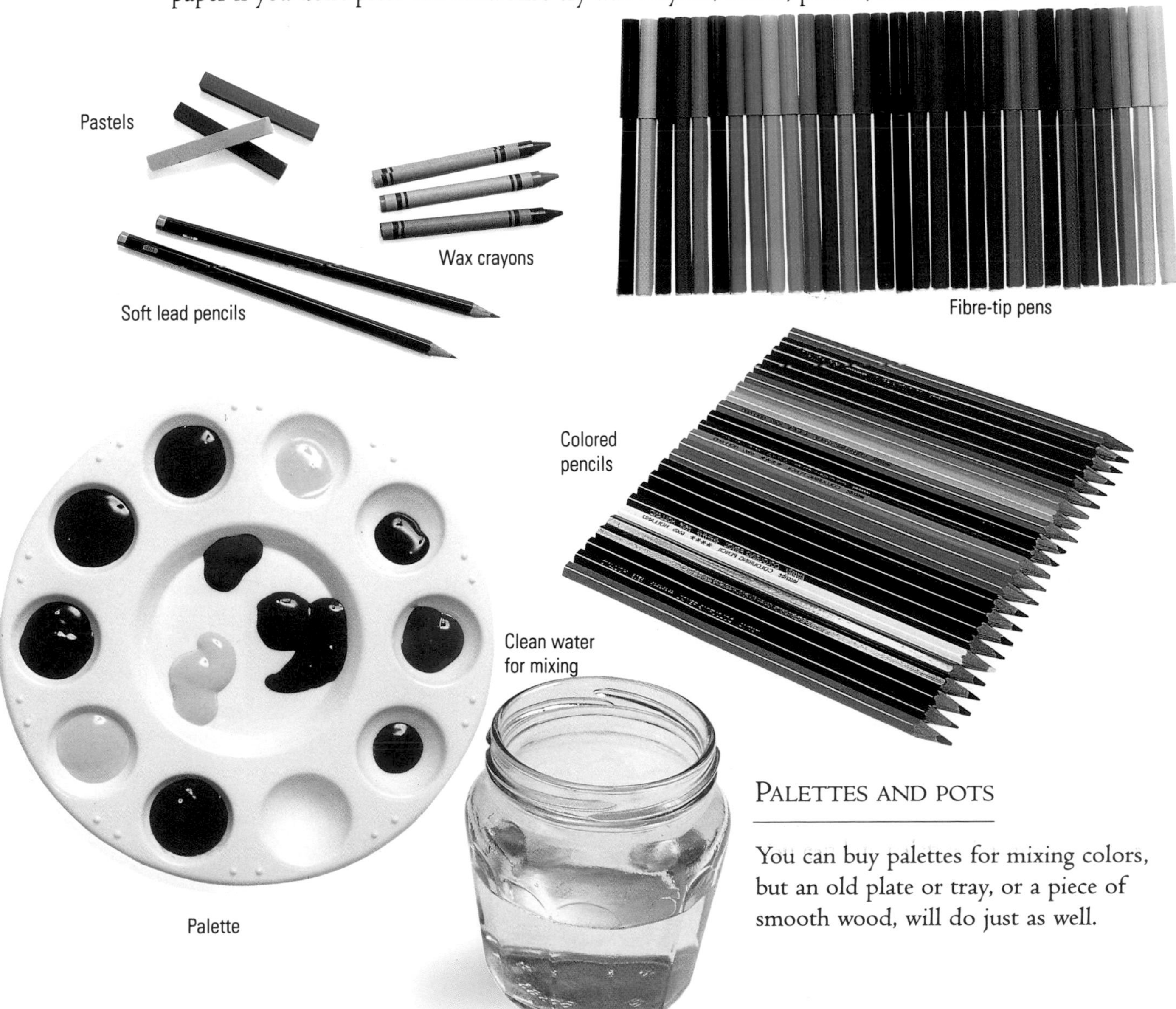

Palettes and pots

You can buy palettes for mixing colors, but an old plate or tray, or a piece of smooth wood, will do just as well.

Keeping notes

YOU'LL WANT TO COLLECT ALL kinds of information to help you with your painting. Get into the habit of carrying a small sketchpad around so that you can jot down ideas and make quick sketches. Collect sketchpads made of different kinds of paper, and you'll have everything you need for painting with different techniques. You can then make a special "portfolio" of your best sketches and paintings.

COLLECTING INFORMATION

You can't always carry painting equipment with you, but you can put a notebook in your pocket! Look out for light effects, colors, and textures. Make quick sketches of scenes you like, so that you can work them up into paintings later. And collect small things you can paste in your notebook – leaves with nice colors, textures or shapes, for example.

PAPER TYPES

Paper is sold in different sizes, colors, thicknesses, and surfaces. You can buy it in sketchpads and in separate sheets. Cartridge paper is smooth, and is good for drawing and painting. Sugar paper is soft and slightly rough. It comes in lots of different colors and is great for pastels, crayons, and charcoal. Watercolor paper is extra thick so it doesn't wrinkle when wet paint is put on it. Start by buying two pads that are recommended for both painting and drawing, one white and one colored.

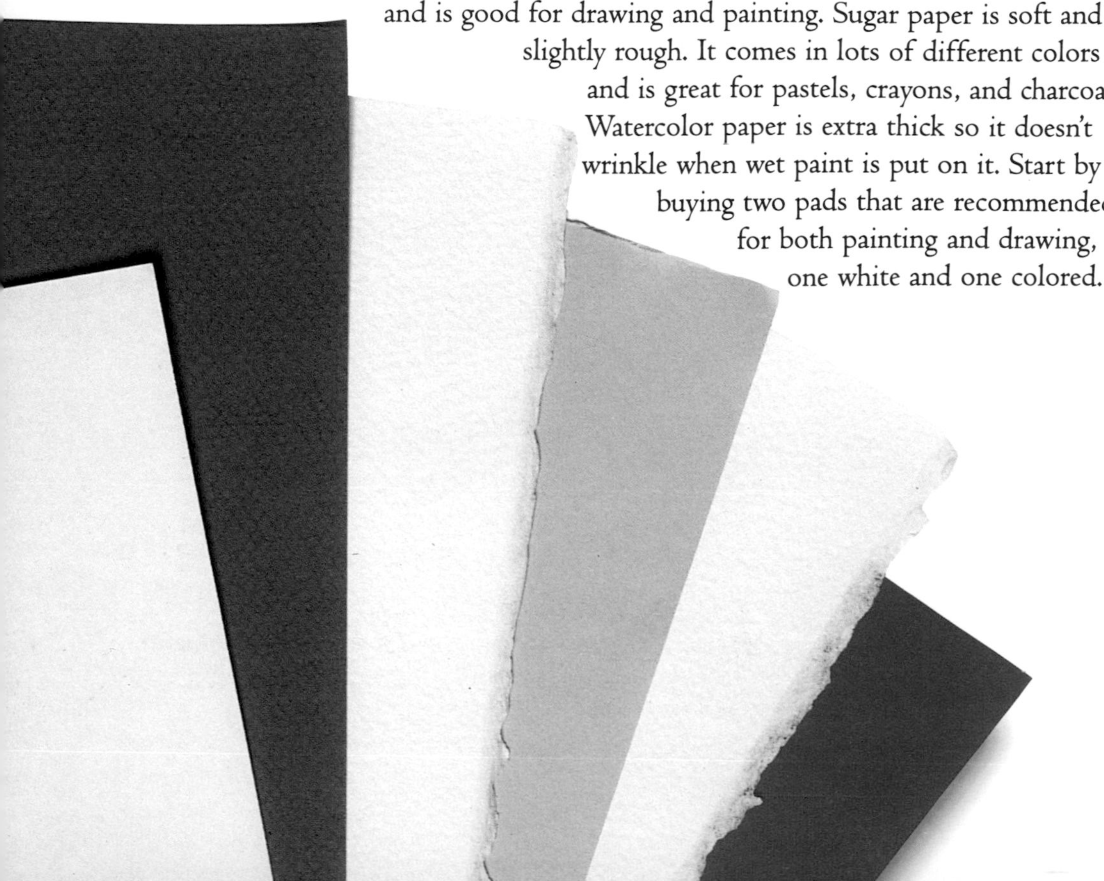

Creating a portfolio

Your best drawings and paintings deserve a proper home, somewhere where they'll be safe from damage until you're ready to show them to people. Artists keep their work in a big folder called a "portfolio." You can make your own quite cheaply.

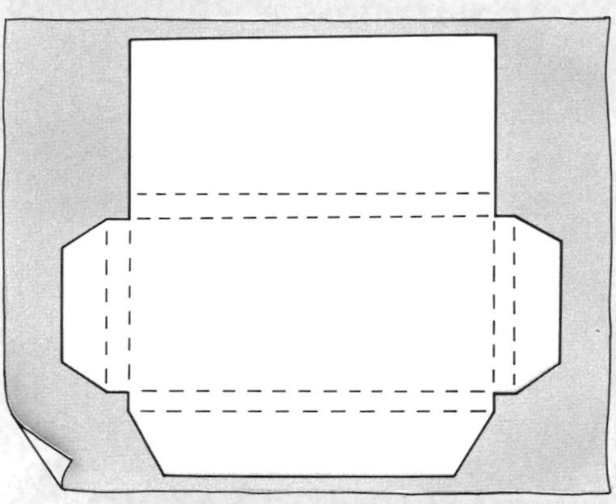

1 Buy some big sheets of thick paper or thin card. Cut the corners out, as shown, to make flaps which will fold right over to make a big envelope. Fold the flaps in along the dotted lines.

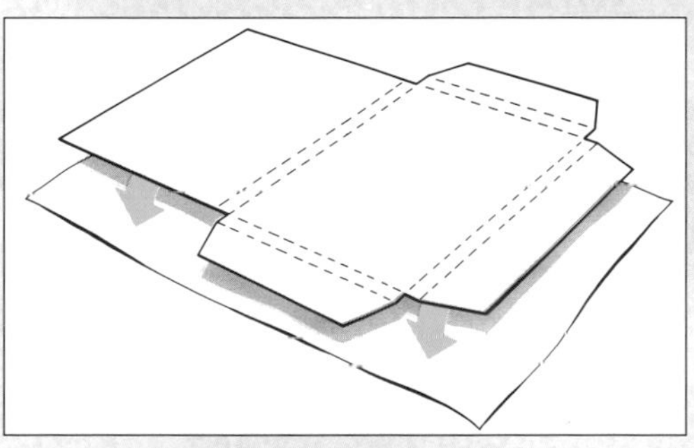

2 Cut another sheet exactly to match the first, and glue them together. The double layer of paper will make the portfolio stronger.

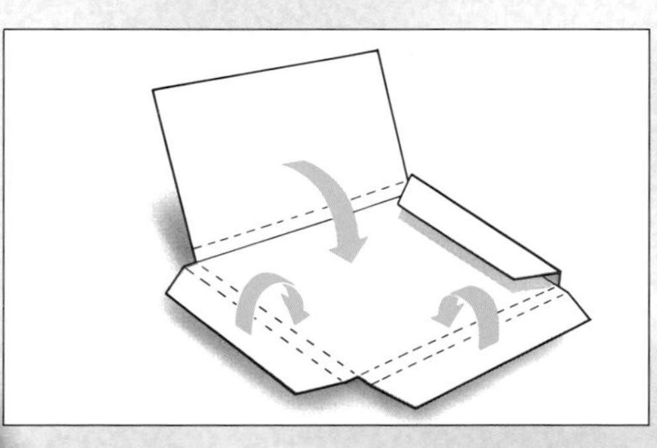

3 Get some strong woven tape from a sewing shop, the sort that won't fray when you cut it. Glue a length firmly on to each side of the portfolio so that you can tie it shut.

◀ *If you like, decorate the outside of the finished portfolio with paintings or prints. As your collection of work builds up, make more portfolios in different sizes and colors.*

All shapes and sizes

IT IS A GOOD IDEA TO THINK ABOUT what you are going to draw before you start. Try drawing things roughly in pencil first to get the arrangement right. For instance, should that tree be in the middle of the paper, or at the side? The way in which a picture is organized is called its "composition." A well-composed picture will be interesting to look at.

Paper Shapes

Make sure that you choose the right size of paper for the picture you are going to paint, and also a piece the right shape. If you are going to paint a wide landscape, use a piece of paper that is wider than it is high. For something tall such as a building or a tree, use paper that is higher than it is wide.

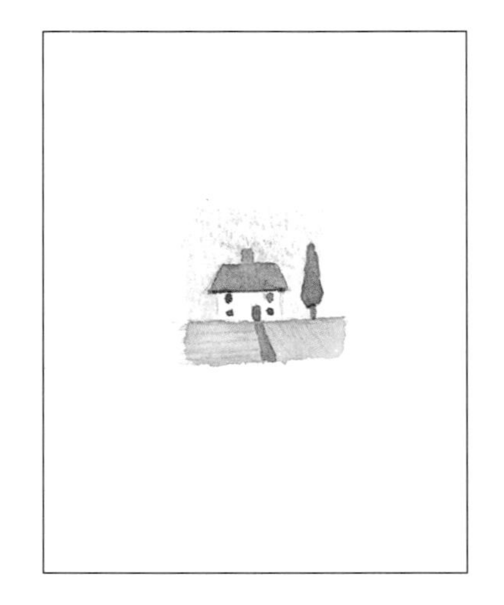

◀ *Try to avoid painting something very small with acres of blank space around it. Think about what you will put round the edges. If you don't want lots of things around a house, for instance, make the house itself bigger – or choose a smaller piece of paper.*

▲ *This tall skyscraper looks a bit boring because it is right in the middle of a wide piece of paper. The walls on each side aren't very interesting, and they take attention away from the building. A higher, narrower piece of paper would be better.*

▲ *This is the right choice of paper size and shape. The picture goes right out to the edges, and there are interesting things over the whole area of the painting, not just in the middle where the trees are.*

◀ *The hull of this boat was drawn large to start with, and then there was not enough room to fit in the sail. If you rough out your drawing in pencil first, you won't make this kind of mistake.*

Thumbs Up

Have you ever seen an artist stretching out an arm and sticking up a thumb? He is checking the size of something in the distance that he wants to paint.

1 The artist is measuring a tree against his thumb. He finds that it is as high as two thumbs – one on top of the other.

2 He measures the size of a figure next to the tree. The person, being much closer, is as high as one thumb. Now he knows to draw the person half the height of the tree.

How to Make a Viewfinder

What You Need
Card
Two paper clips
Ruler
Pencil
Scissors

You can use a viewfinder to help you decide which view to paint. This is a piece of card with a hole in the middle – our one is square, but you could make the hole any shape you like. Hold it in front of your chosen scene and you will see a mini-picture in the hole, just like looking through a camera.

1 Cut a square or rectangle of card into two equal-sized L shapes – an old cereal box will do.

2 Clip the pieces together at the corners to make a square. Using the hand you don't draw with, hold the square in front of you. Rough out the picture inside the square quickly on your paper.

Mixing colors

MIXING COLORS IS ABOUT THE most important thing you'll ever do as a painter, so take time to read these pages and do lots of color experiments. Almost every color you can think of can be made using just three "primary" colors - red, yellow, and blue. Look at scenes in the sunlight and in shadow, and learn to see the different colors that you'll use on paper to recreate the view.

THE COLOR WHEEL

All nine colors in this wheel have been made from the three primary colors in the center. Practice making them with your paints. Start with yellow and add a bit of blue. See how your paint turns green! Mix any of the primary colors with the one next to it and you will get the one shown between them. Then, when you have made the colors on the inner circle, mix each of those with the ones next to them to get the colors on the outer circle.

MAKING COLORS DARKER

Adding black is not usually the best way to make a color darker – it often just makes it look dull. It is better to add a bit of a different, darker, color. You can experiment and see what results you like best.

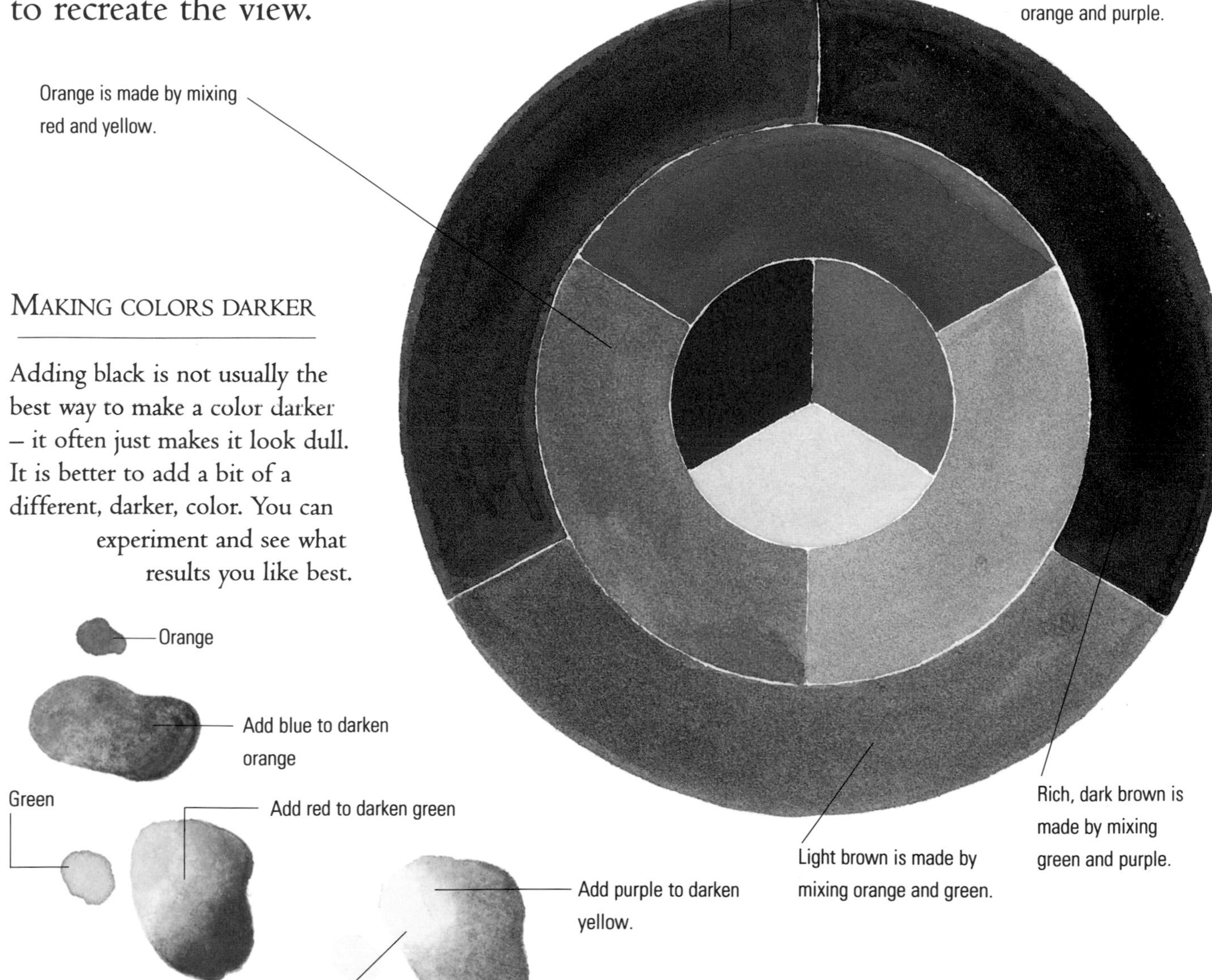

Crayon

Poster paint

Watercolor

Making colors lighter

Getting a lighter shade of color is done differently depending on what kind of paints or crayons you are using. With watercolor, make it thinner by adding more water. With poster paint, add some white, but only a little at a time. If you are using crayons, pastels, or wax crayons, just press more lightly.

▲ *You don't have to mix lots of colors to make a really good painting. This one was made with just two - blue and yellow - plus white. The two main colors mixed togather made the green for the grass, while the white allowed lightening of each color for highlights. Restricting your palette in this way can make extremely effective pictures.*

Seeing tones in color

Look at the two pictures above. One is a color painting, and the other a black-and-white photograph of it. Looking at things without different colors is good practice for learning to see light and dark tones. See if you can paint a simple picture using just black and white, so that you can practice shadows and highlights.

Using colors

THE WAY YOU USE COLOR IN your paintings can have a big effect on their final look. Painting the same scene in "warm" colors and "cool" colors, for example, can completely transform the mood of a picture. Using "complementary" colors (see below) always makes a painting very vibrant and exciting. These rules are simple to learn and most artists find them worthwhile.

▲
Outdoor painters rarely use black to color shadows. They normally use shades of blue, sometimes mixed with the colors that they paint around the shadow. Blue shadows are especially right for snow scenes.

▲
As well as the complementary blue and orange, there are greens and reds. The color wheel tells you that green is made from blue and yellow, so you can see how all the colors in this painting are very closely related to each other.

Complementary colors

The picture on the left was painted using very rich and deep colors that make the scene look very hot. The main colors in the composition are blue and orange. Now look back at the color wheel on page 16. Orange is the secondary color opposite the primary blue: the colors are called "complementary." Artists often use complementary colors for a strong composition.

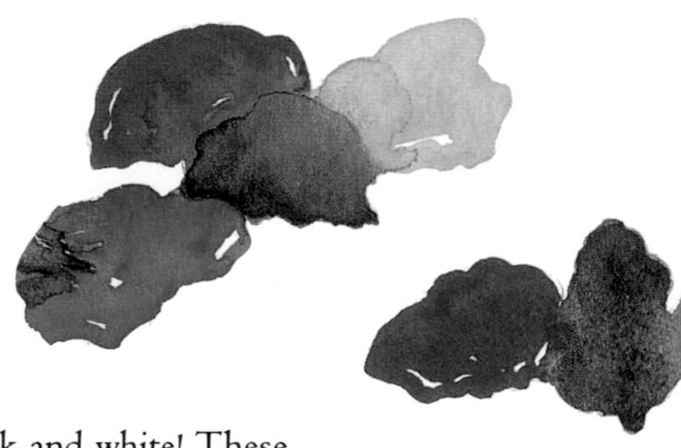

Making grays and browns

Gray doesn't have to be made from black and white! These mixes show how you get interesting darker shades from combining primary and complementary colors.

Many moods

The pictures on this page are all made using restricted color schemes. The primary colors are used with the secondaries made from them, or with their complementary colors. They have a range of feelings, but all are very dramatic and strong.

◀
All three primary colors - blue, yellow, and red - are used here. The blue and yellow, mixed, produce the orange. See how the shadows on the sand contain lots of yellow.

Red is the complementary color of green.

Green is made from blue and yellow.

▲
This forest scene is a study of many different shades of gray and brown. They are made mostly using the greens and yellows in the same picture.

▲
The apple orchard is painted using the "cool" colors - blues and greens. They make the composition harmonious, but the spots of bright red, complementary to the green, brighten it up.

▲
This fire looks really hot! Paint one of your own using the "warm" colors of red, yellow, orange, and orangey brown.

Brush strokes

DIFFERENT BRUSHES CAN GIVE you very different effects. Experiment with them to see what you like, and to give you practice. Always choose the right kind and size of brush for different techniques. If you want to paint colors made up of dots, use a small round brush; for dashes, use a broader one.

PAINTING IN DOTS

For painting in lots of dots, choose fine round-headed brushes. "The Harbour at Bessin Port," by George Seurat, is very striking because of this technique. If you stand back, the colors look solid, but if you go close you can see that each tiny dot is quite separate.

Choose colors for each area that are close in tone, so that you build up a gradual effect.

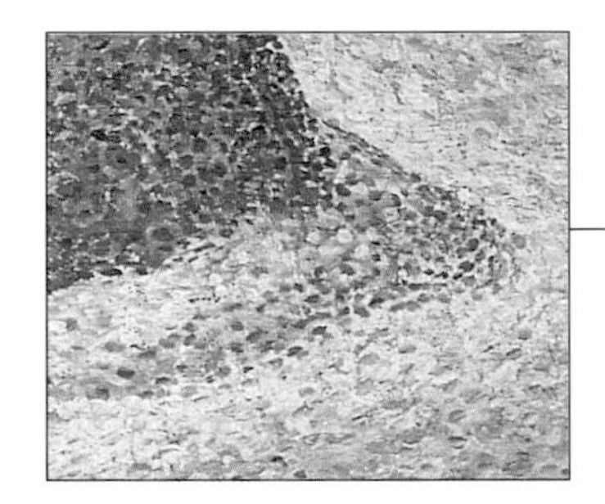

You can vary the length of the dashes, and even their direction.

PAINTING IN DASHES

For quite large dashes, use brushes which end in a square shape, called flats. The painting on the left, by Eli Gallwey, is made up of dashes of different colored paint.

▲ *Use dryish paint on a fine round brush, and let each color dry before you add more.*

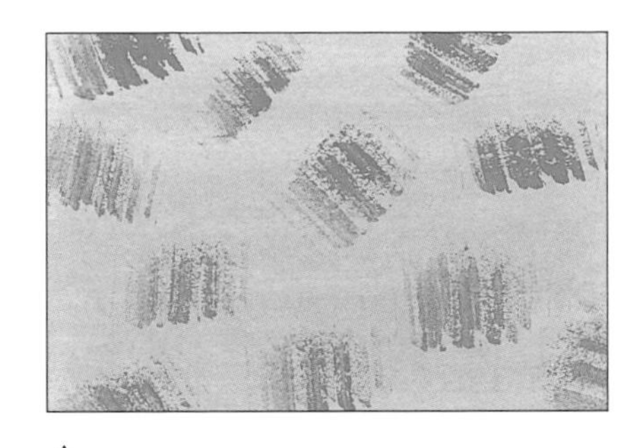

▲ *Use a flat brush, again fairly dry, to make short sweeps across a ground color.*

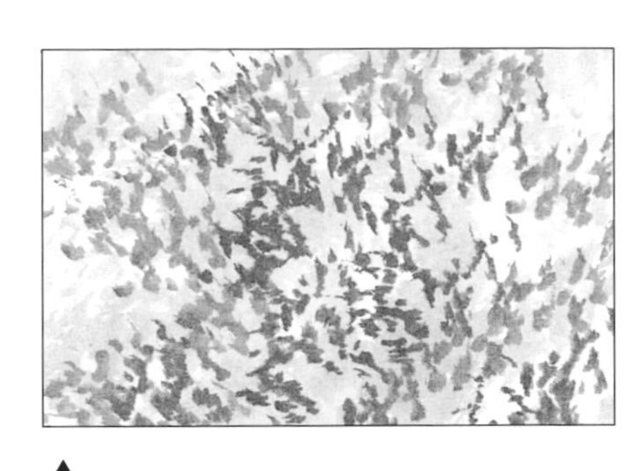

▲ *Use a flat brush, lightly pressed on and lifted up immediately, with the ground still wet.*

PAINTING STIPPLES

Stippling is putting lots of tiny dots on top of another layer of paint. You do it with quite a stiff brush, either round or flat. For this jug of flowers, the blue of the jug was left to dry before the stippling was done. The flowers were stippled while still wet, to mix the colors up more.

Apply the stippling on top of wet paint for a smudgy look.

Put the white stippling on after the blue has dried, so that it stays separate.

Look, no brushes!

YOU DON'T HAVE TO USE BRUSHES OR crayons to make paintings. You can put paint on to paper with all sorts of things – sponges, scraps of fabric, scrunched-up paper, card. Look round your home for old things you could use, particularly materials with an interesting texture which would come through on to the paper.

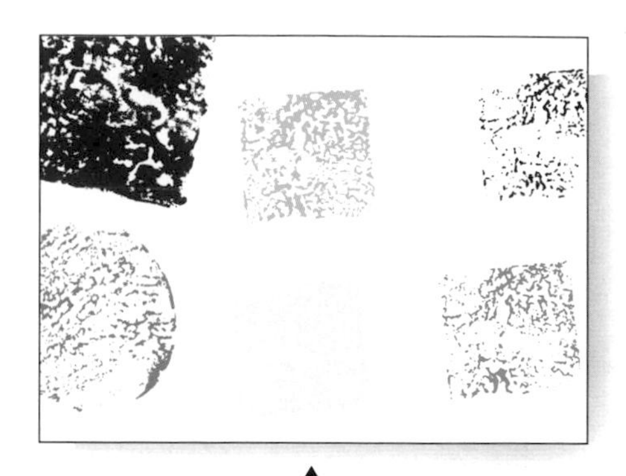

▲ *This picture was made by dabbing paint on with different bits of packaging material.*

DABBING AND SPONGING

Applying paint with a sponge is very easy, and a good way to cover large areas quickly and evenly. Don't let the sponge get too wet with paint, or the texture won't come through. You can also cut up old packaging material into different shapes and use them as little printing blocks.

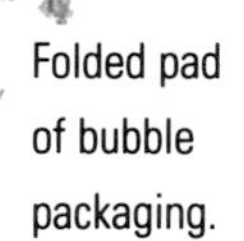

Folded pad of bubble packaging.

Polystyrene packaging cut into shapes.

▲ *Dip a sponge in thick paint and dab or drag it on to the paper. Experiment with different effects as the sponge gets dryer.*

▲ *This flowery meadow was painted without any brushes. The edge of a piece of card was used for the grass, in different greens. When it was dry, the flowers were added on top.*

▲ *Drag dark blue paint on to blue paper for the sea, using kitchen paper. Use small squares cut from polystyrene to block on the cliffs, then dab on white spray with more kitchen paper.*

Use a coarse rag for the trees to give a speckled texture.

◀ *Drag on paint thickly for the grass, roofs, and walls using the side of a piece of stiff card. This gives even blocks of color. When the paint is dry, drag over them again in places with darker color using much less paint, to make shading. Cut a small piece of card to drag for the fence.*

Using pastels

PASTELS ARE MADE SIMPLY OF pigment and gum, and are soft and crumbly. They make brightly colored lines and can also give a delicate, blurry effect if you rub over them with a rag or a fingertip. You can buy pastels made into sticks or pencils. Sticks easily pick up dirt so store them in a box carefully laid side by side.

You cannot easily mix pastels or put them on top of each other to make new colors. However, pastel sets usually have a wide range of shades to choose from.

Putty rubber for erasing pastel marks

Pastel sticks

Use the broad edge of a dark brown stick for the cliff.

Use white strokes and dabs for the froth.

With the thin edge of the stick, use different greens in up-and-down strokes for the grass.

PASTEL TIPS

Pastels look very good on colored paper. Many artists use grey paper to get a soft effect. Black paper makes the colors look really bright.

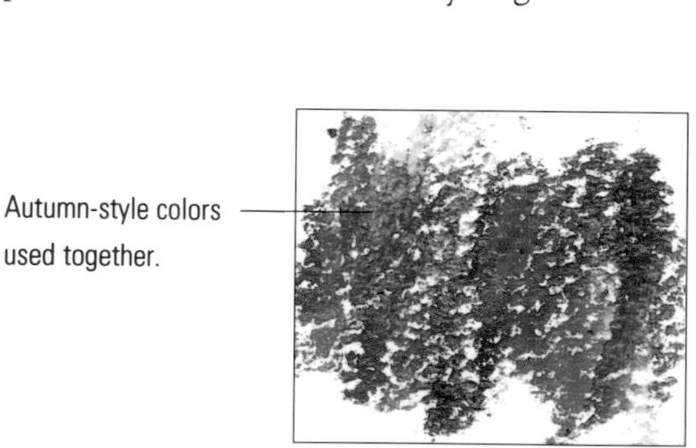

Autumn-style colors used together.

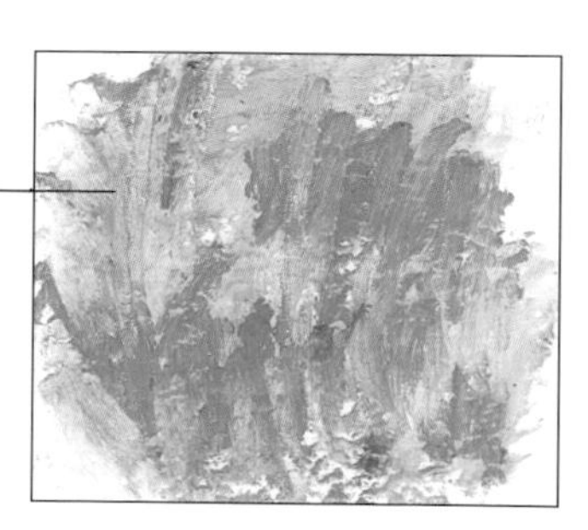

Watery-style colors used together.

▲ *Get a blurred effect by rubbing your pastel marks with a clean dry rag. You can make exciting movement lines in this way. It's also good for doing skies and water.*

This beautiful Christmas tree is easy to draw. Choosing black paper makes the colors of the shining fairy lights very bright.

1 *Draw a trunk in brown. Put in some curved lines for branches, in different shades of green and blue.*

2 *Use a clean dry rag or sponge to rub over the lines you have made. Rub gently in the same direction as the branches. Then add splodges of bright color for the lights.*

3 *Rub gently over the lights, using a circular movement, to give them a soft glow.*

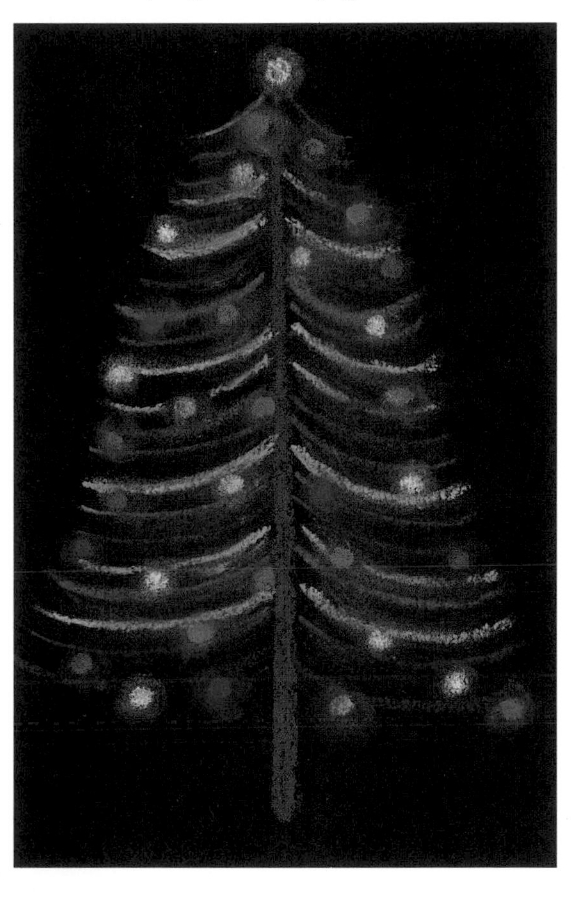

Broad, wavy strokes of blue and white suggest the sea.

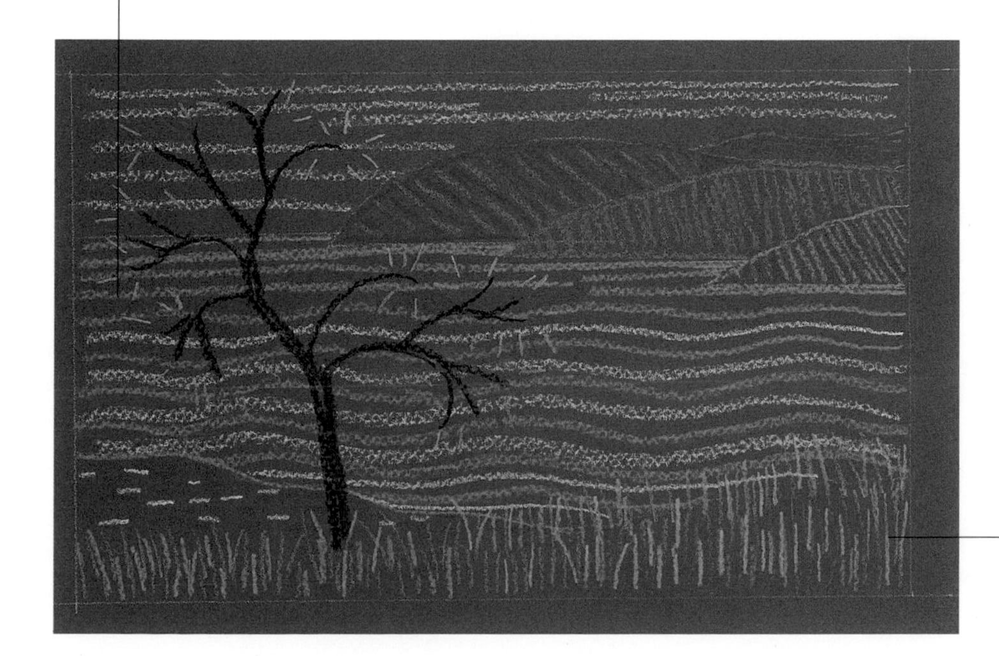

Up-and-down strokes for the grass look good in different greens.

◀ *You can make a lively picture, full of movement, by using small strokes of pastel, with no rubbing or shading. Make your strokes follow the shapes you want to show. For instance, grass is best with strokes that go up and down. Sea is made with wavy strokes going across the page. Use both the thin and broad edges of the pastel to vary the effects.*

Charcoal and chalk

CHARCOAL AND CHALK ARE GREAT FOR doing quick sketches that have sweeping lines and wide areas of light and shade. Both are soft and powdery and can be used to give a textured effect.

Charcoal, made from burnt wood, is very dark gray, black if you use it heavily. You can smudge it with your finger, which makes very good shading. It comes in different thicknesses.

Chalk and chalk pastels are pale and come in many colors. They can look very effective if used on a dark-colored paper, or with charcoal.

Choosing Paper

If you use charcoal or chalk with rough paper, the pattern of the paper's surface will show through. This will give your picture an interesting texture.

Textures

These are just some of the different texture and line effects that you can get with chalk. Try them out yourself.

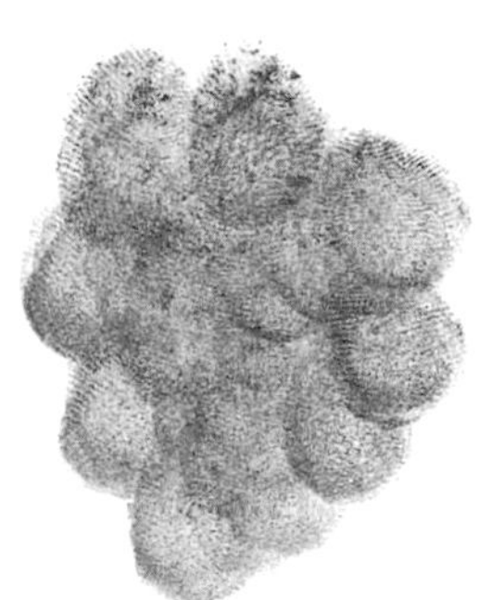

Dabs and dots can be softened by smudging with a finger.

Shapes can be drawn into chalk using an eraser with a fine edge.

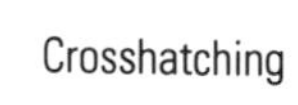

Crosshatching

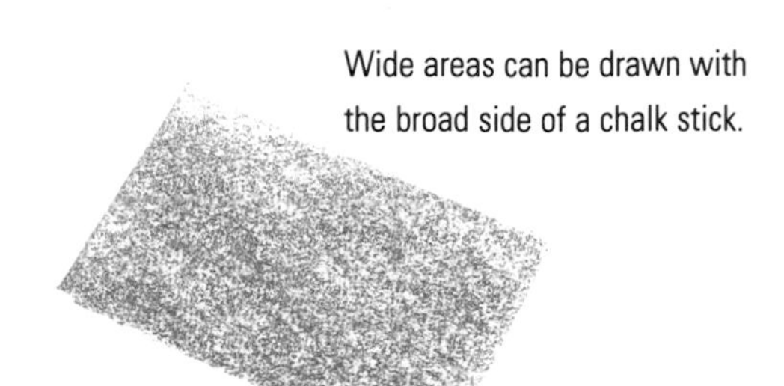

Wide areas can be drawn with the broad side of a chalk stick.

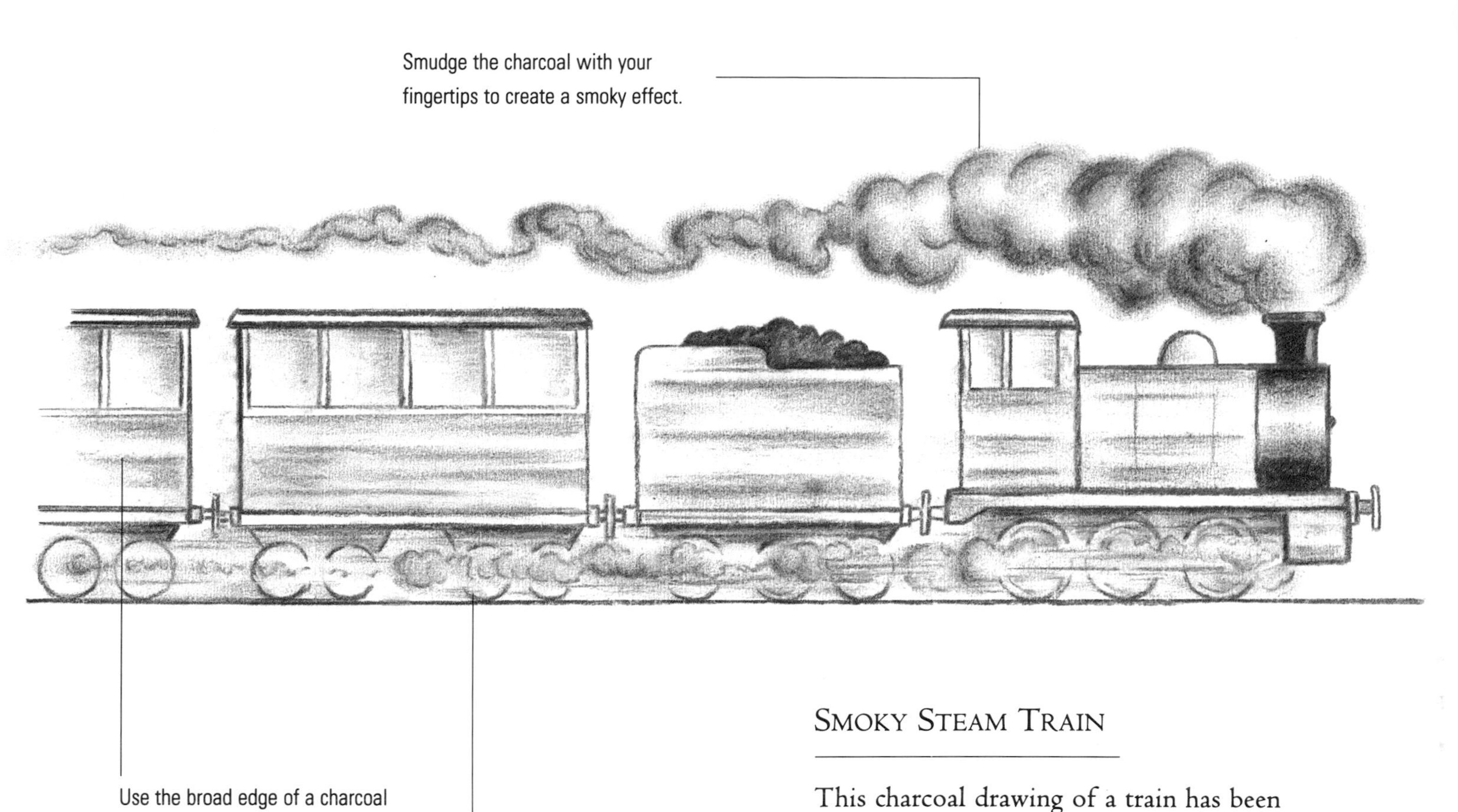

Smoky Steam Train

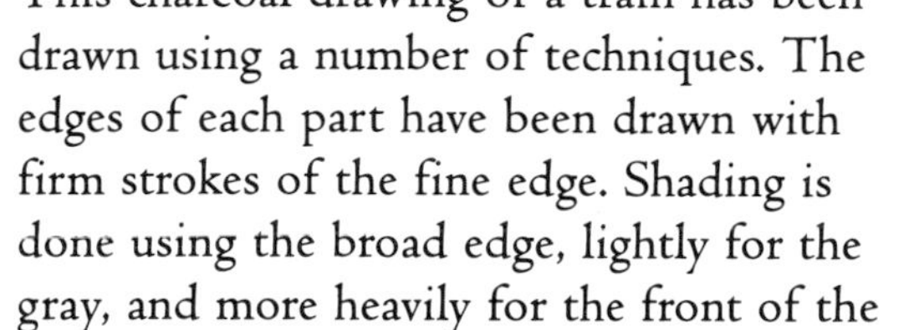

This charcoal drawing of a train has been drawn using a number of techniques. The edges of each part have been drawn with firm strokes of the fine edge. Shading is done using the broad edge, lightly for the gray, and more heavily for the front of the engine. Look how the streaks and smoke puffs by the wheels give a feeling of speed.

Using Charcoal and Chalk

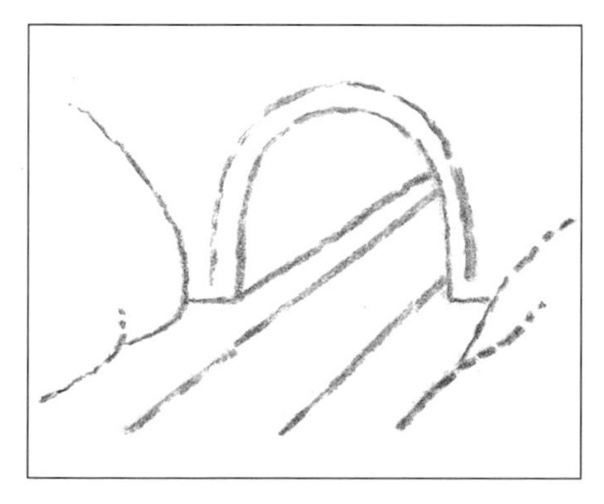

1 *Sketch in the main lines of your picture lightly with the thin edge of the charcoal – the tunnel, the rail track, and the bank.*

2 *Smudge in the dark shadow in the tunnel. Start to add outline detail to the grass and the bricks.*

3 *Using colored chalks, give the bricks a range of colors and make the ground beneath the tracks look rough and stony.*

Putting it in perspective

When you look at a landscape you will see that it stretches away into the distance. Some things look larger because they are nearer, other things look small because they are further away. It can be quite difficult to create this effect on paper. Getting all the parts of your picture the right size in relation to each other, and in the right place so that they look as if they disappear into the distance, is called putting them in perspective.

Parallel Lines

Parallel lines look as if they are joining together as they stretch into the distance. This is an important part of perspective. The further away your vanishing point is, the longer they will take to join.

▲

This photograph would make a good composition for a painting. The furrows of the plowed field, apparently getting narrower as they stretch away, draw the eye into the distance. The contrast between the light and shade on the furrows increases the effect and is very dramatic.

How to Draw a Road

A road makes a good subject for practicing perspective drawing. In reality, everyone knows a road stays about the same width, so the vanishing point in your picture shows very clearly. Here we show you the effect of putting the vanishing point in two different places – in the center and to one side. See which effect you like best.

1 *First start with your horizon line, and put in a pale wash of green and blue for the land and the sky.*

2 *Mark the vanishing point lightly in pencil on the horizon. Here it is in the center.*

3 *Draw lines down from the vanishing point as guides for the road, the sidewalk, and the fence.*

4 *Here is the same picture, with a vanishing point more to the left. See how the trees on the left now line up.*

An outside vanishing point

You can make a vanishing point outside the edge of your picture. To help you, mark it on another piece of paper next to the one you are going to paint on.

Plowed fields

Draw lines coming out of a vanishing point off the page above the horizon line. Use these to guide you to draw plow furrows coming down from the vanishing point. Draw some lines across, too, to show the divisions of the fields. A tractor and a farmhouse, small because they are away in the distance, complete your picture.

Seeing into the distance

HERE ARE SOME OF THE WAYS TO make your pictures look as if they are stretching into the distance. Put objects in perspective and use vanishing points (see pages 28-29). Overlap things, so that one object looks as if it is behind another. Make things big at the front of your picture and smaller at the back. Remember that the further away things are, the less clear their outline.

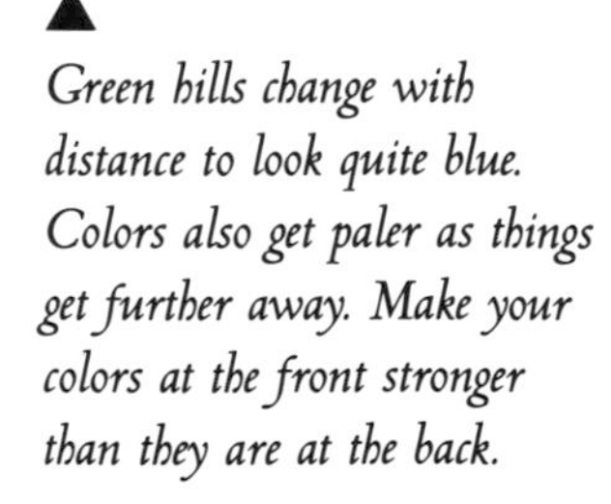

▲ *Green hills change with distance to look quite blue. Colors also get paler as things get further away. Make your colors at the front stronger than they are at the back.*

▲ *Try a picture of a landscape seen from indoors through a window. First paint the window round the edge.*

◀ *Landscape painters rarely use black to color shadows. They normally use shades of blue mixed with the colors that they paint around the shadow. First check which way the shadows lie.*

Blurred Distances

In the foreground, edges are distinct and colors separate, as in the bench in the picture on the left. Further away, in the distant fields, edges get fuzzier and colors tend to look mixed together - the church tower is just a light splodge of brown.

◀
Constable's "A Park Glade" is a view of Dedham Church - but you can only just see it!

Blue Horizon

If you look at a range of grassy hills you will see that the green color tends to turn soft blue the further away it is. Try a picture like the one below. Overlap the hills as they slope towards the water. Start off with strong greens and distinct blades of grass at the front. Add blue and white to the greens as you paint to the back.

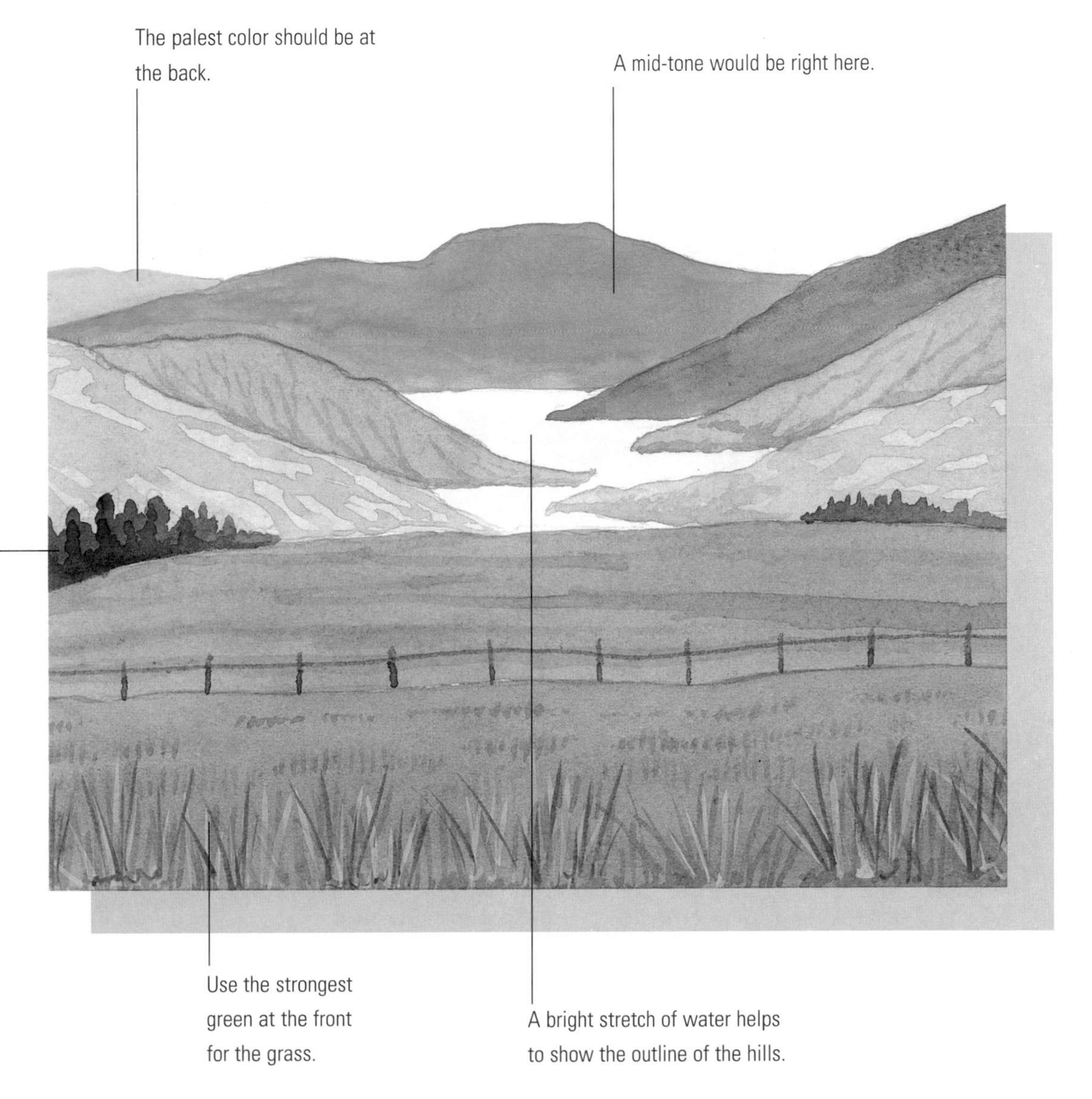

The palest color should be at the back.

A mid-tone would be right here.

Dark green trees help define the slope of the field.

Use the strongest green at the front for the grass.

A bright stretch of water helps to show the outline of the hills.

Looking at light

THE SUN'S LIGHT HAS A VERY important effect on outside scenes and colors. For most of the day the sun is not directly overhead, but shines on things at an angle. The area behind an object is blocked from the light and in shadow. You need to note where the sun is and what directions the shadows fall in. Weather has an effect, too. On an overcast day, not only are there no clear shadows, but the light is softer and more even.

▲
Here are some of the different green colors used to paint this tree. Look how different the greens are on the sunny and the shady sides.

LIGHT AND COLOR

Look at the leaves on a tree. You will see that they are made up of several different greens – some light and some dark. Up close, with the light even, they are mostly the same color, but when light shines on them at different angles from a distance they look different.

▲
The sand on a beach looks all the same color on a dull day, but in strong sunlight shadows make lots of variations.

▲
When the sun is low in the sky, shadows are much more pronounced. The hollows between the dunes look almost black.

Painting by the clock

The same scene looks very different from one hour to the next as the light changes. You can use this effect to make an unusual picture.

Make a preliminary sketch of an outdoor scene. Paint the scene at four different times of the day, carefully noting how the colors change. At early morning and evening, for example, when the sun is low in the sky, the light is more red. Cut your paintings into four quarters. Fit one quarter from each scene together to make a new picture.

The Impressionists

The Impressionists were a group of painters in the late nineteenth century, famous for their studies of the effects of light on color. Look out for their work in galleries and art books.

Claude Monet painted this picture called "Haystacks." He did not use strong outlines but created all the shapes using different colors. Look at the picture from about ten feet away, and the grass and haystacks seem to be solid colors. In fact they are made up of an amazing number of different colors, all created by the effects of light.

Painting shadows

WHEN LIGHT SHINES ON AN object, the object casts a shadow on the ground. If you put shadows into a picture, it helps to make it look more real and gives it a 3D feel. Look carefully at the scene you are painting to work out where the shadows fall. Roughly sketch them when you are planning your picture at the beginning.

See how the side of the block is darker than the to

The back is the darkest because it gets no light.

WHAT IS A SHADOW?

Quite simply, a shadow is the area behind an object that is blocked from the light. It therefore appears as a dark area the same shape as the object.

CHANGING SHADOWS

As the sun moves across the sky, the shadows of a stationary object move, too. Try this painting experiment to see for yourself. Do it on a sunny day, when the shadows are clear and sharp. Put your card figure outside if you can. Indoors, use a table in front of a big window where the sun shines in for most of the day. Sketch the figure and the shape of the shadows at different times.

1 Cut out a simple person shape from a piece of card. Leave extra card at the bottom. Turn this back to make a stand.

2 Stand your figure facing south. In the morning, the sun is in the east, and casts a shadow to the right.

3 At noon, the sun is directly overhead, and slightly to the south. The shadow is very short.

4 By the afternoon, the sun has moved round to the west, and the shadow is cast to the left of the figure.

5 Late in the evening, the shadow is very long and stretched out. This can make very dramatic effects in outdoor painting.

How many shadows?

When only one light is shining, such as the sun, an object will cast only one shadow. If more than one light is shining, shadows become more complicated!

Go outside or look out of a window one evening when there are several street lights or window lights on. There will be lots of different shadows going different ways. Try sketching them quickly and use your sketches to make an interesting painting later on.

The snowman has two shadows because he is standing between two lights.

Shadow Shapes

◀ *Compare the shape of the tree and the shape of the shadow. To make your pictures real, details like this are very important.*

Look at the way the shadows fall on the sidewalk

▲ *Look at the shape of the railings, and see how their shadows have the same shape, but slightly distorted because of the angle from which the light is shining.*

Scary shadows

Shadows sometimes look frightening because they can make mysterious, distorted shapes, especially in the evening when the low sun makes them stretch out longer. You can use this effect to paint a sinister, dramatic picture with mystery shadows that suggest scary monsters!

Using shading

IF YOU LOOK AT AN OBJECT YOU WILL see that some parts of it look dark and some parts look light. This is called tone. It is caused by the way that light falls – the brightest parts are where the light is shining directly on to the object. You add tone by shading the parts of the object that are away from the direct light source. This makes things look very solid.

This side of the house is in shadow.

▲ *This house has been shaded so that one side is darker than the other. It makes clear from which direction the sun is coming, so the house looks realistic.*

USING TONE OUTSIDE

Look carefully at the things you are going to paint or draw. The parts that face away from the sun will have a darker tone than the parts facing the light.

Bright sun makes onc side of the tree very light, and the other strongly shaded.

When the sun is not bright, the differences between light and shade are much less marked.

MODELLING OBJECTS

When you are shading an object, the marks you make should follow its shape. To make something look round, use rounded strokes of your brush.

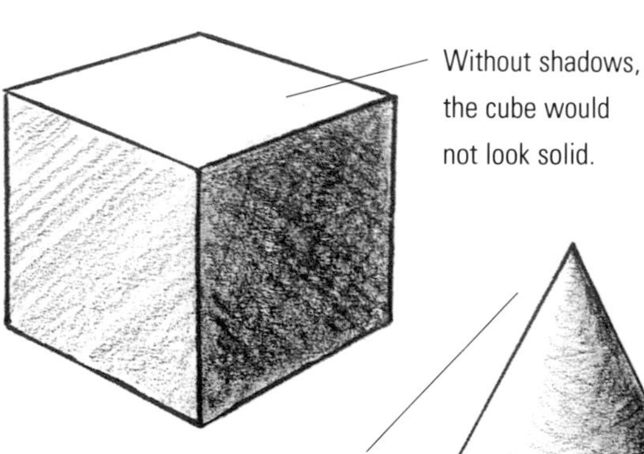

Without shadows, the cube would not look solid.

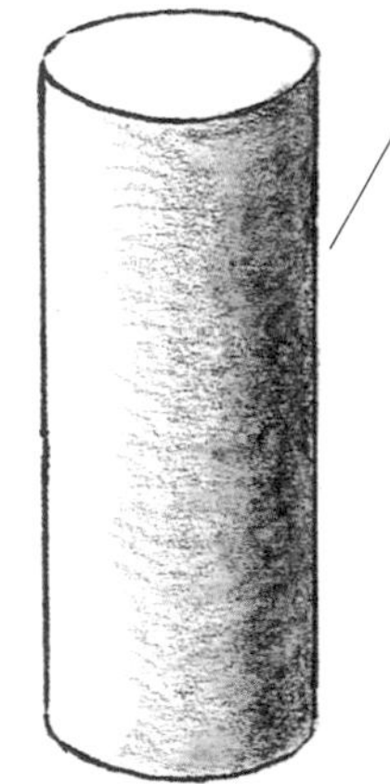

The shading down one edge of the cylinder fades away as it rounds the curve

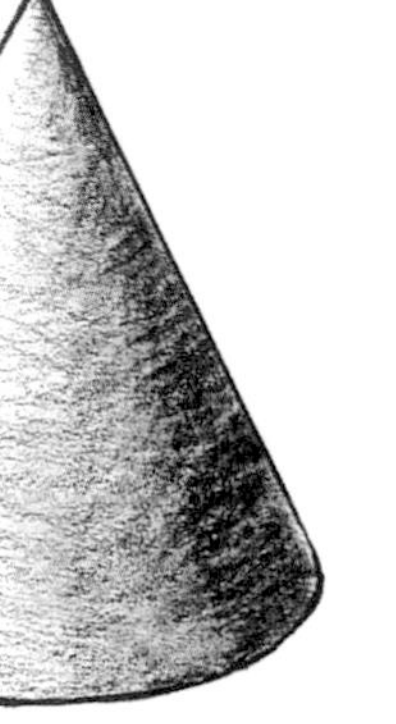

To make a cone shape, use shading down one edge, fading away towards the center.

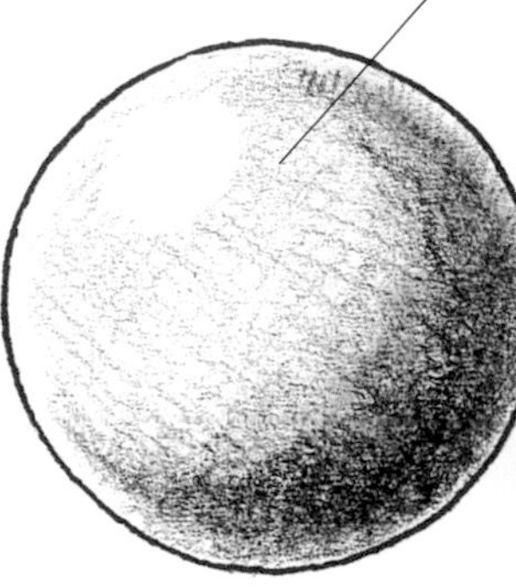

This is the hardest shape to do. Shading fades way towards the center to make a crescent shape.

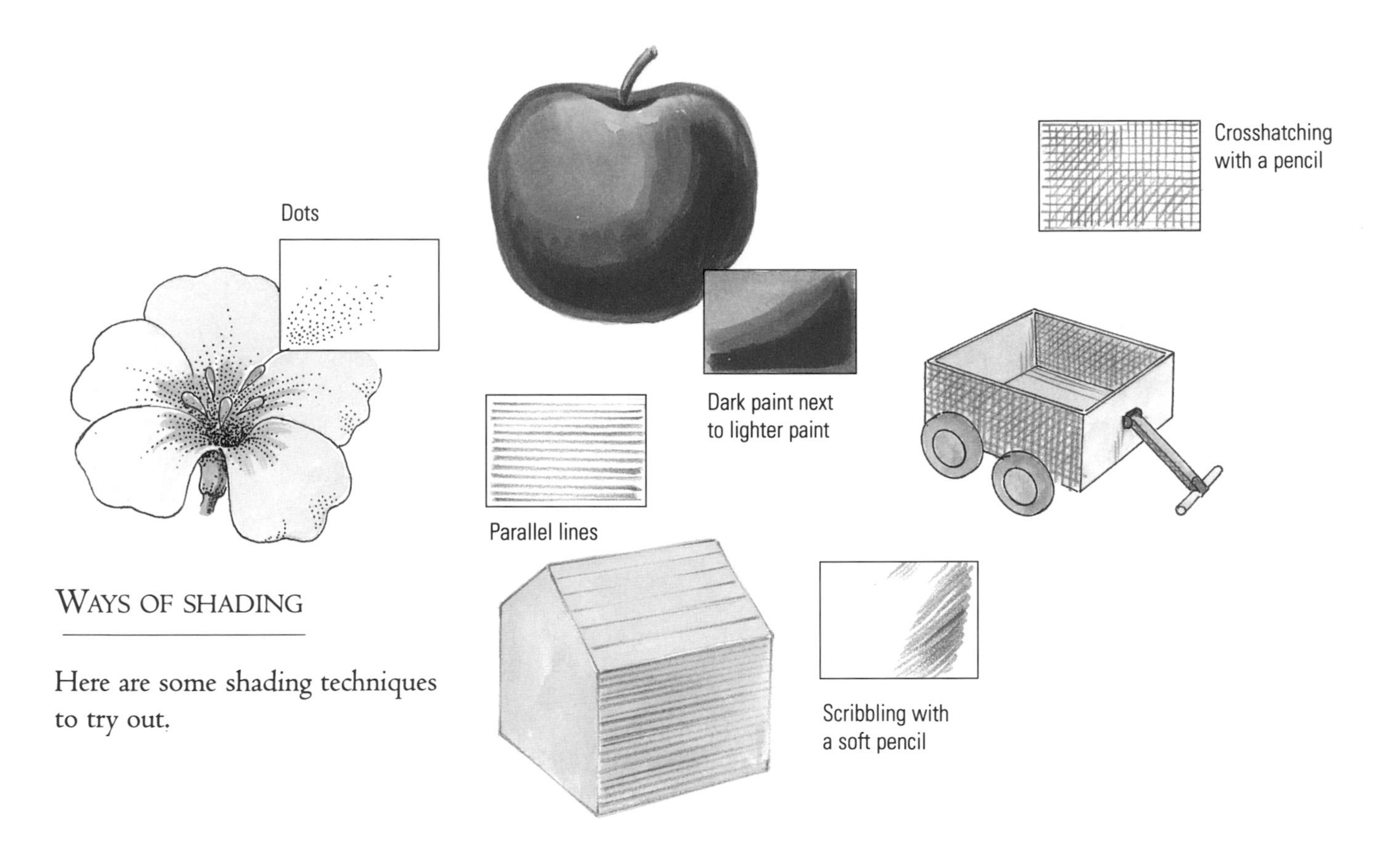

Ways of shading

Here are some shading techniques to try out.

By moonlight

Moonlight creates tone and shadows in the same way as sunlight. Try doing a moonlight picture on dark paper. First work out where the moon is shining from. Then add shading, shadows and highlights in the same way as for a sunny picture.

A landscape in layers

HERE IS AN EASY WAY TO MAKE AN OUTDOOR painting really look as if it is 3D! It is made up of layers, one behind the other, so the distances really look convincing. Look again at the pages on perspective and distance painting for tips. Always make the foreground stronger and more detailed than the faraway parts.

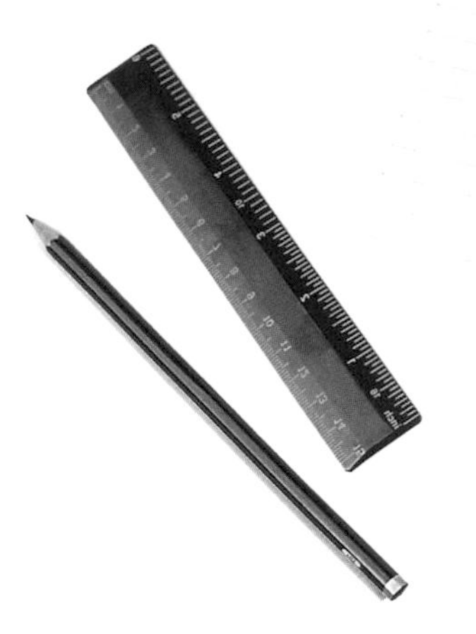

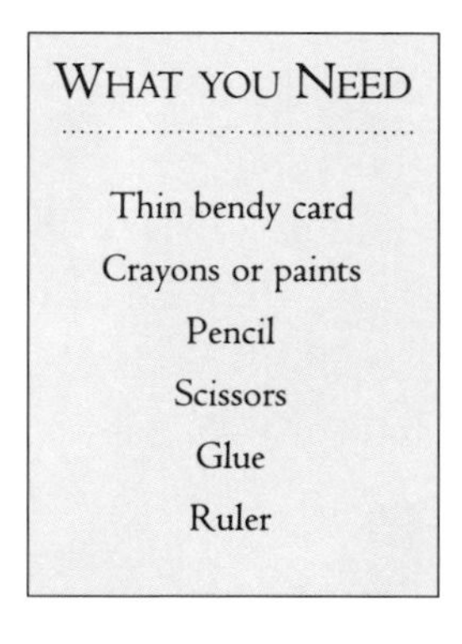

WHAT YOU NEED

Thin bendy card
Crayons or paints
Pencil
Scissors
Glue
Ruler

1 Cut out six rectangles of card each measuring 9 x 7 inches. Cut out two square pieces each measuring 7 x 7 inches.

2 Paint one of the rectangles of card blue for the sky. Cut another rectangle into a frame shape, by cutting out an even hole 8 x 6 inches, which leaves a half-inch frame all the way round. Decorate the frame with your paints any way you like.

3 Use the two square pieces for the sides. Mark them in pencil in seven inch-wide sections. Draw straight lines with a ruler to indicate the sections, and get an adult to score down each line with a sharp knife. Then fold them along the scored lines to make concertina shapes

4 Glue the side pieces to the front of the sky piece – the sky piece forms the back. Then glue the frame to the front.

PUTTING IT ALL TOGETHER

Making this layered painting is almost like constructing a little toy theater! When you have made the back, sides, and front frame (steps 1 to 4 on the left), you'll be left with four rectangles of card. These are used for your painting.

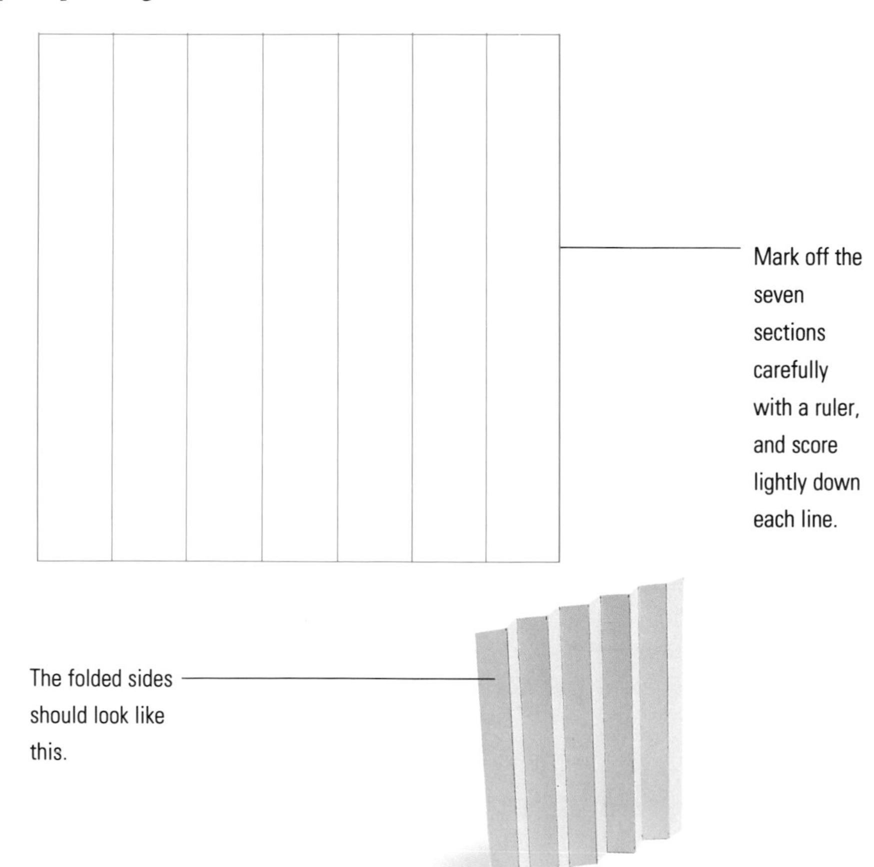

Painting the picture

Use your four rectangles of card to make the picture. First sketch the picture on a single piece of paper for reference. Then decide how to divide it up. Cut out along the top outline of each piece.

▼

When you have finished each piece, put a little glue down the sides of each card. Slot them, in the right order, into the sides of the frame. Push them right down to the bottom and leave them to dry.

Make it flat!

YOU DON'T HAVE TO USE PERSPECTIVE IN a picture or try to make it look realistic if you don't want to. You can paint what you see in your own way. Many painters are more interested in using flat patterns, bright colors, and interesting shapes than in making their paintings look "real." This is called "abstract" painting. When you are painting realistically, you need to keep objects in the right scale. But in abstract paintings, scale does not matter so much. In the picture on the right the leaf, the window of the house and the pond are all the same size!

◀
The artist Paul Klee called this picture "Sea Ghost." You can see two fish, some blue wiggly lines for the water, and brown and green in the background. He didn't use perspective, and he didn't try to make his picture look real. The fun is in working out what is there, and what you think it all means.

◀
Here is a landscape with lots of things you would see outside. There are two different kinds of leaves, a blue sky with clouds, parts of a house, and a garden with a pond and a fence. They don't look realistic, though, because there is no perspective, no scale, and the shapes are arranged to make nice patterns on the page. You could do the same!

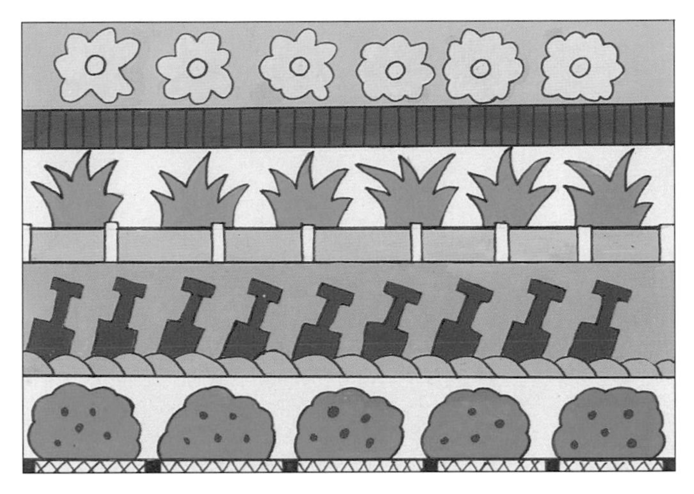

▲
This picture started with soft pencil lines drawn across the page with a ruler. Between the lines, the artist painted rows of things you might see in a garden. Then he made the ruled lines into different kinds of fences.

▲
This scene looks more real than the top one, because it has scale, perspective, and a convincing arrangement. But the shapes are still abstract. Try the idea yourself, using the shapes shown here.

Triangle

Circle

Rectangle

Rhomboid (a rectangle leaning over to one side)

Printing pictures

PATTERNS AND SHAPES LOOK really interesting if you print them. Printing is using an object to transfer the paint to the paper. It is the best method for building up a picture from lots of repeat patterns. If the printing "block" has a texture on it, this will come through, too.

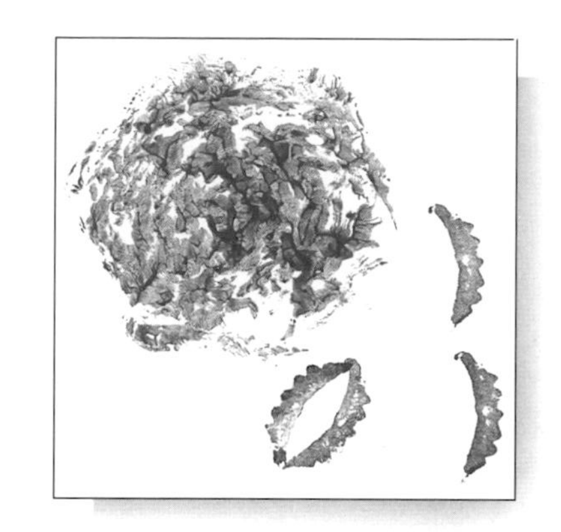

Celery stick

Cabbage leaves

POTATO PRINTING

Potato halves make brilliant printing blocks, and are easy to get hold of. Cutting them out can be quite tricky to start with, so practice with simple shapes, such as the star shown here. Cut a large potato in half cleanly. Let it dry a bit. Then draw your shape on to the cut half with a fine felt-tip pen. With a sharp knife, cut round the outline. Cut the surrounding edges away so that the shape stands out by at least a quarter-inch.

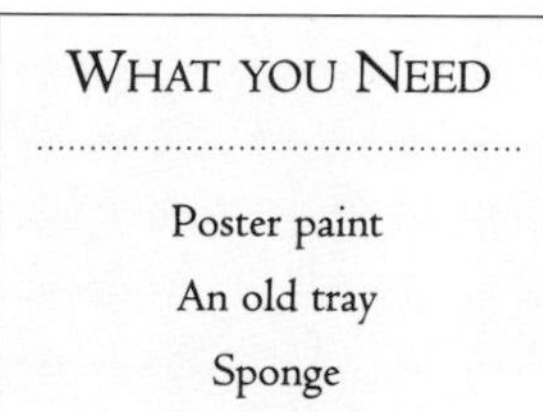

WHAT YOU NEED

Poster paint
An old tray
Sponge
Knife
Old rags

1 Put some paint on to a flat sponge so that it soaks in well. This is your printing pad. If you can, prepare several with different colors.

2 Press the potato block firmly and evenly into the printing pad.

3 Press the inked block firmly on to your paper for a second or two, then lift it off cleanly. You'll be able to make several prints before you need to re-ink your block.

▲ *Mushroom halves make a very attractive shape, with their curved tops and straight stems. Try printing them in different colors.*

Making the most of vegetables

Lots of other vegetables make good printing blocks. Look for ones with interesting textures. Here we are using cabbage leaves, whole celery sticks, pepper rings, thin celery slices, mushroom halves, and halved cauliflower florets. You can either press them into an inked sponge pad, or paint on them with a thick brush. Then print them on paper in the same way as the potato block.

Think thick!

USE EXTRA THICK PAINT TO GIVE YOUR pictures a more interesting surface. Mix powder paints thickly by adding only a little water. If you use paints from a bottle or tube, don't add any water at all – or, instead of water, mix tube paint with fine sand. Try spreading paint on with a palette knife or a plastic picnic knife instead of using a brush.

Always put thick paint on to thick paper or card. Thin paper will tear very easily.

HOW TO MAKE POSTER PAINT EXTRA THICK

- mix it with washing-up liquid and a few drops of water.
- mix it with fine sand, but don't make it too thick to spread over the paper.
- leave your sand overnight to dry. When it is dry, dust off the loose grains.
- mix it with flour and water.

Scrape lines with the edge of your knife.

Dab on leaves for the tree.

▲ *Look at the sky and grass in this farmyard scene. These large areas of thick colors have been put on with a palette knife. If you don't have one, a plastic picnic knife will do just as well.*

▼ *The grainy texture of this sand painting makes the shells look particularly realistic. Instead of mixing paint with sand, you could use thick poster paint on sandpaper for a similar effect.*

◀

This sea scene was created using acrylic paints, which dry very quickly. The boat's sails have been painted in white and gray. Different shades of blue and green are used to make the sea look textured. It is easy to give the water a feeling of movement by adding touches of white paint to the tops of the waves. Notice how the small dabs of red stand out clearly from the rest of the scene.

Splash on white over the blue paint.

Never use a pure black for shadows, but mix it with a little blue.

▼

By using your palette or plastic knife in bold sweeps you can create imaginative land or seascapes.

Dragging and combing

YOU CAN MAKE EVEN lines and patterns in thick paint by dragging things through it. This is a good technique for making waves, waterfalls or patterns in the sky.

WAVES AND STRIPES

These are some of the simple shapes that you can create by dragging a comb through wet, thick paint.

A medium comb used straight.

Cut out different comb shapes from a piece of stiff card or from some old plastic packaging.

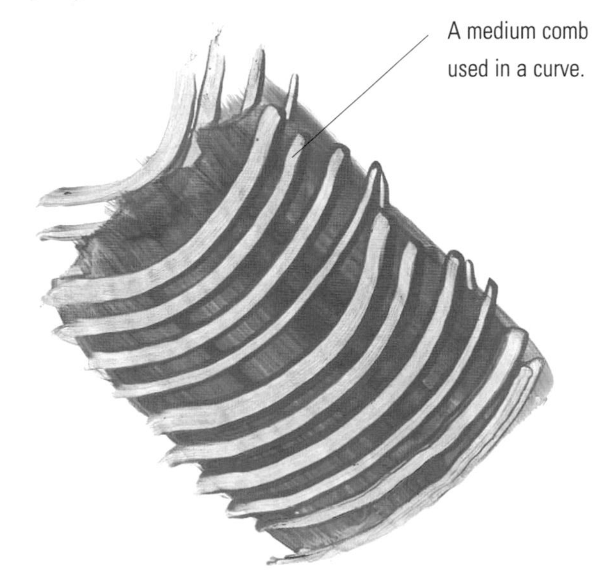

A medium comb used in a curve.

Circles made with the end of a paintbrush.

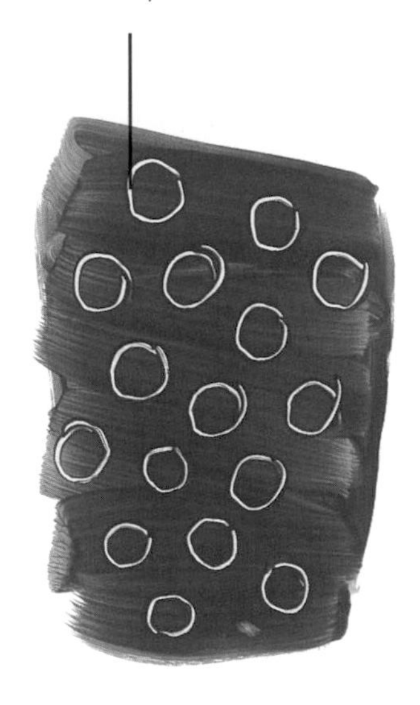

◀ *As well as different-shaped combs, you can drag other things through paint. Try using the ends of pencils and paintbrushes, of different widths. For a very fine effect, you could use paper-clips or nails.*

Making your mark

To make the sea scene below, start with dragging the background areas of yellow and blue. Keep the paint thick. This will give you continuous swirly lines right across the page. Then make the fish, using a range of comb shapes, cut them out and stick them on the sea. We have also made starfish, a shell, and some seaweed to put on the beach.

Waxing and scratching

WAX CRAYONS ARE WATERPROOF. IF YOU paint over them with watery paint they show through because the paint runs off the wax. You can cover wax if the paint is thick enough - use poster paint for this. Then you can scratch through it to show the wax colors beneath. This is ideal for making night pictures or the flickering flames of fires.

▲
Broad diagonal lines of yellow and red wax are good for a fire scene. Cover them with thick black paint and then scratch through to make tongue shapes of fire.

SCRATCHING WAX

Cover the paper with thick lines of wax crayon – use one color or lots of different ones as you like. Then paint thickly over the whole sheet with poster paint. You may need two coats.

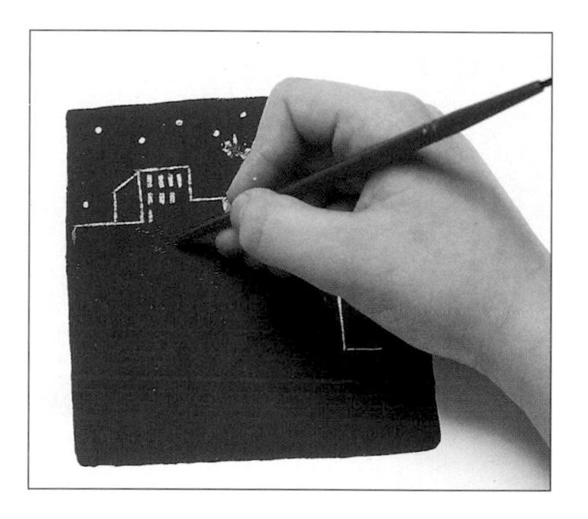

▲
Here, yellow, orange, and red wax was put on first, then thickly covered with dark blue poster paint for a night scene. When the paint is dry, scratch lines through it with the end of your paintbrush.

▶
Use lots of different colored wax crayons beneath dark blue or black paint to make a dazzling firework explosion.

▲
To make this flying night owl, cover the paper with white wax. Paint thick black on top, then scratch out the owl shape. You can then color in the owl with more wax crayons.

Using Watery Paint

If you use watery poster paints, or thin watercolors, on top of the wax, they will run off the wax without needing to be scratched out. This is a very good technique for making clear white outlines or white shading – for example, ripples on water or light clouds in the sky. Don't make the top coat too watery, though, or the paper will crinkle.

1 First draw a light pencil outline of your picture. Draw white wax lines over all your pencil

2 Using thin poster paint or watercolor, start painting in your colors. You'll see all the white outlines showing through.

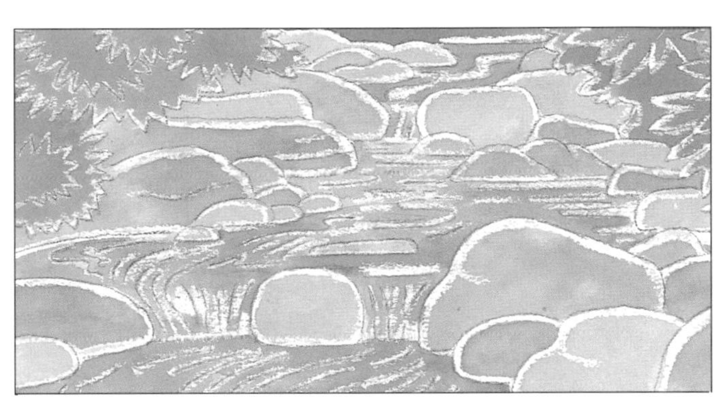

3 Finish with strong greens for the trees, and darken some of the gray stones to add variation. The white outlines look like sunlight on the water and the wet stones.

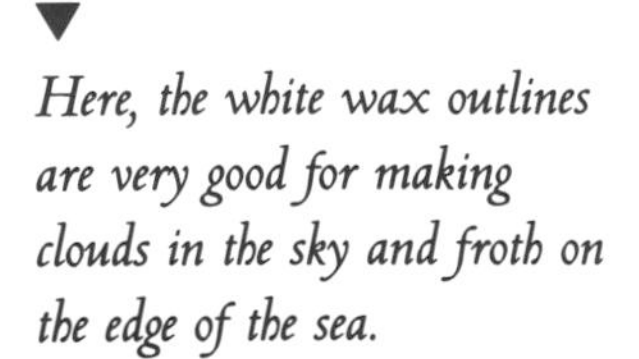

▼
Here, the white wax outlines are very good for making clouds in the sky and froth on the edge of the sea.

Watercolors

WATERCOLOR PAINTS MAKE DELICATE colors that are good for landscapes. You can buy them in tubes or blocks and they are easy to carry around outdoors for making quick color sketches. However, watercolor technique is known to be quite tricky. For one thing, you can't have second thoughts, because there isn't a satisfactory way to correct mistakes once the paint is dry. You should certainly practice indoors first! It's a good idea to start by using photographs – either copy them exactly, or use them to give you ideas.

Always use watercolors with clean water. If you use dirty water you will make a muddy mess! Set up two jars – one for mixing paint and one for cleaning brushes. If you can, borrow some paints first to experiment. If you decide you like using them, you can buy them later.

USING WATERCOLORS

Watercolor artists start off by laying down the lightest colors first. Gradually they build up the darker colors on top.

- You can make colors lighter and thinner by adding more water. If you want them lighter but thick, then add a bit of white.
- If you paint one wet color next to or on top of another wet color they will run together. This creates a soft effect, ideal for painting distant landscapes.
- If you paint a wet dark color on top of a wet light one you will get an uneven line between them when they dry.
- If you put wet paint on top of dry paint, the colors won't run together.

STRETCHING PAPER

You can buy white watercolor paper in separate sheets or in pads. It comes in lots of different thicknesses and surfaces. The easist thing is to buy special thick paper that won't crinkle when you put the wet paint on it. If you use thinner, or professional, watercolor paper you will need to stretch it before you use it.

You stretch watercolor paper by wetting it and leaving it to dry while it is taped to a board. You must let it dry slowly, and not in sunshine or by a fire.

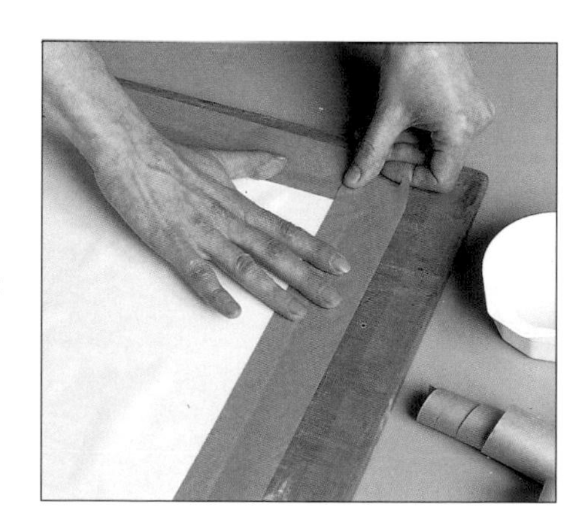

1 Soak a sheet of paper in water for about ten minutes. Then lift it out carefully and lay it on a flat, clean board. Tape the edges of the paper to the board with brown tape called gumstrip. You need to wet the back of the gumstrip to make it sticky.

2 When the paper is completely dry, you can lay on a background wash of a pale color. Leaving the paper taped down, put on the color in broad sweeps with a wide, soft brush. When this background color is dry, you can start painting details.

A WATERCOLOR SKETCH

Artists tend to use watercolor to make a dreamy impression of a scene, rather than a very realistic, detailed picture. Before you start, choose the colors you want to use and lay them within reach.

If you do make a mistake, you can often manage to remove paint while it is still wet by pressing the area gently with a soft, damp sponge. Many famous artists in the past used bread for this trick!

1 Use a thick brush and broad strokes to lay down a pale wash for the sky and another pale wash for the land.

2 While the washes are still wet, add some darker paint to make blurry trees and mountains.

3 When the paint for the groundwork is dry, add details with a fine brush. Once watercolor is dry, you can work on top of it with pastels or chalks for different effects and greater detail.

Watery paint

YOU CAN GET SOME WONDERFUL effects if you put wet paint on to wet paper. The paint dries to give a very even, soft result, which makes good skies and seas. You can use watercolors or watered-down poster paint, but you must stretch the paper first. Otherwise it will go crinkly when it dries.

WORKING WITH TWO COLORS

First wet the paper by painting clean water evenly all over it with a wide, soft brush. Apply a single color and you will get an even wash. Depending on the effect you want, either wait for it to dry, or apply the next color immediately. You need to work pretty quickly!

Put on the second color without too much water on the brush, and brush gently over the wet edges.

Paint in clouds with poster or acrylic paint.

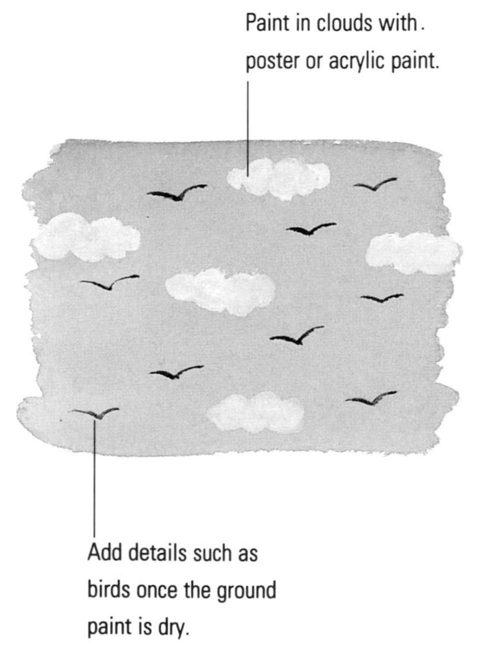

Add details such as birds once the ground paint is dry.

Load a thick brush with the second color and drip it on to the wet ground paint. For a runny effect, tilt the paper slightly.

A GLOWING SUNSET

The warm colors of a sunset sky make a good subject for painting wet on wet. First have all the colors you will want to use for the background ready to hand. Prepare the paper by painting clean water all over it with a wide, soft brush.

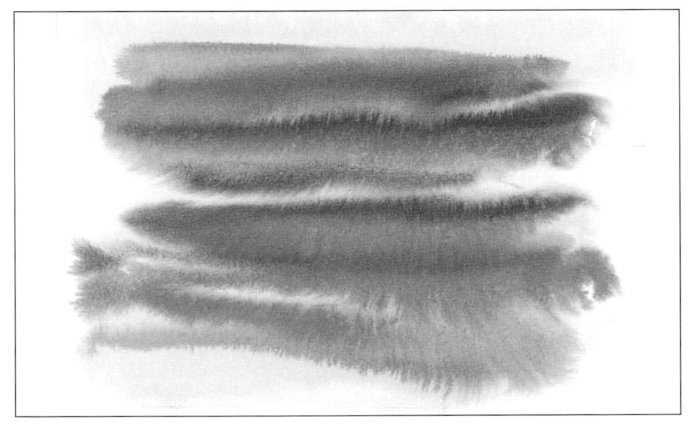

1 *With the paper still wet, apply an even wash of yellow with a wide brush. Then add broad strokes of orangey red.*

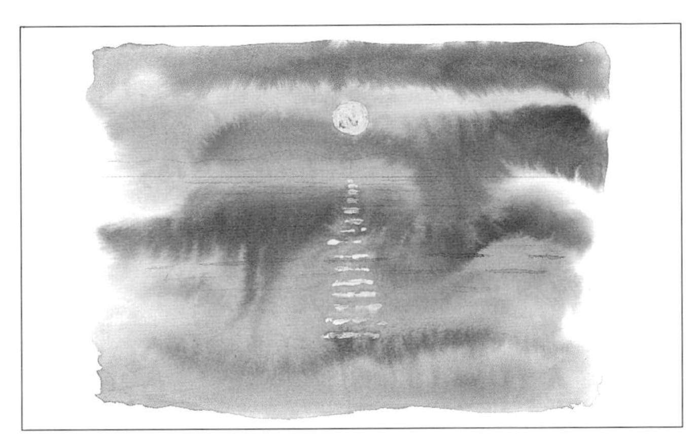

2 *With a clean brush, put in dark blue for the sky, and pale blue for the sea in the foreground. The edges will run together.*

3 *Leave the groundwork colors to dry. Then add details, such as the fishing boats with their reflections, the sun, and blue strokes over the golden water.*

Drawing buildings

YOU CAN DRAW BUILDINGS THAT LOOK flat or you can give them depth by using perspective. Look at pages 28-29 for tips on perspective drawing and practice with the exercise here if you aren't too sure. Plan your picture first. Sketch it in lightly before you start to draw or paint it properly.

3 Add a roof and windows at the side. Remember that the shaded side will be darker than the others.

A BASIC HOUSE SHAPE

Try this perspective exercise. Once you have done it a few times, use the same ideas to make different-shaped houses.

1 Start by using a ruler to draw the house front. Using watercolor, light chalks or pastels, color it a pale stone color. Add a door and windows.

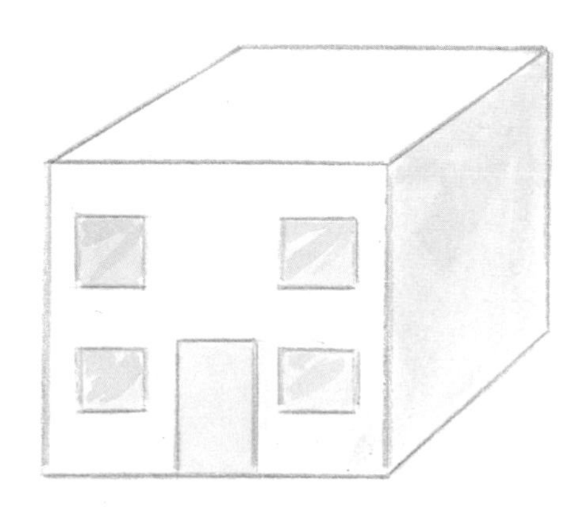

2 Draw in the sides to make a cube. Use lines drawn lightly to a vanishing point if this helps you. You can rub them out afterwards.

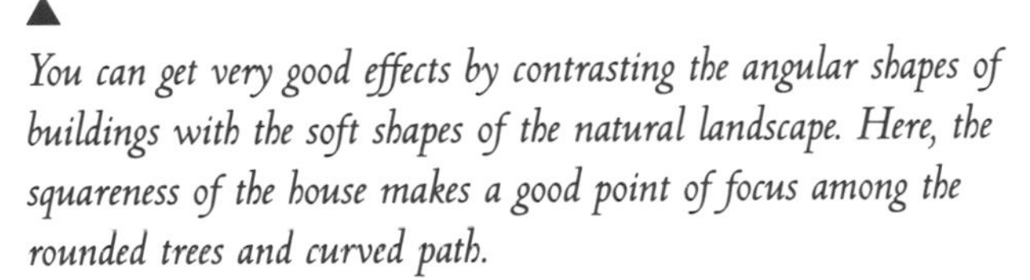

▲
You can get very good effects by contrasting the angular shapes of buildings with the soft shapes of the natural landscape. Here, the squareness of the house makes a good point of focus among the rounded trees and curved path.

▲
You can still give a sense of perspective even if you paint a square building from the front so that the sides don't show. Here, the shadows cast by the overhanging roof, and the shading on the fence and the grass, all help to create a feeling of distance.

4 *Add details to the walls, roof and windows. For extra realism, have the house cast a shadow on one side.*

COMPLICATED SHAPES

If you want to draw a complicated building, it's best to sketch it out first using simple shapes. Try to see what the main shapes are - circles, rectangles, etc. When you've got the basic outline, it's much easier to fill in the details.

▶
Here is a dramatic building shape for you to copy. Sketch it out first using basic shapes. Look how the skyscraper gets narrower at the top, which increases the sense of perspective and makes it look very tall.

Cityscapes

City scenes are full of exciting shapes and patterns. They are ideal for making busy pictures with lots of different textures and brushmarks. Don't be put off thinking they look too difficult – the trick is to look at everything carefully, and see the patterns and shapes in the buildings.

▲
In this picture, the triangular shapes of the distant factory roofs and the tall straight telegraph poles dominate the composition. See what other shapes you can find.

Basic Shapes

In the city there are lots of shapes made up of straight lines. Make a simplified city picture using the shapes you see. Color them with bright strong colors using wax, pastels, or poster paint, or a mixture of all three! Make sure you look closely at the buildings first, and include any distinguishing features, such as odd-shaped windows, towers, and clocks.

▲
This picture makes the city view look flat, although there is perspective and a sense of depth caused by buildings being behind each other. The bright colors make it a lot of fun.

Brickwork

There are several ways of painting brickwork on a building. If you are doing a close-up, you need to show the pattern in detail.

1 Wash over the wall area with flat color. Wait for it to dry.

2 Put dabs of a different color on top.

3 Paint lines around the dabs with pale color to show the mortar.

Use a fine black biro or drawing pen to mark in the outlines and details of the buildings.

Paint soft watery washes over the buildings, sky, and foreground.

Pen and wash

This method combines drawing and painting. A fine pen means you can add lots of detail.

Making a print

If you look down from a high building you'll see many different roof shapes. They are ideal for making a print of a city picture.

What you Need

Thick card
Block of wood or polystyrene
Poster paint
Old plate or tray
Glue
Rags
Paper

1 Cut out a simple roof shape from thick card. Spread glue over the block and press the card down on it.

2 When the glue is dry press the card down into paint mixed in a plate or a tray.

3 Press the card down several times on the paper. Wipe it with a damp rag before changing colors. Draw details with a pen

Industrial scenes

ONCE YOU HAVE PRACTICED DRAWING AND painting buildings separately, you can start putting them all together in different kinds of views. Don't just think about people's houses and apartments. Town centers full of shops make good subjects, and so do industrial scenes, such as factories, warehouses, and power stations. These often have very dramatic outlines, and interesting machinery to paint. You can experiment with different lighting - try painting a factory at night under floodlights!

▲
Sketch out the outline of two or three skylines. Paint alternate ones in black, one behind the other, to give the effect of a big city.

◀
Factories, power stations, building sites, and docks make exciting outdoor pictures. Use charcoal and chalk smudged with your finger to make a smoky scene.

▼
A silhouette is the outline of a shape without any inside details. It is a good way to do building skylines and machinery. Try a black silhouette scene on white paper or a white silhouette scene on black paper. Draw the outline first in pencil or paint it with a fine brush, then fill it in.

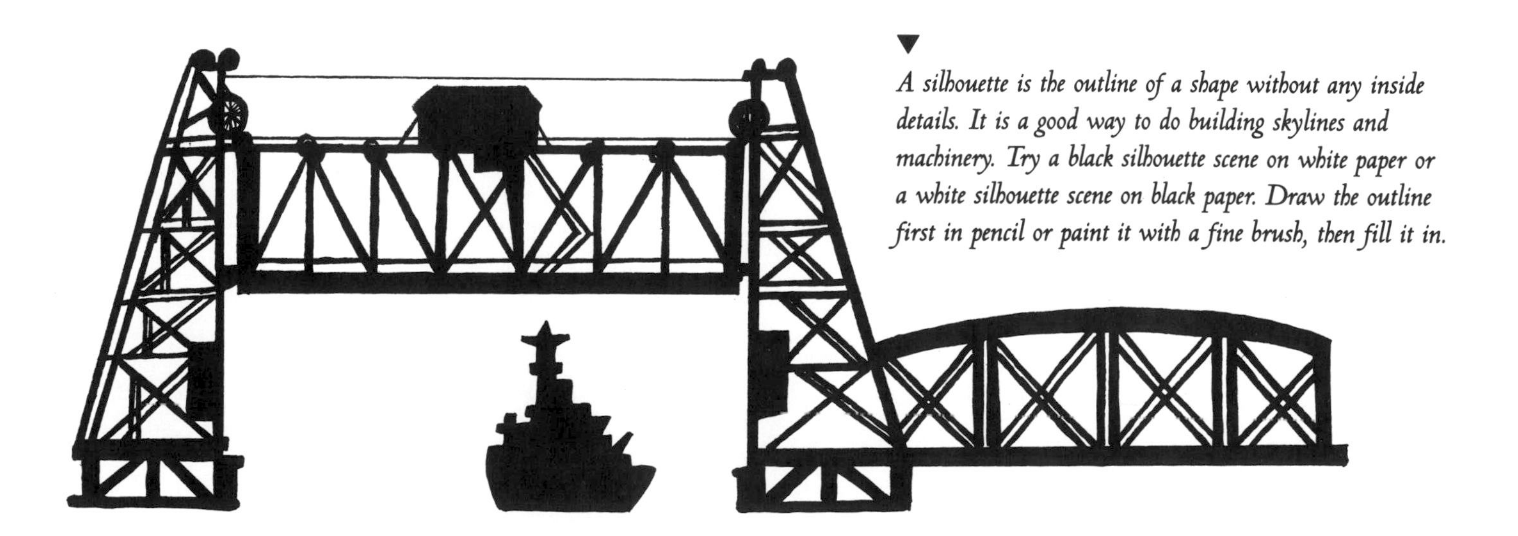

Night in the city is a time for sparkling lights and excitement. Paint or color it brightly on dark paper – choose dark blue for a night-time feel. For greater excitement, this scene has been painted with all the up-and-down lines curved in a "fish-eye" view, to imitate the distortion you would get through a camera lens. Afterwards, you can glue on some glitter or sequins for an even more sparkling picture. Use some glitterpaint for an extra glow.

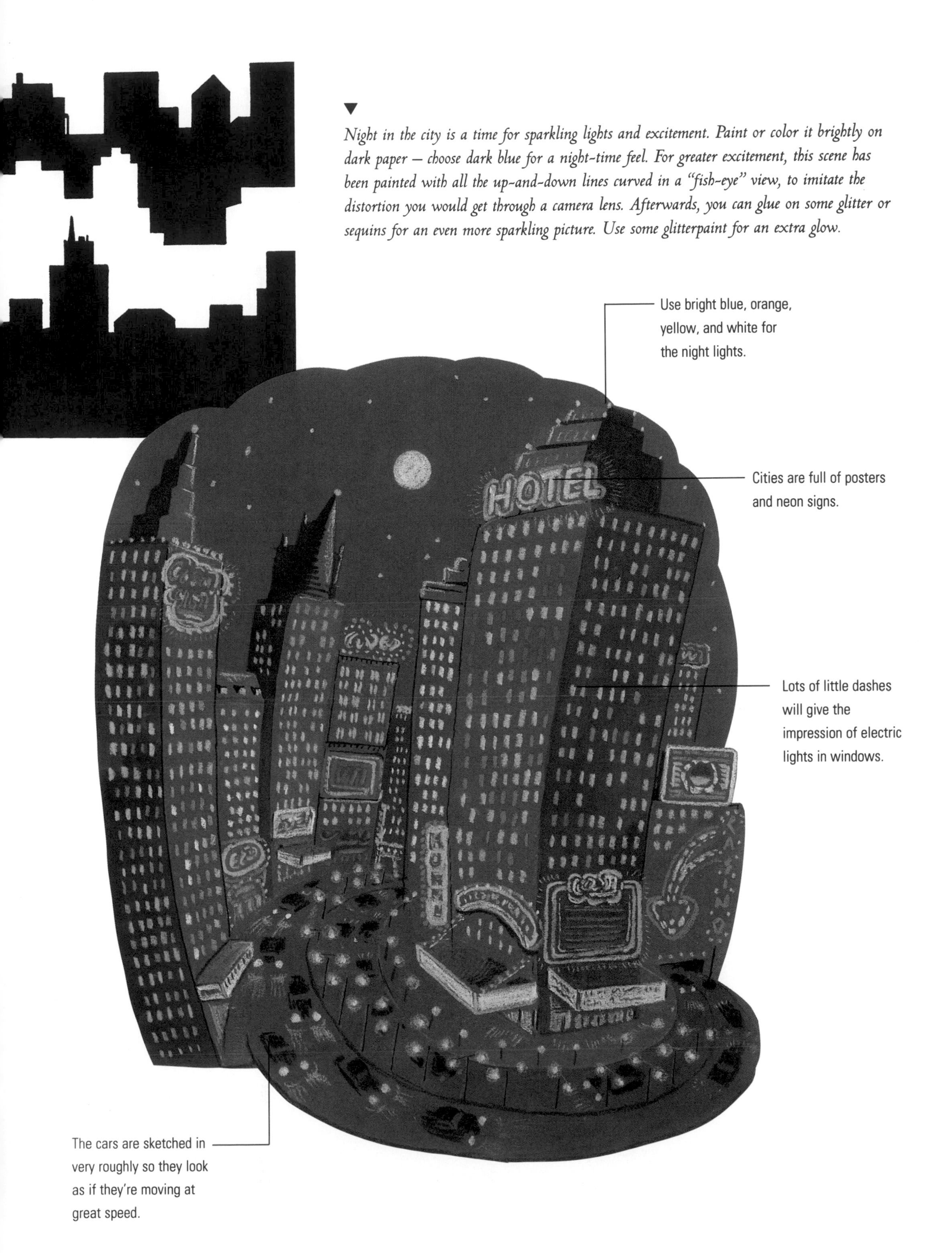

Use bright blue, orange, yellow, and white for the night lights.

Cities are full of posters and neon signs.

Lots of little dashes will give the impression of electric lights in windows.

The cars are sketched in very roughly so they look as if they're moving at great speed.

Painting the sky

YOU CAN USE SKY TO CREATE a mood in a picture. For instance, it could be calm, clear and sunny, or dark and threatening. Skies can form a very important part of outdoor painting. Start by planning out your picture and then painting in at least some of the sky first. That way you can get the right mood before you go on to details and, if you're not happy with your sky, you can start again with a different idea!

▲
Start with broad strokes of strong watercolor blue. Gradually add more white as you get nearer the land.

CLEAR SKIES

For a clear sky, paint in horizontal lines with a thick brush. Start at the top and work downwards, gradually changing color as you go down. The sky should look palest on the horizon line.

▲
Skies aren't always blue! Try an evening sky with threatening gray clouds and a pink sunset.

PAINTING A VAN GOGH SKY

The painter Van Gogh lived in the nineteenth century. He had a unique way of painting, using very small brush strokes in many different closely related colors. These give a wonderful feeling of movement, with swirls and dots of thick bright paint.

It is an extremely effective method for doing skies, as you can see from this picture of his called "The Starry Night." All the stars have such big glows they look like huge planets. Here we give you some tips so that you can try the idea for yourself.

Making clouds

Clouds come in lots of different colors, shapes, and sizes. Here are some ideas for basic shapes, using a range of techniques.

▲ *Paint a blue sky with runny poster or watercolor paint. While it's still wet, dab on a soft rag or dry brush to remove patches of paint to make cloud shapes.*

▲ *Try painting or crayoning on white paper, leaving spaces in the shape of clouds.*

▲ *Start with an even blue background and paint on fluffy white clouds. Then add gray to the undersides of the clouds to make them look rainy.*

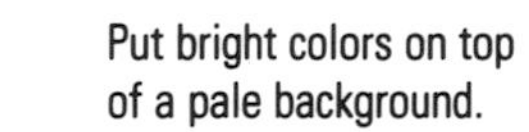

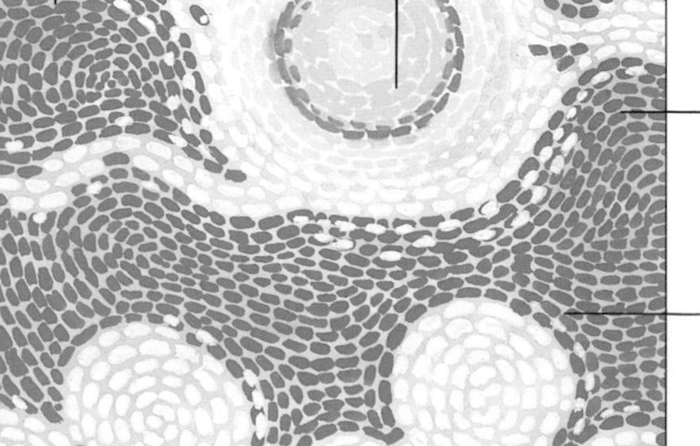

Winter weather

GETTING DRAMATIC WEATHER EFFECTS IN your paintings can be great fun. Rain, wind, fog and snow can be just as exciting to paint as bright, sunny days. You can use a range of techniques, such as smudgy charcoal, chalks and pastels, and watercolors. Colored paper is a good choice for dramatic effects. Remember to use shading to give your paintings form, even if your scene has no direct sunlight.

RAIN

You don't need to draw in every raindrop. Just suggest rain falling by drawing slanted lines on the top of a scene.

Draw rain lines with charcoal on top of a painted background.

Smudge the lines with your finger or a rag.

FOG AND MIST

Aim to convey the idea that you can only dimly make things out. Don't put in too much detail, but concentrate on shapes.

Rub lightly over a painting with the side of a piece of white chalk. This creates an effect of rolling mist.

Fill in the basic shapes. Keep thin lines very pale, so that they look indistinct.

Sponge or paint pale gray and white paint all over the sheet to form the background.

Make foreground objects stronger and darker than those in the background.

Wind

You can't see wind, but you can work out which direction it is blowing in by showing what it does to things such as trees, flags, hats, and people's clothes. Make sure that everything in your picture is being blown in the same direction.

Give the kite a dancing tail.

Make sure all the trees lean the same way.

The girl's skirt and hair must blow the same way as the trees.

Make strong blue shadows to show a sunny day in winter. They must all go the same way.

Use white chalk to make snow on colored paper. Show other details in different colored chalks.

Snow

If you use white paper, you can paint in only the objects, and leave areas unpainted for the snow. Shadows will make the snow look deep – paint them in shades of blue.

Use an old toothbrush to spatter white paint to make a snowstorm.

Ways with water

WATER CAN LOOK VERY DIFFERENT depending on the time of day, the light, and the weather. Some water moves fast with lots of ripples or waves. If it is in a stream with lots of pebbles and stones, it will break up into different channels, with swirls and white froth. Some water is calm and still with different-colored reflections on the surface.

Water always reflects what is above it. Remember to put some of the surrounding colors into it, especially the color of the sky.

Vertical lines show a deep waterfall, with crosshatching at the bottom to show a cloud of spray.

DRAWING WATER WITH A PENCIL

Don't think you need colors to portray water! Careful pencil shading can suggest many different kinds of water. If you leave areas of the paper white, they will act as highlights to help give a feeling of depth or movement.

Fine shading and white areas show a large expanse of calm water.

Dark lines show shaded areas.

Zigzag lines going forward show reflections.

Crosshatching in little flicks shows rough water.

Painting reflections

The way you paint reflections will show what kind of water is in your picture. It could be full of movement, or very calm and still.

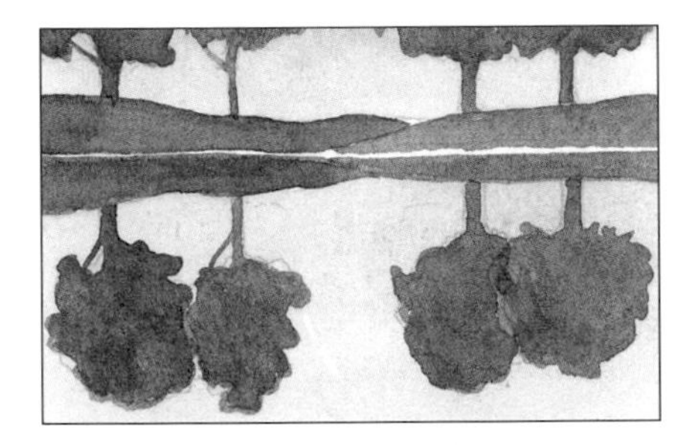

1 In completely calm water, objects are reflected almost perfectly, upside down. The colors are the same, too.

2 When there is a little movement in the water, reflections will be ripply, and colors lighter than the object itself.

3 These reflections are even more broken up, with a little white in them to show the way the light catches the ripples.

4 Putting in a white zigzag line stretching off to the horizon gives the idea of a reflection from the sun – even if you can't actually see the sun itself.

Sea picture

If you build up your picture gradually, you can get just the effect of movement you want in the water. First you should decide where your horizon line is going to be.

1 Paint a background of one color for the sea, up to the horizon line. Add a paler wash for the sky, and a sailing boat if you like.

2 Gradually add short strokes of other colors, to represent ripples and broken-up reflections. Long, straight strokes will suggest calm water.

Making waves

THE SEA IS ALWAYS MOVING, EVEN on the calmest day. You need to add waves or ripples to show how the light is caught and reflected off the water. If you draw a shoreline, the ripples or waves should follow the same shape. Stormy seas are full of crashing waves and spray. Calm seas will have clear reflections of boats and the sky.

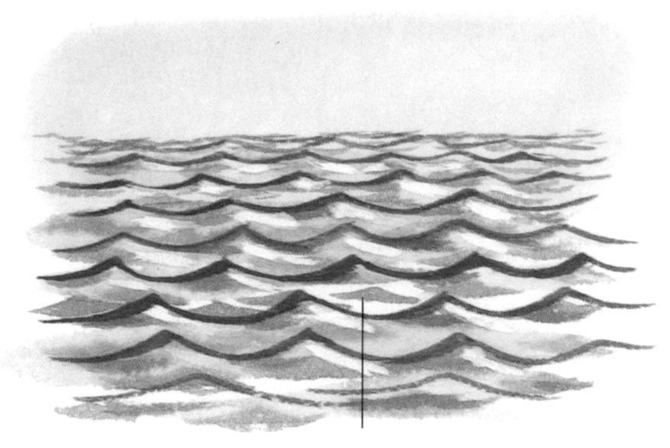

Wave shapes with crests touched in with white show lots of little ripples. Make sure all the waves go the same way.

Sea shapes

There are lots of shapes of lines you can make for waves, to convey different kinds of seas and weathers. Practice them using all your different pencils, crayons, and paints.

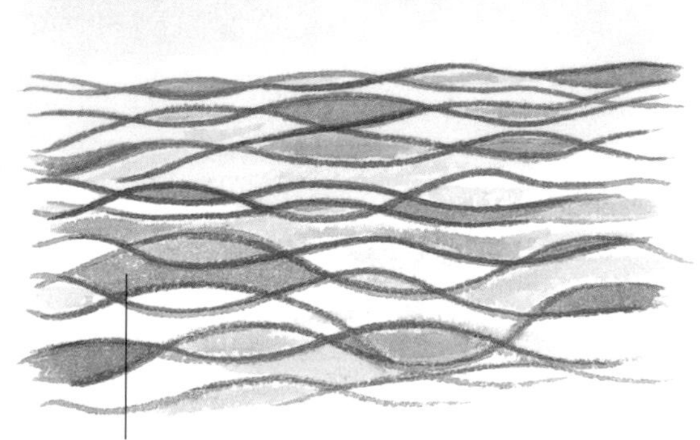

Wavy lines filled in with blues and greens create a more abstract idea of the sea.

Lots of little dashes in blue and green ink suggest a lively, constantly moving sea.

Broad strokes made with chalk pressed down on its side give the idea of a calm, almost waveless, sea.

ROUGH SEAS

To make a storm picture, try using charcoal and chalk smudged together, or thick paint dragged into wave shapes with the edge of a piece of cardboard.

1 First put on your background with even watercolor paints. Then put on a few blobs of different, sea colors. The blobs must be of thick paint, not too runny.

2 Using the edge of a piece of card, drag the blobs in curves to make wave shapes. The colors will all mix together.

3 When the sea colors are dry, paint the tips of the waves with white, and splatter on more white with a toothrush to make sea spray.

SUNSET SEAS

At sunset, the water reflects the red and orange colors of the sun, in a broad band at the front and getting narrower towards the vanishing point on the horizon. You can put in these reflections even if the sun has disappeared from the picture.

Use white and paler shades of the sky colors for the setting sun's reflection in the water.

Foreground objects, like the shoreline, the trees, and the boat, will appear in silhouette against the brightness of the sun's glow.

Flowers

FLOWERS HAVE INSPIRED OUTDOOR painters for many hundreds of years. You can paint or draw them realistically or use them to make imaginative abstract designs. They can be painted in delicate watercolors or bold, bright poster paint. Start by looking carefully at their different shapes and colors.

▲
If you put different watercolors together while wet, they will run together and smudge slightly, giving a very delicate effect.

BASIC FLOWER SHAPES

Some flowers grow in simple shapes, and others are very complicated. Whichever they are, it helps to start with simplified shapes when you draw them. Look at all the flowers you can find and see how many fit into these shapes. Make sketches of other shapes for yourself.

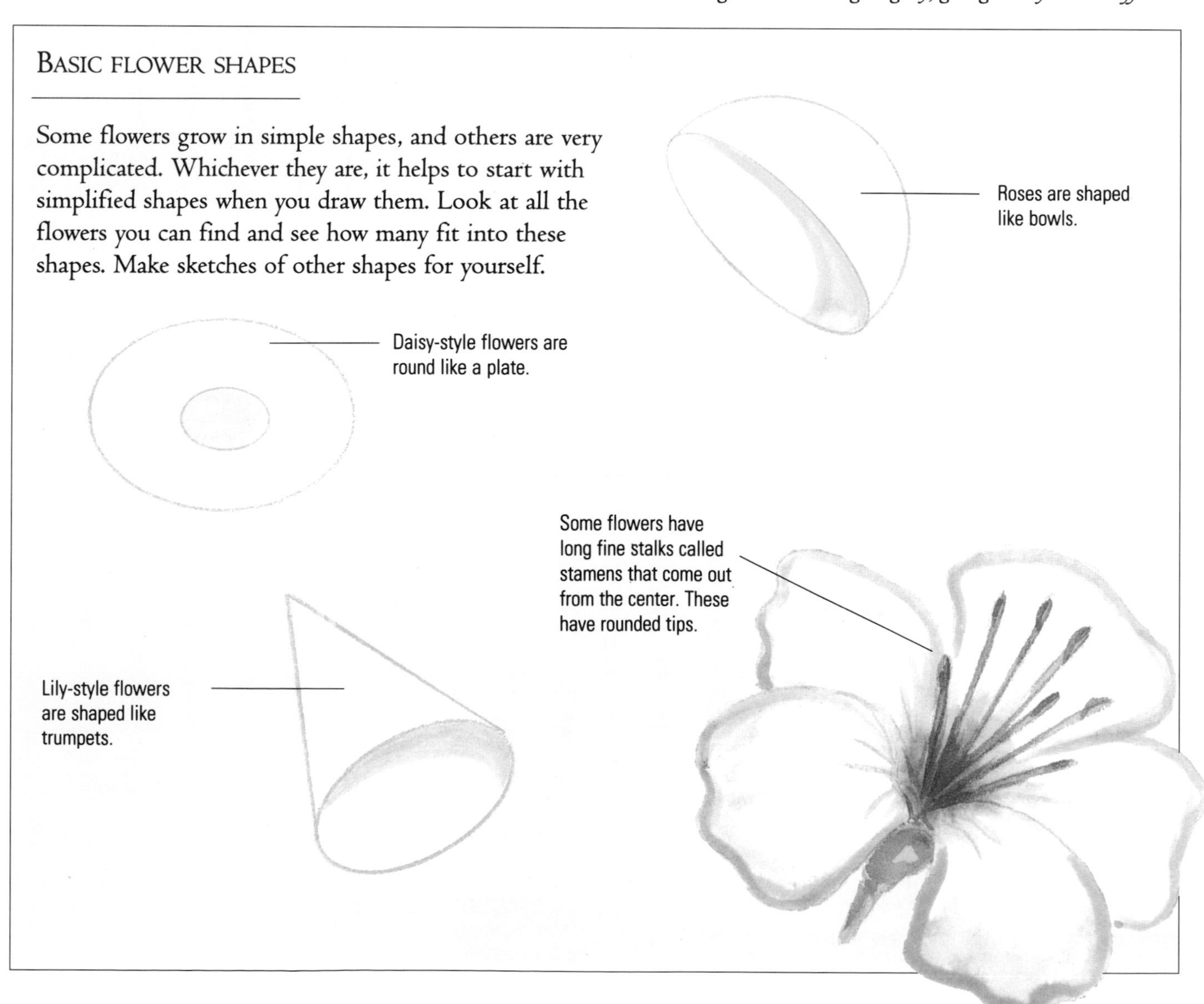

Flowers in the Landscape

You can position flowers in outdoor paintings to help you create different points of view. Remember the rules of perspective – things look bigger the nearer they are.

▲

This is a view from the middle distance, with the flowers mostly the same size, but relatively much bigger then the trees.

▲

Here is a view from much nearer the ground. Because the flowers are much closer, see how they are bigger and more detailed.

▲

This view is from high up on a hill. The flowers are so tiny that they are just dots of different color, without any detail.

Flowers Step by Step

If you want to paint a flower realistically, it is best to build it up gradually. This daisy is done using poster paint.

Start with a fine pencil outline.

Put fine shading around the top petals to separate them from the layer below.

Add detail to the center, the leaves, and the outside edges.

Use big brushes and thick, brightly colored paint. Let each layer of paint dry before you put on the next.

Make sure that the shaded parts – of the bowl and the leaves – are all on the same side, and that the light casts a shadow.

Flowers in Strong Lighting

If you paint flowers against a very dark background with bright colors, they will really glow. This is a different approach from the daisy. It doesn't try for realistic detail, but gets the effect by the right shapes and colors, and realistic shadows and highlights.

More flower ideas

ONCE YOU HAVE MASTERED THE basic shapes and colors of flowers, and practiced different painting techniques, you can go on to more adventurous things. Here we show you how to make flower "paintings" out of paper, and how to paint in oriental and abstract styles.

FLOWERS FROM PAPER

These beautiful flowers are very easy to make with pieces of colored paper. First sketch out your flower shapes and plan what colors to use. Then cut out the different shapes. When you have successfully copied these, try making up your own!

◄
Cut out your shapes from each piece of colored paper. Glue the big pieces at the front together first, then add the separate leaves and petals to the back.

FIELDS OF FLOWERS

Flowers can either be close up, and shown in detail, or part of a bigger landscape. Look at the poppies in the picture on the left, by the French Impressionist Claude Monet (for more about the Impressionists, see page 33). The ones in the foreground are made of two shades of red, to show light and shade. Further back, they are just one color. The artist has made them look just like poppies, but without painting any detail such as stems.

Oriental flowers

In China and Japan artists use pale, washy watercolors or inks to make very delicate, simple pictures of flowers and trees. Much of the paper is often left unpainted. You can get a similar effect by using cream or white watercolor paper.

Occasionally add stronger colors or black to give the picture variety.

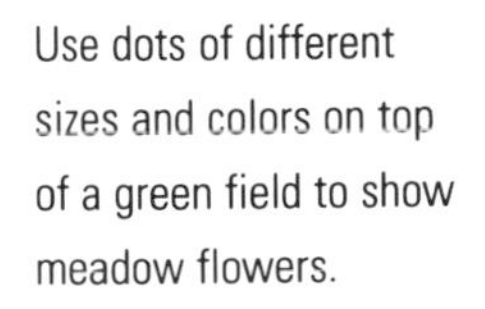

Use dots of different sizes and colors on top of a green field to show meadow flowers.

Use mostly delicate colors like gray and pale green. Keep the paint thin and watery, and the shapes very simple, with short brush strokes.

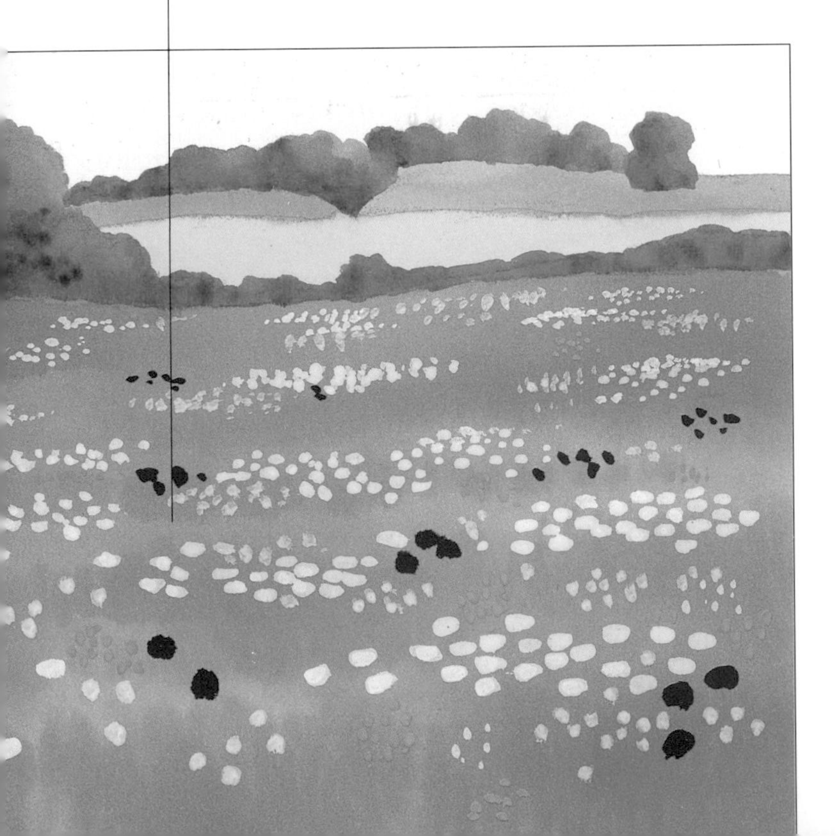

Flower patterns

Flower shapes and colors make good abstract patterns. If you want to do stripes, start with fine ruled pencil marks to help you keep them straight. You won't be able to see the pencil marks when you have finished painting.

Trees

NO TWO TREES ARE THE SAME. They grow in all kinds of shapes and sizes. Their colors change with the seasons, the time of day, the weather, and the light of the sun or moon.

Sometimes they look dark and threatening; sometimes they look bright and colorful. They make an ideal subject for painting or drawing at any time of the year.

▲ *Leaves in the Fall are among the most beautiful and colorful things you'll ever want to paint. See how patterns are made in these maple leaves in different colors that follow the shape of the veins. Try copying part of this photograph using your paints – mix the colors*

WHAT TO LOOK AT

Start by looking at lots of different trees and outlining their general shapes, both the trunk and the branches. Here are some common shapes – see if you can find others.

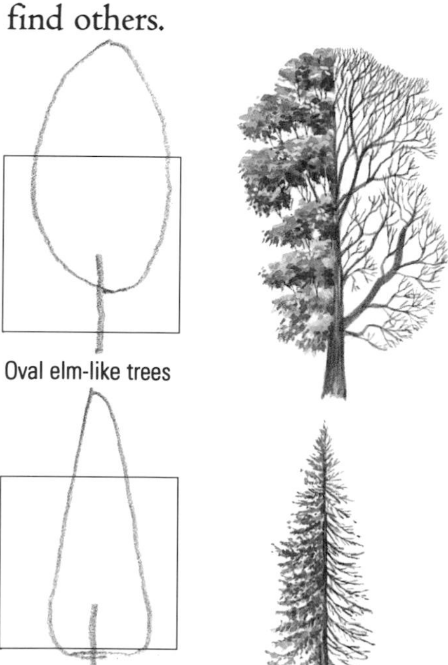

Oval elm-like trees

Tall fir-like trees

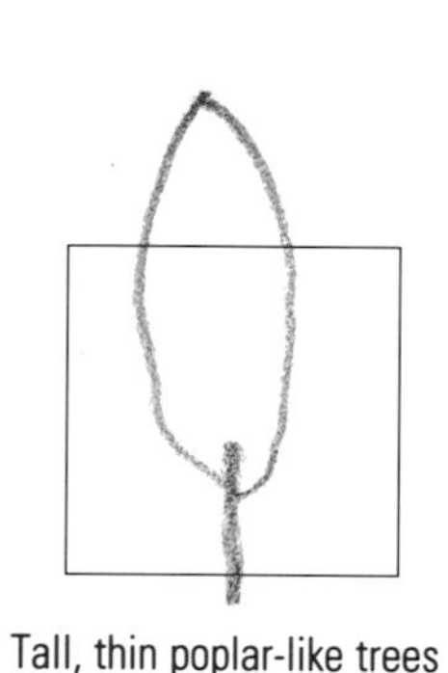

Tall, thin poplar-like trees

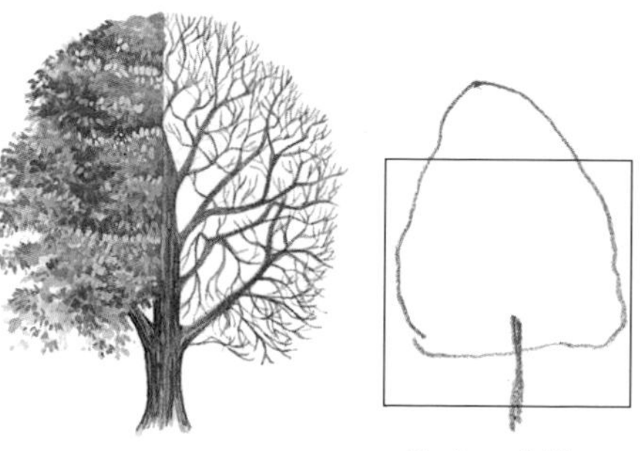

Bushy oak-like trees

LEAVES

Leaves are not only different shapes and sizes, but very different colors. They range from golden to bluey greens and in the Fall they can be glorious reds, yellows, and browns. Look carefully at the shapes, and see which shape belongs to which tree.

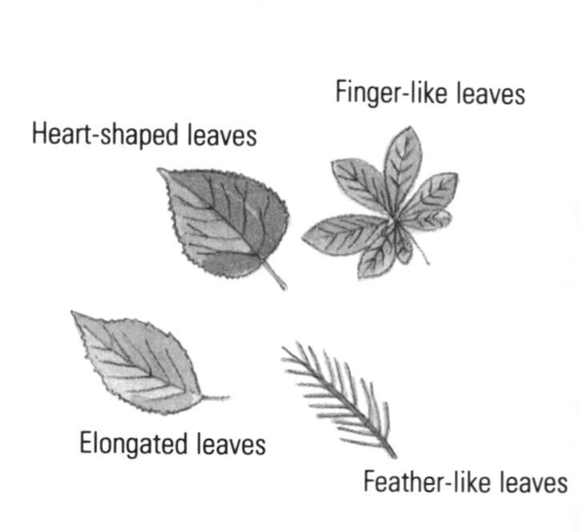

Painting a tree in stages

One of the best ways to paint trees is to build up the paint gradually. Choose your colors and sketch your outline first. If you want your tree to look realistic, make sure its shape, leaf shape and color all match up. You can either look at the trees around you, or check picture books for more ideas.

Outline the tree's shape with watery paint and a thin brush. Then paint in some shaded areas of foliage, and strengthen the color of the trunk. Paint in the sky around the tree and in any gaps between the branches. When the paint is dry, finish off by adding more light and dark to show the effects of the light on the leaves.

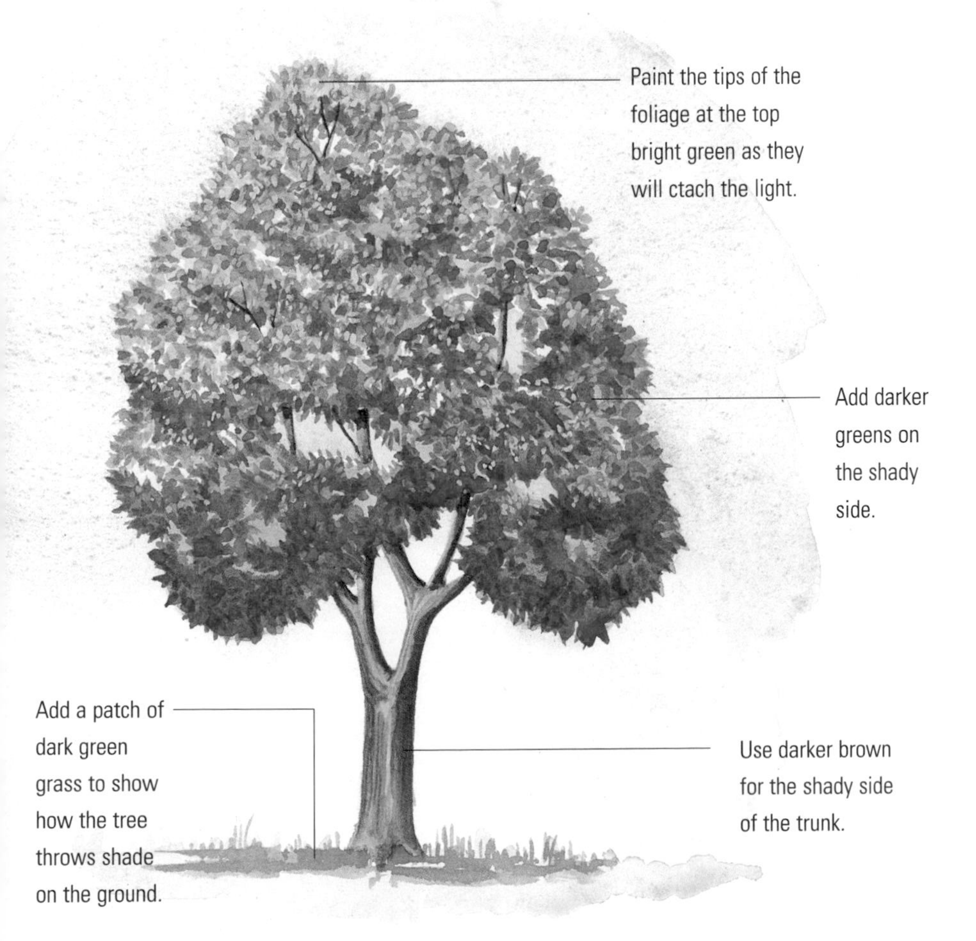

Using trees to show distance

When you are painting or drawing a landscape you can use trees to help you create a sense of depth. If you are painting a wood, overlap the trees slightly, and shade each one differently. Make the trees in the front bigger than those further away.

Tackling tree trunks

Look at the trunks of trees as well as their foliage. Bark can be really interesting to draw and paint. See what kind of patterns and colors it has, and use paints or crayons to practice drawing different kinds.

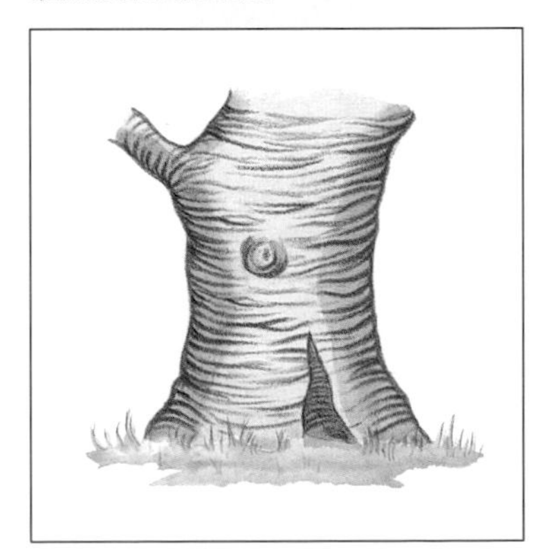

Special tree effects

LOOK AT TREES AT DIFFERENT times of the day and the year, and see how varied they are. Deciduous trees lose their leaves in winter, when you can see their shape in the branches. Evergreens keep their leaves, but the color changes. The leaves aren't the only important part! Think about blossoms and fruits as well.

SPONGING LEAVES

You can make a tree look convincing without painting leaves in great detail. Paint two colors for the foliage. While they are still wet, blot off excess paint with kitchen paper or tissue. This will mix the colors together.

When the greens are dry, dab on darker colors with a sponge

TREES FOR ALL SEASONS

You can have fun painting the same tree as it appears at different times of year. Start with the winter view of a tree that loses its leaves, so that you can see the shape clearly in the branches. Sketch this first, and you can copy the sketch as the first step for all your other ones.

Fruit trees will have pretty blossom in spring, thick green leaves in the summer, and bright fruits in the Fall. Or you can paint a tree like a maple, which has beautiful glowing colors in the Fall.

Spiky shapes with a straw

One way to make different colors blend together well is to blow paint through a straw. This makes the paint go off in different directions into exciting shapes. For trees, choose different greens, browns, and yellows that go together well. If you want all the colors to stay separate, let each one dry before you do the next; if you want them to mix together, work with them wet. You can use this technique for lots of different subjects.

1 *Start with watery paint and put a blob on the page with your brush. Then blow on to the paint through a straw (not too hard!) to make it spread.*

2 *Add different colors, one by one, and repeat the straw blowing. When the blotches have all dried, you can add more details with a dryish brush.*

A tree silhouette

Draw or paint around the outline of a tree, leaving the white space for the tree itself. Plan the outline and draw it carefully in pencil before you start. Use a bright, strong color so that the tree shape will stand out.

Dead trees

Dead trees are spiky and jagged. Try drawing them with a soft black pencil or smudgy charcoal on white paper. For a dramatic, more abstract effect, you can also try using white or pale colored chalks on dark paper.

Think BIG!

WHY NOT TRY A HUGE painting? You can put it on your wall so that it looks like a mural - or even paint a mural directly on the wall if you're allowed! The trick with really big paintings is to plan them first small, using an ordinary sheet of drawing paper. Then you "scale them up," which means transferring the plan to the final size.

SCALING

First sketch out your painting in pencil in the usual way. It's a good idea at this stage to paint a small version, too. This is because it is much easier to decide on the colors and the composition at a small scale. Also, it doesn't matter too much if you make a mistake!

When you have completed the small version and the paint has dried, rule a squared grid on the painting. If you prefer, you can use a separate piece of tracing paper for the grid, and lay it over the painting, taping them together so the grid doesn't slip. This means you do not spoil the small painting, and you can re-use the grid for another project.

▼

Decide on a unit of measurement - say, two inches - and mark the measurements carefully on all four sides of your painting or tracing paper overlay. Then join the marks together with a ruler, to make two-inch squares all over.

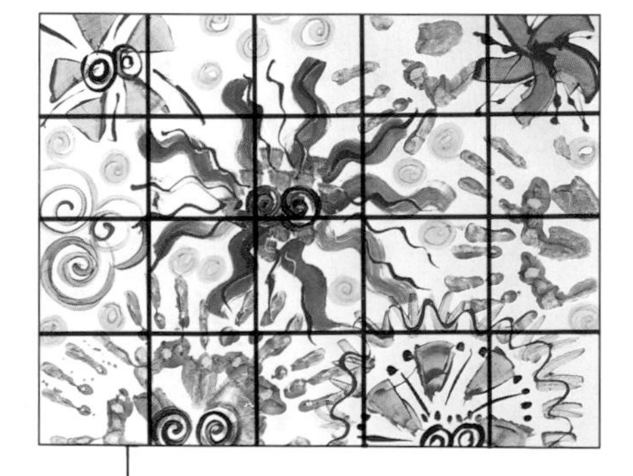

Use a ruler to join your marks so that the grid is straight.

▲

Use wallpaper lining for big sheets of paper, and join several widths together if you need to. Draw a grid very lightly on it in pencil, with the same number of squares, but much bigger than the original squares, depending on how big you want your final painting to be. Copy your painting carefully, square by square, in a rough pencil sketch. When you are satisfied, put on the color, referring to your small version for help.

Big painting ideas

Here are examples of big paintings and murals done outside. See how the composition should be kept fairly simple when you are painting on a large scale. You'll need spray-paints, or very big brushes, such as wallpaper and decorating brushes. Or have fun smearing the paint on using your fingers and hands.

◀ *The spray-paint colors in this mural really glow, and the texture of the wall is a valuable part of the painting.*

◀ ▲ *In the mural of the boy dancing on the piano keys, the supports of the outside wall have been used as a part of the composition. In the city silhouette, the simple, strong shapes show up well on the blank wall beneath the windows – keeping to only three colors plus black has added to the effect.*

Painting on glass

GLASS IS AN EXCELLENT THING TO paint on, since the light shines through it, making the colors glow. You've probably seen pictures on clear plastic for hanging in front of your window - they're often made to look like stained-glass windows. Here we show you how to make your own!

To make a background color, glue a whole sheet of tissue paper over the acetate, and paint it. Then continue with your collage. The light will shine through the background color, making it look very bright.

▲
Use different colored tissue papers and cut them out to make a collage painting. Glue them carefully on to acetate to make a bright, glowing picture.

PRETEND GLASS PAINTING!

In case you don't have a window you're allowed to paint on, you can get the same result by using clear plastic. You can buy this in stationers and art supplies shops - it is called acetate and is not very expensive.

If you arrange the tissue paper so that it makes layers, you can create deeper lines of color which act as shading.

Painting on glass

To paint directly on to a window, use thick poster paint. Mix the paint with some dishwashing liquid instead of water - this makes it easy to wipe off again. You may get drips: wipe them off quickly with a damp rag, and paint over the gap again. If you use "glow in the dark" paints, you can even enjoy your painting at night!

▲
These exotic birds were painted with thick paints, in layers of color. Let each layer dry before you add the next. Finally, add some sparkly gold or silver. You will get a different

▼
Paint an exotic beach scene on your window to cheer yourself up in winter! Look at pages 44-45 for tips on how to do the sea by dragging thick paint with a comb. You can also use the end of your paintbrush to scratch lines out of the

Textured rubbings

YOU'VE PROBABLY HEARD OF BRASS rubbing, when you lay a piece of paper over an engraved brass and rub all over it with a crayon to make the pattern come through. You can do exactly the same with textured objects such as leaves, tree bark, bricks, and stones. Use wax crayons, chalks, and charcoal, and experiment with colored papers. Cut out your rubbings and make them into collages.

Charcoal gives a dark, smoky effect.

Experimental Textures

Use medium thickness paper to make rubbings of leaves. If the pattern doesn't come through very well, try thinner paper. Don't use really thin paper, because it might tear. Try charcoal, and different-colored wax crayons.

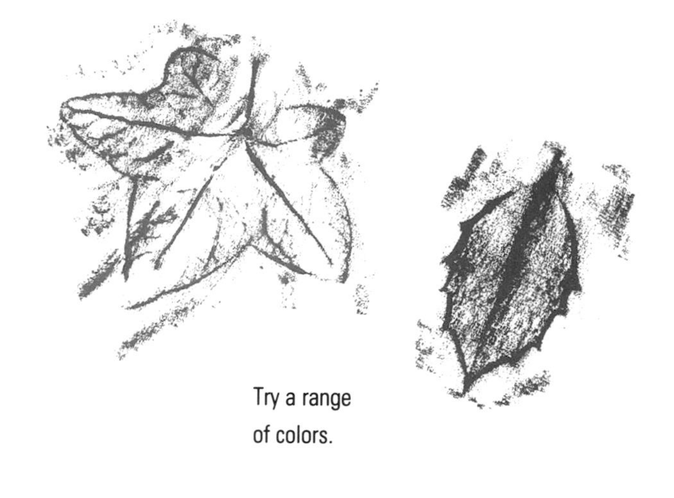

Try a range of colors.

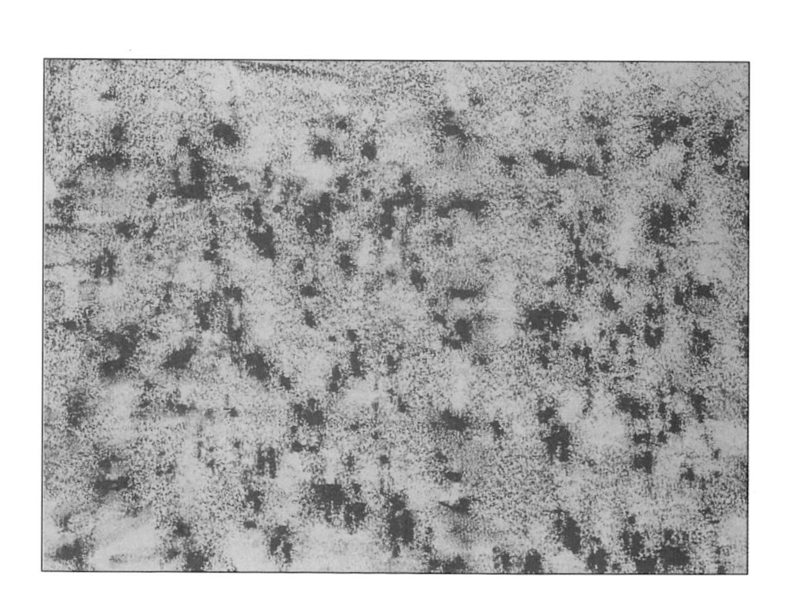

▲ ▶ *These rubbings were made using rough-textured pieces of tree bark and colored chalks.*

Collage rubbings

Make lots of different rubbings in bright colors and paste them on colored paper to make a collage. You don't have to aim for a realistic arrangement if you don't want to – you can make exciting abstract pictures.

◀
This arrangement of rubbings makes a pretty pattern against the red background. Always plan how you are going to combine colors before you start.

▲
This picture was made with rubbings of leaves and bark. The colors were chosen so that the finished arrangement looks like trees and grasses.

◀
Here is a lovely tree which stands out against the dark background. It is fun to make rubbings that match up with what you are going to create in your collage. Here, leaf rubbings make the leaves, and a bark rubbing the trunk.

Ancient art

FOR THOUSANDS OF YEARS people have painted scenes of the outdoors. Many ancient civilizations thought that the landscape and animals around them had magical powers. They painted what they saw in order to collect some of the magic. You can easily paint in some of the same ways, like dabbing and splattering.

▲
Pictures of hands made by Native Americans on a rock in New Mexico.

Making your own Hand Print

Hands have been used as a decoration and a subject for painting since ancient times. Here we show you how to make a print in the old way. If you do this on your own, you will only be able to make one hand print at a time. It's more fun to get a friend to help you, and take it in turns to make prints of both your hands.

1 *Lay the paper flat, and put one hand firmly on the center, palm down, with the fingers spread out.*

2 *Shake the powder all round your hand, making sure it goes between your fingers.*

3 *Lift your hand off quickly and cleanly. There'll be powder on it, so take care not to let it fall on to your print.*

4 *If you want to keep the print, fix the powder firmly in place by spraying the paper all over evenly with aerosol fixer.*

▲
On the left we show you how to make a hand print exactly the same way as this one, painted many years ago in a cave in Australia. For this, the artist probably made a pale powder from soft stone, to show up against the brown surface.

What you Need

Black powder paint
Coarse sugar paper
Spray fixer

STONE AGE STYLE PAINTING

Stone Age people lived over 20,000 years ago. They painted pictures on cave walls, showing animals that they hunted. They made their paints from different colored earth and pieces of burnt wood, getting brown, yellow, orange, red, and black. The picture on the left shows a deer from a cave at Altamira, Spain. You can easily recreate Stone Age painting by following these simple steps.

WHAT YOU NEED

Thick paper
Poster paint
Cotton wool
Charcoal or black wax crayon
Rough and fine sandpaper

1 *Paint a cream background. Use cotton wool to lightly dab on some patches of reddy-brown and grey. When the paint is dry rub it over lightly with fine sandpaper to make it look like stone.*

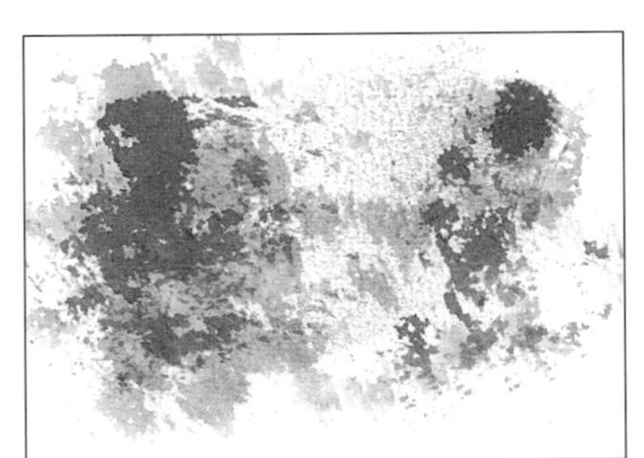

2 *Draw a simple animal shape in charcoal or black wax. Fill it in with cotton-wool dabs of reddy-brown. When the paint dries, sandpaper the painting to make it look patchy and old.*

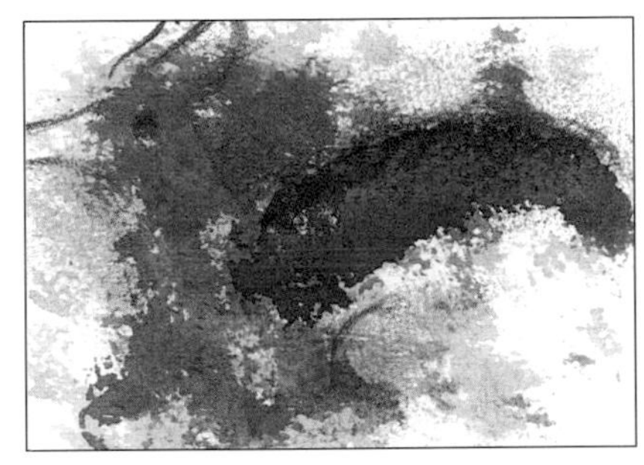

NATIVE AMERICAN PAINTING

Native Americans used painting to tell stories of their outdoor adventures. Their colors were made from plants and earth, but you can get a similar effect by using watercolor pencils or paint. The artists often used symbols for objects, based on simple abstract drawings of them. We've shown some for hailstones, lightning, mountains, and rainbows. Try copying them to make your own Native American painting.

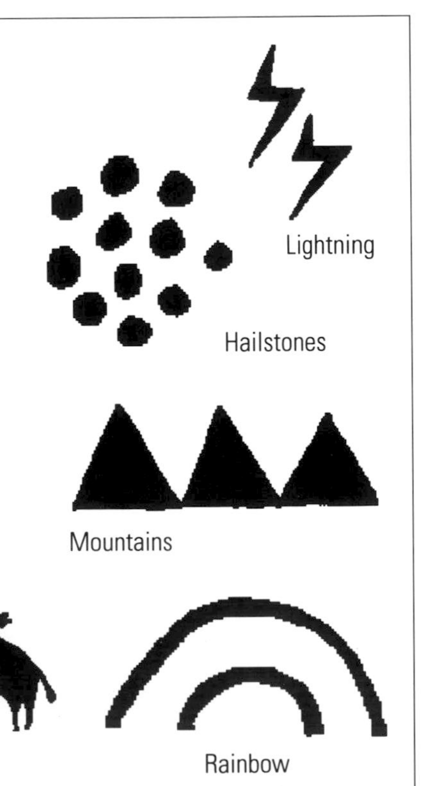

Buffalo

Colorful collages

YOU CAN BE VERY INVENTIVE MAKING pictures from all kinds of unusual materials. As well as paper and fabric - which are great for different colors and textures - collect objects from where you live or from holidays in the country or at the beach.

These clouds are made from scraps of white lace.

You can buy ready-made fabric flowers at department stores. Or make your own!

THE MATERIAL WORLD

Fabric gives a wonderful range of colors and textures for an outdoor picture. Plan your picture first, then choose the right colors for each part of it. Aim for appropriate textures, too - e.g. soft green fabric for the hills which you can fold.

WHAT YOU NEED

Glue
Stiff card
Large fabric pieces for background
Smaller fabric scraps for objects

1 Start by sketching your picture in soft pencil. Use stiff card or thick paper so that it won't tear when you glue things to it.

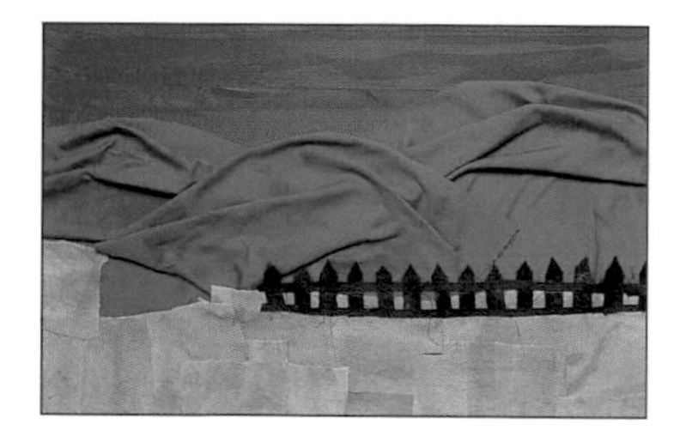

2 Cut out the large background pieces of fabric. Glue them on to the card. Make folds in the green fabric for the hills.

3 If you like, paint shading on top of the fabric to help give a sense of depth. Use watery paint so that you don't hide the original color.

The trees are stuck separately on to card so they don't tear.

▲ *When you have sketched out your picture and glued everything in place, you can add great depth and atmosphere by painting varnish all over it so that it shines. This is especially good on a dark background color.*

Paper Art

This colorful outdoor picture was made from scraps of different papers. Use tissue paper, old newspapers (you can paint or crayon colors on them), and clothes cut out of magazines.

Trash Art

A space picture makes a great choice for using a kinds of shiny objects. Try sequins and glittery beads on a thread, pins and safety pins, old metal fasteners, bits of zipper, nails and screws, nuts and bolts - the list is endless!

Working with photographs

YOUR CAMERA IS A VERY USEFUL ACCESSORY for painting the outdoors. It's much quicker to take a snapshot than paint a picture! So take shots to help you later, with things like lighting effects, the positions of shadows, and perspective. You can also use your favorite shots as part of your paintings. You can paint fantasy backgrounds for familiar things or people, and make collages out of photographs you have taken yourself or cut out of magazines.

PHOTO PICTURES

Why not make an exotic background for your own home? This would make an amusing greetings card to send to your friends! Cut out your home from a photograph, then sketch out the background you want to paint. Trace in the outline of the building and paint a bit inside the outline so that no edges will show. Then glue the photograph in the space.

▲
Put your friends and family in some unexpected places! Paint the mountain scene first, then glue the figures on top of it. To add realism, put in shadows so that the people really look part of the scene.

Photo collages

Lots of famous artists have made collages out of different photographs taken from papers and magazines. You can do the same, putting in some photos of your own if you like. Use thick paper or card that won't tear when glued, and try different background colors. Like any painting, plan it first, thinking about colors and composition. Then just lay the photographs in place to have a final check before you paste them down.

◀
Collages can be made from all sorts of things — this one like the picture below has come from torn up magazines.

▼
This collage was made with background papers of plain color or slightly patterned, with details such as the house and the tiled pot of flowers taken from magazines. The birds were drawn afterwards with black pen.

Still life collages

TWIGS, FLOWERS, LEAVES, AND BARK ARE USUALLY easy to collect. Look out for seashells, too, and other things from the beach. You can even use dried things from the kitchen, such as pasta shapes, pulses, and beans. Combine your "found objects" with painting for a varied and original effect.

FLOWER PICTURES

Plan a flower painting using real flowers, stems, bits of bark, and twigs. Ordinary flowers that have died can look very striking, but for the longest-lasting result use pressed, dried flowers in bright colors.

1 Sketch your outlines first on a spare piece of paper. This makes a guide for you to copy so that you'll have no pencil marks on the finished picture.

2 Glue all your collected bits on to stiff card or thick paper, using your sketch as a guide. See how the twigs can be arranged to give different effects.

3 Add a painted background in watery paint and, if you like, some painted flowers as well. Painting some of the twigs gold will really make the picture glow.

◀ *Dried pasta, grains, beans, and pulses make wonderfully colorful pictures – and they don't cost much! Use a combination of colored pasta, and shapes that you paint yourself, especially gold and silver.*

▶ *This one is very easy! Simply collect lots of different shells from the beach and paint a sea background of high waves. If you like, add sand as well. Make shapes on the paper in glue, and sprinkle sand on before the glue dries. You can collect different colored sand from some beaches.*

◀ *If you collect fir branches, fir cones and twigs, you can make a whole forest scene. Arrange the twigs in the shape of fir trees, and design a forest floor of fallen twigs and cones. Choose deep blue card for a night sky and add silver stars. Glittery gold and silver paint will make the scene look moonlit.*